The Financial Security Bible

The Financial Security Bible

Mike Summey

MEDIA

Published 2018 by Gildan Media LLC
aka G&D Media
www.GandDmedia.com

Copyright © 2016, 2018 The Financial Security Bible

By Mike Summey

ISBN: 978-1-7225-0033-7

Contents

PART VI. GETTING STARTED—PUTTING IT ALL TOGETHER

Why This Book, Why Now?

All of the money in the world is no use to a man or his country if he spends it as fast as he makes it.
All he has left is his bills and the reputation for being a fool.
—Rudyard Kipling

I believe that the greatest injustice successful people can do to their fellow man is to go to their graves and take with them the knowledge that brought them success. I come from a humble background, have limited formal education, and yet I have been blessed with a good life and much financial success and happiness.

Success means different things to different people. To some it is social status, to others it is relationships with family and friends, and to still others it may be a certain standard of living or financial status. There are those who would measure success in terms of spiritual involvement, musical ability, or athletic talents. In this book, I will not be debating the definition of success; I'll just go ahead and tell you now that the ideas and principles contained in this book will help you be more successful at whatever you choose, whether it is making money, managing finances and building wealth, or just being happy—things that when done honestly and effectively will enhance all other aspects of your life.

People "work" for different reasons. If you're a wage earner, you know first and foremost that you work to provide the basics of life: food, clothing, and shelter. Everyone needs these basics to survive, but beyond them lie worlds of possibilities that can either inspire optimism or produce pessimism. How one views the future probably has as much to do with his or her happiness and success as any other factor. Granted, difficulties and disappointments of the past can affect the way you see things, but you must realize that each of these experiences contain life lessons, which can be used to make life better. Your attitude and actions can't change the past; they can only impact the future. It's easy to fall into an "Oh woe is me!" frame of mind that can ruin the rest of your life. This book will help you prevent that from happening.

From past experience, I've learned that people you meet on the ladder of success fall into one of two categories. The first type, if they're above you, they're trying to stomp your fingers and loosen your grip on the ladder, and if they're below you, they're pulling your ankles and trying to drag you down a few rungs. The second type, if they're below you, can't wait to give you a boost up to make more room on the next rung for themselves, or if they're above you, they're reaching down to help you up, hoping you will give them a boost. Which type are you? Are you open to learning, or are you jealous and envious around successful people? Do you believe financial success is something you create, or do you think it is something that must be taken from someone else?

In this great country of ours, I believe anyone can build wealth and be happy if he or she really wants to. Life hands problems to all of us; the question is, do you treat these as impediments to success or opportunities for accomplishment? When you encounter difficulties, does your rigid thinking turn them into excuses to fail, or do they open your mind to seek the knowledge required to overcome them and keep you moving ahead? Do you measure your success against the success of others, or do you measure it against how you performed yesterday. In other words, are YOU getting better or not?

If I measured my financial success against that of Bill Gates, Donald Trump, or Warren Buffett, I'd probably consider myself a miserable failure. However, when I measure it against what would normally be expected from a kid who grew up in a broken home in the poverty-stricken coalfields of Southern West Virginia, one who doesn't have a college degree and had to make it on his own from the tender age of 15, I stack up pretty well. I've gone from wondering where I would get my next meal to being able to enjoy a comfortable retirement since age 50, and I've done it without partners, without investors, and without winning the lottery. By these standards, most anyone would agree that I must have learned a few things along the way.

As you read this book, you'll find it packed with ideas and tips on how ordinary working people can achieve extraordinary success. You'll learn the difference between building wealth and earning a living. You'll discover the value of patience and persistence. You'll pick up ideas on how to make your current income go further, plus ways to increase it. You'll learn about destructive debt, the proper way to use credit, and how to get out of debt if you're already in trouble. I'll cover all this and more.

The Financial Security Bible is my contribution to helping you climb the ladder of success, but if you're already well up that ladder; I hope it helps you climb faster and encourages you to help others improve their lives. That's why I'm committed to helping as many people as possible build wealth and be happy. Here's to a brighter future for all of us! Now let's move on and get you started on your journey to wealth and happiness.

PART I

Beginning the Journey!

You are about to embark on a journey that will challenge your thinking, upset the status quo, and change your life. Many self-help books are based on research and theory and read much like textbooks. This book also includes research and theory, but what sets it apart from so many of the others is that I will open my heart and mind to share many personal stories; some very emotional, some painful, and some downright funny that have helped me develop a unique way of thinking about financial success and happiness.

In this section I will define what financial success is, what it isn't, and the positive effects it can have on your life when you understand how to use it. Financial success is not something magical, it doesn't require a college degree to understand, and it proves that you don't have to be born with money to enjoy financial independence. What it will prove to you is that **ordinary people can achieve extraordinary success.**

In this section, I will define the difference between the Lifestyle of Success, the Lifestyle of Failure and the Lifestyle of Ordinary. As you read about the similarities and differences between these lifestyles, it will encourage you to identify the traits and characteristics you possess and help you determine which of these lifestyles you are living. Until you establish where you are, you can't set a course to get you where you want to be. If you're in Pittsburgh and you want to go to Dallas, it doesn't make much sense to map out a route to get there from Orlando. Likewise, if your goal is financial independence, and you're currently in debt, have poor credit and no job, it doesn't do you much good to study how someone with great credit, cash in the bank, and a good job would do it.

As you journey through this book, you will be able to pinpoint your position in life and determine the course of action you need to take to reach your goal of financial independence. As I share my journey from a very modest background to achieving financial independence, you will see that I encountered many of the same obstacles you encounter and what I did to overcome them. You'll learn that I relied on patience and persistence, rather than luck; that setting aside time to learn each day had more to do with my success than any specific events. You'll also learn that I haven't done anything you can't do if you really want to.

Achieving financial success is not an event; it's a course of action. What you'll find in this text is how to learn from day-to day-events and use common sense to build a successful financial future. Whether it's having to earn the money for your first bicycle, building a business, learning to fly airplanes, or becoming a millionaire, you can't arrive unless you're willing to take the journey.

Yes, life is a journey. It consists of a changing, shifting series of events that ultimately leads us all to the same place ... death. While that's a sobering thought, the amount of joy and excitement, and of accomplishment and reward, and the peace of mind we get from the journey depends on our willingness to keep learning new skills and seeking additional knowledge. Since we all know what our final outcome here on Earth will be, shouldn't we focus on doing or not doing things between birth and death that will make our life more enjoyable rather than more miserable? And the beauty of it all is that we get to decide how much or how little of the trip we enjoy. It all starts with our mindset: how we approach problems, how we react to outside influences, how well we control our emotions, and what we decide we want from life. We get to choose whether we face the future filled with excitement and anticipation or whether we view it with fear and despair.

My goal with this book is to help you to establish a roadmap to wealth and financial independence that you will feel comfortable traveling. That's important, because your willingness to follow the map will be strongly influenced by how much you enjoy the trip and how soon you are able to arrive at the destination. In all walks of life, there are people excelling and people failing. Although sophisticated financial planning and exceptional investment knowledge can help, achieving financial success doesn't require these. Following simple commonsense principles has created more millionaires than all the gimmicks combined. When you finish this book, I want you to say, "Wow, I can do that!" Now turn the page, and let's get started.

Preparing for Your Journey!

One of the things that constantly astound me about life in this great country is not so much the great contrast between the rich and poor, but the astonishing contrast between the successful and the unsuccessful. Some people seem to achieve great wealth with seemingly little effort, while all too many are unable to survive without the help of others. And this is the wealthiest country the world has ever known!

All people are created equal, we are told. Look through the maternity ward window at your local hospital and look at the newborn babies. Can you tell which of them will be successful? I doubt it. They all look physically much the same, and they all have many more brain cells than they will ever use. Which one will be building an empire of wealth and influence, and which one will be standing on a street corner saying, "I'm homeless. Can you spare some change?" It's really hard to tell, isn't it?

Why do some people zoom down the highway of financial success, while others end up as road kill on life's economic highway? That's what happens to so many well-meaning, hardworking individuals. Sometimes it's shortsightedness. They spend more money on casino gambling or lottery tickets than it would take to build a safe and secure financial future. Others are so cautious they are afraid to take any risks at all; they want a sure thing. Although their styles are vastly different, the results are often the same: they are rarely able to build wealth and achieve financial security.

Is the willingness to take risks a key to financial success? That sounds right. Most wealthy people will tell stories of the giant risk they took on the way to success. Beware of coming to that conclusion. It's deceptive, because we always hear about the people who successfully take risks; we don't hear about the thousands who take similar risks and lose. We hear about the $10 million lottery winner, but we don't hear about the many millions more who lost a dollar trying to win. What I'm going to teach you is that the willingness to take informed risks is the key to developing financial independence, not simply the willingness to take risks.

In this book, you're going to learn about the characteristics of informed risk taking and why it is so different from just blind risk taking. I'm going to teach you how changing the way you think will change your life and especially your financial future. In fact, until you change the way you think, you're never going to change either your life or your financial future. I've heard it said that doing the same things today that you did yesterday and expecting different results is a good definition of insanity. Think about it, the same actions usually produce the same results. It takes different actions to produce different results.

Take a different approach. Instead of thinking, "What do I have to do to become rich?," start thinking, "What am I doing wrong that's keeping me from already being rich?" The United States is the greatest economic engine the world has ever produced. If you're not doing well financially in this country, it's your fault. This country is filled with economic opportunities that people throughout the rest of the world have only dreamed about in past centuries. Not since Venice was the most powerful merchant state in Europe during the Middle Ages has this kind of opportunity existed. And the incredible thing about America is that the opportunity to build wealth exists for everyone, not just a privileged few. If you're not financially successful in this country, you're doing something fundamentally wrong, and the first step to improving your future is changing the way you think.

You read a book by starting at the beginning and reading through to the end. You build a life by starting at the end – deciding what you want to become – and then mapping out a route that will take you where you want to go.

Those who are destined to become road kill on life's financial highway probably fall into one of two categories. If you pay a visit to the Financial Road Kill Café and read the menu, you'll see that most dishes are made from tortoises and hares.

Hares get run over because they are always in too much of a hurry to stop and look both directions before bolting into the road. They are the folks who want quick financial success with little or no effort. They are the people who buy into every get-rich-quick scheme that comes along. They aren't interested in the hassles and responsibilities that come with building financial success. They want big success, and they want it now. They're the ones who continue to buy lottery tickets, play slot machines, and bet on the horses in spite of the fact that they've already lost a small fortune over the years. They are firmly convinced their big hit is just around the corner.

You've heard them talk. They have a friend named Joe who has an uncle who has a son-in-law who lives in another state that once won a million dollars in the lottery. These are the people who are easily seduced by the siren song of instant riches. I'll even confess that I feel a little giddy when I see that the Powerball Lottery prize has reached over $300 million. Somebody has to win it. Why not me? Wouldn't it be great to have all that money! It causes the right side of my brain to take off on a delicious fantasy that could easily drown out the logical-thinking left side of my brain when it screams, "You idiot, don't you realize that for the prize to be $300 million, there are probably way over 300 million losing tickets." Anyone with an ounce of common sense knows that the odds are absurdly against you. I was recently listening to a radio ad for the lottery, and it contained a quick disclaimer stating that the odds of winning were one in 195,000,000. That's not informed risk-taking, and it's not for me!

Hares don't seem to realize that when they are running in a dozen different directions and always looking for that "lucky break," they are asking to get run over. These are people who are failing to take advantage of the genuine opportunities to achieve true financial independence that exist in this country.

The tortoises, on the other hand, religiously get up and go to work five, sometimes six or seven days a week, receive a regular paycheck, pay their house payments, car payments, and credit card bills on time and choose to save a portion of their salary each month rather than wasting money gambling. They are much more conservative than the hares, and as a result, they don't take a lot of chances. They plan for the future, make regular deposits to company-sponsored retirement plans or IRA accounts, invest in mutual funds, buy a few shares of stock, and keep a respectable amount of cash in the bank. They are convinced that by continuing to invest a portion of their earned income, it will assure them of a safe and secure income in retirement. Twenty, 30, and 40 years ago that wasn't such a bad plan. You could get a good education, go to work for a large company, religiously contribute to their profit-sharing and retirement plans, and retire with enough income to live comfortably, but not today. Depending on corporate pension plans to see you through is Pollyanna thinking these days. Look at what happened with companies like Enron, K-Mart, WorldCom, and even some of the nation's largest financial institutions. Tens of thousands of good hardworking people saw their futures eradicated by corporate greed or incompetence.

Eagles are different! That's why you won't find them on the menu at

The Road Kill Café. Unlike the tortoises and hares that make up the vast majority of the financial road kill, the financial eagles soar above it all. Their lofty perspective gives them wisdom. They see tortoises and hares scurrying about in their own little worlds unable to see the big picture. The Financial Road Kill Cafe is full of tortoises and hares, but for two very different reasons. The hares tend to bolt into the roadway without looking, often right under the wheels of oncoming traffic. Tortoises, on the other hand, ease onto the road, not realizing that there's a semi truck two miles down the road that will run over them because they move so slowly. Some will even venture halfway across the road, pull their head in their shell, and just sit there. Maybe they're trying to decide whether to go ahead and cross to the other side or come back to the side where they started.

People who are failing financially can nearly always be classified as tortoises or hares. Those fitting the hares' mold are always rushing into get-rich-quick schemes and never develop a long-term financial strategy. I've watched tortoises agonize for days or weeks over a decision, only to second-guess themselves after making it, change their mind, and fail to see it through. They are like the tortoise frozen in the path of a speeding semi truck, not knowing whether to advance or retreat.

Have you ever seen an eagle hit by a truck? It just doesn't happen! A soaring eagle doesn't dive into oncoming traffic, because he views things from a different perspective. As he soars over the countryside, he can see the cars coming from a greater distance. Although he moves at faster pace, he does so with the knowledge that comes from knowing his surroundings and acting with the wisdom that comes with seeing the big picture. Financially successful people are like this. They develop the ability to look beyond the end of their noses, to anticipate pitfalls and avoid them, but they also plan a strategy to deal with setbacks in case they do arise.

The tortoises and hares of the world share thoughts such as, "Those people were luckier or smarter than me. They were in the right place at the right time. If I'd had the same opportunities they had, I'd be more successful too. If I had their courage, I'd be as wealthy as they are." Some of these types of people would rather make excuses than put forth the effort that success requires. Others put forth the effort but are like ditch diggers sweating in the hot sun with pick and shovel, while a backhoe sits idle because they won't take the time to learn to use it. They have yet to learn that nearly all luck is nothing more than the intersection of preparation and opportunity. The tortoises and hares spend more time looking for excuses than it would take to solve most problems.

They have discovered that making excuses takes much less effort than developing financial strategies and making them work.

There's no doubt that it is difficult to admit that what they have been doing in the past was wrong and taking responsibility for it is not pleasant. The fear of accepting responsibility for their financial shortcomings causes these people to continue trying to cross the same highway. Of course, the results never change, and they ultimately end up as more economic road kill.

The concept of wealth building is foreign to most people because personal financial literacy isn't a top priority of our educational system. We graduate students who can plot the course of a rocket to the moon, but they can't balance their checkbooks. This is a real shame, because all people need to know how to prepare a budget, pay their bills, and deal with credit whether they plan to be a ditch digger or a doctor. In this book I'm going to share the basic commonsense principles that have enabled me to achieve financial independence long before I become eligible for Social Security. I'm going to show you how anyone can build wealth and do so in an honest and honorable way.

While the concept is simple, it does require you to look at life from a different perspective. If you develop the ability to anticipate problems and prepare to deal with them when they arise, you will always enjoy more success than those who are surprised by problems and don't have a clue what to do next when confronted with them.

In this book I'm going to explore what it takes to develop this ability and show you how it can guide your life decisions in ways that will lead you to achieve financial independence. We all have bad things happen to us occasionally, but if we realize that there are valuable lessons embedded in negative experiences, we can turn them into learning experiences that would make us stronger. A big part of developing the ability to anticipate and deal with problems is learning to distill positive lessons from what appear to be negative experiences. Throughout life, we are faced with the age-old question, "Is the glass half full or half empty?" Those with positive outlooks on life see the glass as half full, while negative thinkers see it as half empty. (As my college-educated children pointed out to me, this assumes that you want the glass to be full. If it were half-full of hard-to-dispose-of toxic waste, you might want it to be empty!) Step one in developing the proper thinking is to look for the good in life, not the bad. Nurture the good things, learn from the bad things, and, above all, take personal responsibility for the mistakes that you make. When you start taking personal responsibility for the decisions you make and accept what happens as a result of them, you are on your way.

Building wealth and achieving financial success isn't difficult, but it does require the right mindset. One thing I learned early in life is that it requires making a commitment to what I call the three Ds of success: Desire, Discipline, and Dedication. Desire comes from having goals that create a burning desire to accomplish them. Goals shouldn't be confused with wishes. Goals get accomplished, while wishes breed excuses. Desire is increased when you constantly measure the results of the decisions you make, against your distance from the goals you set. In other words, are you closer to your goals today than you were yesterday? Truly successful people don't measure themselves against others; they measure themselves against the way they were last week, last month, or last year. Seeing their progress gives them tremendous desire to get better with each passing day. Discipline is what keeps you consistently making small decisions that are designed to move you closer to your goals. These could be as simple as getting out of bed when the alarm goes off rather than hitting the snooze button and losing another half hour of productive time. Dedication is continuing to move toward your goals long enough to see them accomplished. Anyone can be a quitter. That takes no talent. When you commit to persevering with a course of action until it is brought to a successful conclusion, you will learn the true value of accomplishment.

Throughout this book, I will be sharing thoughts, actions, and experiences from my own life that have enabled me to develop an uncanny ability to think two, three, or even four steps beyond the decision I have to make at the moment. Success or failure in life is all about choices. Every day we are faced with numerous choices. Getting out of bed or hitting the snooze button on the alarm is the first choice many people have to make. Looking just two steps ahead might involve thinking about what would happen if you choose to get up versus what might happen if you choose to hit the snooze button.

Let's quickly explore these choices. I want you to understand that all choices have consequences. If you get up early, you may be able to avoid rush-hour traffic, get to work early, and find a better parking spot. All good! But it might also mean driving in the dark and having a higher risk for an accident, which could damage your automobile or even cause you to get injured. All bad! Now, let's look a third step ahead. If you get to work early, you will probably get more accomplished, impress your supervisor, and set yourself up for a raise. Or, your promptness might result in jealousy from co-workers who criticize you for always parking up front, clocking in early, and making them look bad. Can you see how each decision has both positive and negative results?

Let's look at your other initial choice. Suppose you decide to hit the snooze button and catch that extra few winks of sleep. What might happen? You may get up and not have time for proper grooming before heading out into rush-hour traffic, where it takes you twice as long to make the trip to work. You may have to settle for a parking spot in the far side of the lot and eventually clock in to work late. All bad...for you! Or you might feel more rested and arrive at work to pats on the back from your co-workers who will love you because you kept them from being the last one to get to work. All good...for them!

As you can see, both decisions can have positive and negative implications, but some will enhance your success, and some won't. When faced with these choices, you need to look out for yourself and your family. You have to realize that you are not making choices to the detriment of others, but ones that will enhance your own financial future. Choose to succeed! In other words, do what's right even if others don't want to join you. Financial success comes from being a leader, not remaining an obscure member of the crowd.

As you read, you will learn that I wasn't born into a life of wealth and influence. I wasn't blessed (or cursed) with a formal education or born with a silver spoon in my mouth. I had to pull myself up from poor surroundings, with little help from others, in order to achieve success. Throughout this book I will share many personal and sometimes painful experiences that enabled me to develop a mindset that would bring this success.

I began my journey in the poverty-stricken coalfields of Southern West Virginia to become a financially independent real estate investor, author, and public speaker. The voyage took me from door-to-door encyclopedia sales, to construction worker, to factory worker, and to many years in the politically charged billboard business. The consistent application of the common-sense principles I will describe in later chapters proved to me that ordinary people can achieve extraordinary success. Now let's move on to the next chapter so I can start sharing some of these experiences.

Key points from this chapter:

- Don't be so short sighted that you take unreasonable risks and waste your life chasing get-rich-quick schemes.

- Don't be so cautious that you're unwilling to take any risks.

- Learn how to take informed risks.

- Don't think, "What must I do to become rich?" Instead think, "What am I doing wrong that is keeping me from already being rich in this, the wealthiest country the world has ever known."

- You read a book from beginning to end, but you build a life from the end to the beginning. You decide what you want from life and then develop a plan to get it.

- To avoid becoming road kill on life's financial highway, don't race into things with little thought like the hare or move too slowly and indecisively like the tortoise.

- Develop the perspective of an eagle; look at the big picture and then swoop in to take advantage of opportunities when they arise.

- Learn to distill positive lessons from otherwise bad experiences.

- Nurture the good things and learn from the bad things.

- Take personal responsibility for both your successes and your failures.

- Commit to the three Ds of success: Desire, Discipline, and Dedication.

2

The Lifestyle of Success

Let me begin by saying that I readily acknowledge that success means different things to different people, but I want you to know from the beginning that throughout this book when I refer to success, I'll mainly be talking about financial success.

If you ask a monk if he is successful, he might reply, "Yes, because I feel closer to God than ever before." If you asked a baseball player if he is successful, he would tell you how many home runs he has hit, or how many no-hitters he has pitched. I doubt if he would tell you about how much money he's making from a businesses he might own. Ask a mother if she's successful, and she may tell you how well her children are doing in school. Ask an alcoholic if he is successful, and he might say, "Yes, I've been sober now for 92 days."

Yes, success comes in many forms, but for the purpose of this book, my goal is to teach you how to develop the thinking that is required to achieve financial independence. I'm going to stay focused on teaching you how ordinary people can achieve extraordinary wealth. So you puritans out there who are successfully bright and broke, I'm not talking about you. If you're happy working 40 hours a week, 50 weeks a year, for 40 years and then ending up with nothing more to show for it than a worn-out body and a Social Security check, God bless you. However, if you want to get off this 40-50-40 plan of life and become financially independent while you're still young enough to enjoy it, then you are holding in your hands the guidebook that can give you a roadmap to success.

What is this lifestyle of success? Is there something magical about it? Are some people just luckier than others? Isn't it amazing that you can drive down streets in America and find neighbors, living side by side, both earning the same income, yet one has a lovely well maintained home, nice clothing, new cars, and all the trappings of success, while the other lives in a house that needs painting, wears hand-me-down clothing, drives an old clunker, and is always broke? Why? What does one do that the other doesn't?

Over the next few chapters I am going to define the differences between the Lifestyle of Success, the Lifestyle of Failure, and the Lifestyle of Ordinary, and do so in a way that will help you determine which lifestyle you are currently living. Let's begin with the Lifestyle of Success.

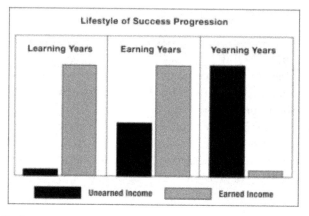

Fig. 1

The graph in Figure 1 above shows the growth process that occurs when we live this Lifestyle of Success. The left, or vertical, axis of the graph represents income, while the bottom horizontal axis represents time. For simplicity, I have divided time into three phases. The first phase corresponds to youth, the middle phase represents middle age or peak earning years, and the final phase signifies retirement years. As is noted, I call these phases the Learning Years, the Earning Years, and the Yearning Years. I'll talk more about this later.

The columns in the graph represent income. There are two columns in each phase. The one on the left represents unearned or investment income, money for which you don't have to trade your time or labor to earn. The column on the right in each phase represents earned income, or what you work for.

First, let's look at the youth phase. Notice that during this period, nearly all income is earned income, and there is very little, if any, unearned income. That's the way most people begin life as adults. They have to get a job and work for money to pay the bills and provide sustenance. Their standard of living is determined by what they can earn.

For those people living the Lifestyle of Success, the middle portion of the graph shows what happens as they move into their peak Earning Years. As you can see, earned income is still high, but unearned or investment income is beginning to show an increase. This indicates that people living this lifestyle are still working full time, but they have begun making investments that are starting to generate money for which they don't have to work.

Finally, as you can see from the graph, when they reach their retirement years, they are able to have the same amount of income from their investments and not have to work. That's a nice thought isn't it? Not only is it a nice thought, it's what happens when you live the Lifestyle of Success. But, once again, what is this Lifestyle of Success? Let's use another graph to illustrate what you have to do in order to live this lifestyle.

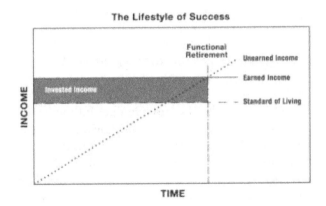

Fig. 2

As in Figure 1, the left or vertical axis represents money, and the bottom or horizontal axis represents time. I do not show specific numbers on either axis, because this graph is designed to illustrate a concept, not specific amounts of money or periods of time.

The horizontal line at the top is labeled "Earned Income" and it represents the earnings from your job. Notice it is constant over time because it represents your earnings, whatever they might be. Whether you make a little or a lot, it's the amount you earn working. The horizontal line below it is titled "Standard of Living" and it represents the money you spend to maintain the lifestyle in which you are living. The example in this graph depicts someone who may be living the Lifestyle of Success, because the standard of living line is under the Earned Income line.

The shaded area between the Earned Income line and the Standard of Living line is labeled Invested Income. It represents the amount of money you have to invest after paying your bills. When this money is invested, it creates the diagonal third line on the graph titled "Unearned Income." This is the amount of money your investments are earning. It is money for which you don't have to trade time or labor.

This may seem like an oversimplification of how to achieve financial success, but let's take a closer look at the concept. You will notice that in the beginning, the Unearned Income line starts at zero. Unless you are fortunate enough to have a trust fund or inheritance bestowed upon you, you will start just as I did, with no investments and lucky to have a job.

What's important at this stage of life is not so much what you make, but what you spend. If you discipline yourself to live on less than you make and invest the difference, no matter how small it may be, you will begin to start seeing some Unearned Income. If you continue this practice and leave the Unearned Income alone and allow it to compound, what starts out as a tiny trickle, gradually becomes a flowing stream of income and the Unearned Income line on the graph continues to grow.

As you saw in Figure 1, by the time you get into your true Earning Years, your Unearned Income begins to become a significant portion of your overall income. By allowing this Unearned Income to stay invested and continuing to compound, it creates a snowball effect. The money from your Earned Income that you are continuing to invest, together with the Unearned Income that is accruing, makes the time it takes for your investments to double grow shorter and shorter. What may take 10 years to double the first time, may double again in six years and again in four years, etc.

For those of you who are thinking that this is the tortoise way to financial success, you're right. It's a slow and methodical way to wealth, but it works. What I am discussing here is the "concept" of wealth building, not the speed. I'll get into ways to speed up the process later, but for now I want to be sure you understand that the one absolute rule for wealth building is, "You can't spend everything you make. You have to invest for success." This rule forms the basis of developing the proper thinking or mindset it takes to become financially independent.

When you establish a lifelong commitment to investing, the Unearned Income line will continue to grow until eventually it will equal or exceed your Earned Income. This is the point, as noted on the graph, that I call Functional Retirement. This is when you reach the point at which you can continue to live the lifestyle to which you are accustomed without ever having to work for money again. There is no age associated with Functional Retirement. It can come at age 25 or 35 or 45 or 55 and it does not have anything to do with whether you quit your job or not. It is merely the point in life at which you could give up your job if that's what you wanted to do.

I set a goal at age 20 to become a millionaire by age 30 and retire by age 50 and was able to reach both of these goals. (I'll talk more about the importance of goals later.) What I didn't understand when I set this goal was the difference between quitting work and Functional Retirement. Today, I'm as busy as ever, but I'm doing what I want to do, not things I have to do to earn a living. Big difference, both mentally and physically!

Today, with all the get-rich-quick schemes being advertised, there seems to be a common thread that runs through all of them. That thread is being able to quit your job. Developing a success-oriented mindset is not about quitting your job; it's about having a more productive and rewarding life. Many people love their jobs; what they hate is the fact that they have to work to survive. Life is so much more rewarding when you do things because you want to, not because you have to.

Even if you aren't an economist, you can see from Figure 2 that if you discipline yourself to live on less than what you make and invest the difference, gradually over time the unearned income from your investments can grow until it equals or exceeds what you earn on your job. When this happens, you have many options. For example, you can choose to continue working and increase your standard of living. You can choose to stop working and maintain the same standard of living for the rest of your life. You can choose to work part time and still increase your standard of living, but at a slower rate. You can choose to quit working, increase your standard of living by a portion of what you have been investing, and continue to invest the difference so that your unearned income still continues to grow. You can choose to keep the same standard of living, continue to work, and invest for several more years, and then both quit your job and substantially increase your standard of living. The options are numerous.

But, you say, "How can we invest when we can barely pay our bills now?" Answer: It's simple! You reduce your standard of living for a period of time just as you would if suddenly your income was cut by 10, 15, or 20 percent and you couldn't find another job to replace your loss. Is it easy? NO! Is it possible? ABSOLUTELY! Are you willing to do it voluntarily? MAYBE . . . MAYBE NOT!

I know that it's hard when you're first getting started. When I decided to change my life, I did two things: I cut spending to a bare minimum and looked for ways to increase my income. What prompted these changes? They were the direct result of having a specific goal that was written and included a timetable. I'll discuss this goal in more detail later, but for now I mention it only to emphasize the importance goals play in helping you change your thinking. Without goals, you have nothing against which to measure your progress. With nothing to guide you, it's virtually impossible to know whether you are on the right track or not.

As Lewis Carroll wrote in *Alice in Wonderland*, when Alice asked, **"Would you tell me please, which way I ought to go from here?"**

"That depends a good deal on where you want to get to," said the Cat.

"I don't much care where . . ." said Alice.

"Then it doesn't matter which way you go," said the Cat.

That's the dilemma faced by so many people. It's as if they want to arrive without taking the journey. The problem is, life doesn't work that way. Until you decide what you want from life and strive to get it, you're stuck with whatever life hands you. Goals give you a sense of direction that insulates you from the confusion that comes with all the free advice that is available today. The Internet can be a blessing or a curse. It's a blessing if you know what you want from life and use it as a research tool to hone the skills needed to accomplish your goals, but it can be a curse if you lack a sense of direction and use it to allow yourself to be swayed and influenced by what everyone else is doing. In the latter case, it's too easy to climb on someone else's wagon that may be going in the wrong direction.

That's where the three Ds of success that I mentioned in the first chapter come into play. It's sad to say, but unless you have goals that produce a strong Desire for a better life, the Discipline to take the steps necessary to achieve them, and the Dedication to stick with it long enough to succeed, you probably won't enjoy The Lifestyle of Success.

But, you say, "Money isn't everything. I want to be happy too." To which I respond, "Is one mutually exclusive of the other, or have we just been brainwashed into thinking so?" Are our only two choices in life to be rich and miserable or poor and happy? Couldn't we be well off but happy? Seriously, I'm amazed at the number of people who equate riches with misery. But, if you look at your own personal experiences, have you encountered more miserable poor people or more miserable rich people? Could it be that the sacrifices those who achieve financial success make in the beginning are viewed as misery by people who aren't willing to make sacrifices? How many times have you heard someone say, "I'm going to enjoy all I can today, because there is no guarantee I'll even be here tomorrow, let alone 10 or 20 years from now?" Before you make a statement like this, consider whether it is a valid statement or an excuse born out of jealousy by people who lack the Desire, Discipline, and Dedication required to achieve financial success.

But, you say, "If it's so easy, why isn't everyone doing it?" Well, that's a good question, and in order to answer it, I want you to explore some other lifestyles that people live and see if you can determine the similarities and differences that set them apart from those living the Lifestyle of Success. With that said, let's move on to the next chapter in which I will analyze the most destructive of these lifestyles, the Lifestyle of Failure.

Key points from this chapter:

- Success means many things to many people. In this book, I'm primarily talking about financial success.
- Don't rely on the 40-50-40 plan of life where you work 40 hours a week, 50 weeks a year, for 40 years and end up with only Social Security on which to retire.
- Begin developing goals that will give you a passion for accomplishment.
- The lifestyle of success requires limiting your spending during your earning years so you can build investments that will produce money for which you don't have to work later in life.
- Functional retirement doesn't mean that you have to quit working. You may work with more passion and vigor than ever before because it means you can do what you want to do, rather than having to do what someone else expects you to do.
- Even if you are struggling financially, you can still save a little for investments by adjusting your lifestyle.
- The amount you save is not as important as developing the habit of saving.
- In the beginning, focus on both spending cuts and increasing earning.
- Begin developing the three Ds of success: the Desire for a better life that is strong enough to keep you inspired, the Discipline to take the

steps necessary to achieve success, and the Dedication to stick with it until you succeed.

- Don't think of wealth and happiness as being mutually exclusive . . . they aren't!

3

The Lifestyle of Failure

It goes without saying that no one sets out in life to be a failure. Think back to all those dreams you had as a child about growing up and one day becoming a prosperous adult. Sure, back in elementary school we all had thoughts like that, even those of us who grew up dirt poor. We knew that when we grew up and got out on our own we would get a good job, find our niche in life, and be successful. Then about the time we entered middle school, we started looking around and saw that many adults weren't living that dream. Maybe it was even our own parents who were struggling. I remember times as a child when I wanted a second glass of milk at dinner only to be told one was enough. If I wanted more, I could drink water. Our grocery budget was very limited; we had to make it stretch. When we couldn't afford fresh milk, we had to settle for mixing water with powdered milk and drink that.

By the time I got to high school and knew it wouldn't be long before I had to face the world, it would have been easy to start collecting excuses; companies were downsizing rather than hiring, jobs were going overseas, prices were going up faster than wages, and the only good jobs required a college degree and college was just too expensive.

This dose of reality brought many reactions. Some young friends of mine with bleak outlooks on the future turned to drugs and alcohol to mask their fears and cover up perceived inadequacies. Others quit school and got a menial job so they could buy cars or chase the latest fads. Even those who finished high school and went on to college were bombarded with credit card offers and the lure of easy money. The sad part about all of these things is that they unknowingly start many young people down a road destined to lead to a Lifestyle of Failure.

In the last chapter, I graphed the Lifestyle of Success and explained how it worked. Now let's do the same with the Lifestyle of Failure.

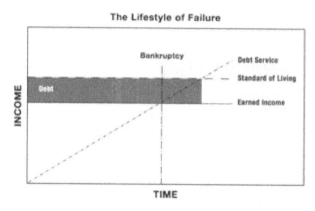

Fig. 3

If you go back and review the graph in Figure 2 and compare it with the one above, you will notice that they look very much alike. Both have a spread between earned income and standard of living, and what is done with the difference between the two creates a diagonal line here just as it did in the Lifestyle of Success graph.

Although the graphs look the same, the difference is huge. Instead of the gap between earned income and standard of living being income to invest, in Figure 3 it represents debt. Instead of the diagonal line representing a growing stream of unearned income, here it represents the increasing burden of debt service. And most importantly, instead of the point where the diagonal line intersects the earned income line representing functional retirement, here it represents bankruptcy or the point at which you can no longer make the payments on your debts.

As I said in the beginning, no one sets out to become a failure in life, so how do so many people get themselves into this pattern of overspending that leads to a Lifestyle of Failure? Well, believe it or not, it's easy, and credit cards are one of the major contributors. Do you realize that each time you charge more to a credit card than you can pay off at the end of the month, you lower your standard of living for the next month and each month thereafter until it is paid? Let me give you an example.

Assume that you earn $3,000 per month and are living a lifestyle that takes it all. If one month you spend an extra $1,000 and put it on your credit card, not only do you not have the money to pay it off at the end of the month, but in order to make the minimum payment, you have to give up something you have been accustomed to buying with your $3,000 or start charging that too. Let's assume that the minimum payment is 2% of the outstanding balance, which would be only $20. If you're like most people, whatever you were buying with this $20, you don't do without it; you just charge it on the credit card. No big deal, right? Well, let's see.

At this point, you think, "No big deal!" I paid off $20 and charged $20, so I'm even. Wrong! If the interest rate on the card is 18%, $15 of the payment went to the bank to cover the interest they charged for the use of their money. That means that you only paid the balance down by $5, but you charged $20. You're not even, because now your outstanding balance has grown to $1,015.

Let's assume that the next month you do the same thing and pay the minimum payment, but in order to continue enjoying your same standard of living, you once again charge an amount equal to the minimum payment back to the credit card so you don't have to give up anything. This time the payment is $20.30 with $15.22 going to interest, and only $5.08 being applied to the outstanding debt. After making this payment, your balance has now risen to $1,030.22, and in just two months, you have paid out $30.22 for which you have received absolutely nothing. If you continue this same scenario for just one year, making the minimum payments and charging back the same amount so you could maintain the same standard of living, you will pay payments of more than $260 and your balance will go up to nearly $1,200. Do this for another year, and you will pay out an additional $312 and end up owing $1,430. The sad part is, in just two years you will have paid out over $570 and your debt will have increased by $430, all because you overspent by $1,000 one month and weren't willing to reduce your standard of living until you could pay it back. Not only will you have gotten nothing for the $570 you've paid out, your minimum payment will have grown from the original $20 to more than $28.

The reason I say credit card debt lowers your standard of living is because it's not until you decide to start doing without some of the things you are accustomed to having and stop charging them back to the card that the balance begins to go down. What's really scary is the fact that if you never added another charge after the initial $1,000 and continue to pay $20 per month, you will have to do without whatever you were buying with this $20 for nearly eight years before the debt will be paid off. Many people never figure this out and continue to sink deeper and deeper in debt.

In the above example, I'm only talking about $1,000 in credit card charges. I know people with $10,000, $20,000, $30,000, and more outstanding on their credit cards, and they still can't understand why they are struggling to keep their heads above water. Unfortunately, these are the same people who continue to make the minimum payments month after month and keep charging more. Imagine how depressing it must be to work hard all month and then have to shell out $400, $500, $600, or more of your hard-earned money to make credit card payments for which you get nothing?

Many people continue to charge until they are unable to keep making the payments and are forced to file bankruptcy. The really sad part is that after bankruptcy clears their debts, they often find themselves right back in the same dilemma within a few years. In spite of ruining their credit and losing nearly everything they owned, some people still haven't learned to adjust their spending in order to live within their means.

Others think they are solving the problem by getting a debt consolidation loan. As my friend Jim Rohn says, "A debt consolidation loan is when you take several very hard-to-make payments and convert them into one impossible-to-make payment."

The problem of debt service eating into lifestyle is not restricted to poor people. During the recent real estate boom, millions of people refinanced their homes to get cash. Even after refinancing with a new first mortgage, they piled on additional debt with home equity loans or home equity lines of credit. At the peak of the boom, people were treating their homes like an ATM machine.

When the crash finally hit, many people were devastated. Caught in the throes of the worst recession since The Great Depression, millions lost their jobs and found themselves buried in debt they couldn't repay. Foreclosures exploded, and real estate values plummeted. Homeowners who thought they were rich when the money spigots were wide open had their dreams shattered when they lost their homes.

Refinancing real estate to raise capital to invest in additional income-producing ventures is fine, but doing it just to get spending money is foolish. Pulling cash out of your investments to pay for consumable items would be comparable to a farmer eating his seed corn.

The problem is not confined to young people who are just getting started, either. I received an email from a gentleman in his 40s asking for some advice on purchasing a real estate investment. In his email he remarked that his income was approximately $100,000 annually, his credit scores were good, but that he had over $50,000 in credit card debt. My response to him was to suggest that he get rid of the credit card debt before doing anything else. There are few investments that will provide a better return and solidify your credit rating more than paying off credit card debt.

I use this credit card example to illustrate the destructive effects of consumer debt. That's debt, other than a home mortgage, that you have to pay from your earnings. Many people, especially young people in college, become ensnared in the trap laid by credit card companies while they are still in school. From the day they arrive on campus, they are bombarded with credit card solicitations that offer the lure of easy money.

To many college freshmen, probably away from home for the first time, these credit card offers are their first experience with credit. Suddenly, they are in college, dreaming of the high-paying jobs they will have when they graduate, and these dreams are solidified by the fact that they are now being offered credit, not by one bank, but by several. They think, wow! It can't get much better than that.

When I was a young man just getting started in life, I mistakenly thought that the more credit cards I had the better my credit rating would be. Although I was smart enough not to run up big balances on them, at one point I had more than 60 cards. They included everything from bank cards to department store cards, oil company cards, and others. I thought it was cool to pull out my wallet and have this long string of credit cards drop out in plastic sleeves. I soon learned that the availability of all that unsecured credit hurt rather than helped my ability to obtain credit for important things like real estate investments. Today, I use two bank cards exclusively, one for business-related purchases and one for personal items; but most importantly, I don't use them as credit cards, I use them as convenience cards, which means I pay them in full each month. It gives me the convenience of having to write only one check instead of many.

As I researched this problem, I was continuously amazed at the number of college students and other young people who, like me in my early years, had six, eight, 10, or more credit cards. I found one young man who at age 23 proudly showed me his 53 credit cards. I was also amazed at how quickly they learn to borrow from one card to make the payment on another when they find money a little tight, which is most of the time for college students.

When I talk with students, I find that few of them express much concern about running up their credit card balances. The standard response I frequently hear is, "Yeah, I know it's bad, but as soon as I finish school and get a job, the first thing I'm going to do is pay off my credit cards." Their intentions are good, but the problem is, just when they think they will be ready to start paying off these debts, they are hit with the realities of life. Suddenly they have rent to pay; groceries, clothes, furniture, cars, insurance and other things to buy, and the regular monthly expenses of electricity, telephone, water, cable TV, Internet, and more kick in. In addition to all of these expenses, many also have student loans to repay. The fact is, paying off debts accrued while still in school isn't as easy as they thought it would be. They often find that what they thought were a few minor credit card bills have ensnared them in a trap of revolving consumer debt that takes years to repay.

While discussing this phenomenon with my friend Michael LeBoeuf, PhD, author of *The Millionaire in You,* he made an interesting point. He said, "Times have really changed since my college days. I remember that first day when I was registering for school; it seemed that everywhere I turned, there were attractive young ladies with sandwich board signs hanging across their shoulders advertising the brand of cigarettes of which they were passing out samples. If the tobacco companies were to try that today, they would be hit with lawsuits and tossed off campus. What I can't understand is why no one seems to equate the way credit card companies are hooking young people on debt with the way tobacco companies tried to hook them on cigarettes 40 years ago. Just go on any college campus on orientation day and look at the banks soliciting young people to open accounts with them and to apply for their credit cards."

But, it's not just college students that get strapped with consumer debt; even kids still in high school fall victim. For them, the culprit is most often car loans. Sure, it's all young people's dream to get their first car and have the freedom that comes with mobility. But once again, their wants are often greater than their ability to pay. As I like to say, they have Champagne taste on a beer budget. Many times, high school students actually drop out of school in order to get a job so they can make payments on a car. In fact, if you discuss this subject with high school principals, they will tell you that buying a car is one of the biggest reasons that kids drop out of school. I know a bit about school dropouts. (My son Jason is the author of *Be Cool, Stay in School.* He founded the "Be School, Stay in School" program that earned him a citation presented by President Clinton in the oval office of the White House for his work in encouraging high school students to stay in school and graduate.)

If they are able to keep up the car payments, these youngsters also become targets of the credit card companies. The fact that they are responsibly handling the loan on a vehicle makes them a prime target for more credit. This often results in their getting sucked into the same vicious debt spiral in which many college students find themselves.

Back in the 1970s when the age for legal responsibility was lowered from 21 to 18, young people hailed it as a great victory for their generation. "If we're old enough to die in Vietnam for our country, we should be treated as adults," they would cry. Guess who was behind that change? The big banks! Before lowering the age that young people could be held legally responsible for their debts, people in that age bracket could default on huge debts and the banks had no legal recourse against them. It wasn't the triumph young people thought it was; it was in fact a windfall for the banks.

No one starts out to be a financial failure, just as no one sets out to become a drug addict. It just grows on them little by little, bit by bit, until the hold becomes so tight it takes professional help and a strong will to break the addiction. Why do we as a society allow this to happen? Could it be that credit has become so universally accepted that we no longer teach children how destructive it can be?

Granted, not everyone gets caught so deeply in the financial quagmire I have just discussed that it leads them to bankruptcy; in reality, only a few do. I don't have any hard facts to back up this statement, but I believe that only 3 to 5 percent of the people in America actually enjoy the Lifestyle of Success I outlined in the last chapter. I also believe that only a similar percentage suffers the disgrace of the Lifestyle of Failure I have discussed in this chapter. If that's the case, what happens to the other 90-plus percent of the population? That's a good question, and to answer it, let's move on to the next chapter where I will discuss the lifestyle I believe most people follow: I call it the Lifestyle of Ordinary.

Key points from this chapter:

- When we are young, we all dream of becoming wealthy, but those dreams can be easily hijacked by growing consumer debt as we mature.

- Using a credit card instead of paying cash is so easy to do, but it can cost you dearly if you use it to make purchases you can't repay when the next statement comes due.

- Don't refinance your property to get spending money. Only do it to raise more capital to invest.

- Paying down credit card debt is one of the best investments you can make. Paying off balances on which you are being charged 18% interest or more, is the same as making an investment that earns an 18% return.

- Students should be counseled about the dangers of easy credit before they are sent off to college.

26

- Credit cards can get students hooked on debt the way that tobacco companies used to get them hooked on cigarettes.

4

The Lifestyle of Ordinary

Ah, the Lifestyle of Ordinary: how should I describe it? Safe, secure, dependable, steady, stable, reliable, responsible, conscientious, trustworthy, sensible, and mature, or should I just sum it all up and call it ORDINARY. This is the lifestyle most people live. "So, what's wrong with that," you ask? Nothing, if you're content to be ordinary, work all your life, and then draw your Social Security or company retirement. But, if you want to achieve financial independence, you have to understand the differences between the Lifestyle of Success and the Lifestyle of Ordinary. The vast majority of people living the Lifestyle of Ordinary actually think they are living the Lifestyle of Success. They pay their bills on time, their credit is good, and they can show you bank and investment accounts to support their claim. So, what's the difference?

Remember back in Chapter 2 when I talked about the 40-50-40 plan of life? These are people who work 40 hours a week, 50 weeks a year for 40 years, and end up with little more to show for it than a worn-out body and a Social Security check? These are the people living the Lifestyle of Ordinary. All those adjectives I used in the first sentence of this chapter describe this plan pretty well. The people living this lifestyle are the solid citizens who work hard and handle their affairs impeccably but just can't seem to get a break. They are convinced they are doing everything right, but for some reason their ship never seems to come in. Although they live within their means, have investment accounts, IRAs, 401ks, and all the trappings of the Lifestyle of Success, they just can't seem to make it to the good life that comes with financial independence. Why? What do they do that keeps them from reaching this goal? That's what this chapter is about.

Just as I did in the previous two chapters, I can graph the Lifestyle of Ordinary. Figure 4 below shows the overall behavior of people living this lifestyle. I will explain this in detail, and then later in the chapter I will show you how those who enjoy the Lifestyle of Success avoid the missteps made by average people.

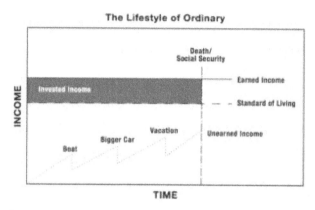

Fig. 4

Once again, the vertical axis represents income and the horizontal axis represents time. In this example, you can see that people living the Lifestyle of Ordinary live a standard of living below their earned income and invest the difference. Just as with the Lifestyle of Success, this creates a diagonal line representing unearned income. So far so good!

The unearned income line is growing, just as it should, but then it takes a dip labeled "boat." This happens when Mr. Ordinary discovers that he can pay his bills on time and has money in the bank, so he decides he can afford to buy a new boat. Problem is, he dips into the funds he's investing for financial independence to pay for the boat. This reduces his investments and causes his unearned income to take a dip also, but he still has money in the bank and everything seems fine. More time passes, his investments continue to grow, and he continues to pay his bills in a timely fashion, so he feels he has earned the right to have a bigger, more expensive car. Once again, he dips into his invested funds to buy the car, investments drop, and unearned income takes another dip.

My good friend Roger Dawson recalls a neighbor who asked him to show him how to get started investing in rental properties. Roger showed him how to buy his first house. A few months later he was talking about buying a second house and kicking his investment program into second gear. Roger and his son drove by the neighbor's house one day, and he was in his front yard hosing down a huge motor home. "Why would you buy this?" Roger asked him. "You were doing so well investing." His neighbor told him, "I really wanted to buy that second home, but I saw this motor home, and I wanted it even more!" As they drove away, Roger's son John, who was six at the time, said, "Now that was dumb!" If a six-year-old can understand the concept, it can't be that hard! As my friend Jim Rohn says, "Don't buy your second car until you've bought your second piece of real estate. Because cars go down in value, while real estate goes up."

This same scenario plays out over and over again in Mr. Ordinary's life. If it's not a boat or bigger car, it's a vacation, bigger house, country club membership, airplane, vacation home, you name it. As this continues, Mr. Ordinary is viewed as a prominent member of the community, a person of means, and one who lives life to the fullest. He likes this newfound feeling of importance, which makes it easier to continue his behavior. It's not until the latter stages of his working career that he looks at his situation and realizes that death or Social Security is going to precede financial independence. Not a very pleasant realization!

Yes, Mr. Ordinary has some unearned income to supplement his retirement, but not enough, even with Social Security added, to sustain the lifestyle he has been accustomed to living. Now he starts making excuses. He says to himself, "I'm retired now, and I really don't need this big a house anymore," so he downsizes. He says, "I'm not working anymore, so I don't really need three cars," so he sells two. And so it goes, as his lifestyle shrinks to fit his meager retirement income.

Believe it or not, those who develop the discipline to live the Lifestyle of Success actually get to do more in retirement than they did during their working years and often get to retire much earlier than Mr. Ordinary, and you know why? Because they learned the secret of the Lifestyle of Success, and yes, I can show this secret on a graph too.

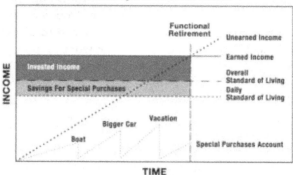

Fig. 5

When you see it on a graph, it's pretty simple, isn't it? The secret is to segregate your funds and understand that your standard of living is made up of two parts. One is the daily standard of living or what it takes to live from week to week, things like groceries, utilities, rent or house payments, gasoline, and other regularly occurring expenses. The other is your overall standard of living, which includes those large periodic purchases and annual expenses that are in addition to day-to-day living costs. Mr. Ordinary fails to plan for this second part and has to dip into retirement funds for the bigger purchases.

In Figure 5, you can see that with the exception of the special purchases account, it is the same as the graph of the Lifestyle of Success in Figure 1. The difference is, understanding how big purchases fit into your overall standard of living. Standard of living is what it costs you to live today. If you live in a big house, drive a fancy car, have a boat or airplane, the cost of all of these amenities figures into your overall standard of living and has to be paid for from your earned income before you can set aside money to invest to achieve financial independence.

About now, you're probably thinking, "How can I have the things I want and still plan for financial independence?" It's called patience, and with few exceptions, patience means saving for these purchases instead of going out and financing them. It requires setting up separate accounts to accumulate money for the large purchases and another in which to invest funds that will ultimately produce the unearned income required to achieve financial independence. One guides you in determining when to buy that new car, take that expensive vacation, and buy the boat you want or make any of the other large expenditures that improve your standard of living today. The investment account is off-limits. You don't touch it except in a dire emergency!

To do this, you have to become a master at deferred gratification! Let's face it; most people live in an "I want it now" society. A now-defunct department store, Montgomery Ward, used to have the slogan: Want it! Charge it! Easy credit was the way they built their markets. Not only were they making 18% interest on charge accounts, they were building a mailing list of people who could walk into their stores and say: Charge it! This massive effort to get people to go into debt eventually was slowed by the federal government's putting some brakes on it when it passed a law that said if you're going to offer credit, you must make the terms of the credit clear in your advertisements.

Deferred gratification means training yourself to think, I want it, but I don't need it now. Thinking this way isn't easy because American marketers are masters at getting us to want stuff that we don't need. That almost sank the US auto industry in the 1970s. The industry became so good at marketing cars that companies didn't have to build good cars anymore. Americans would buy anything. General Motors could say to their advertising agency, "Can we stick a Cadillac emblem on a Buick and call it a Cadillac?" Sure, the geniuses on Madison Avenue would tell them; we can sell that! The problem was that the Japanese were making better and more reliable automobiles and holding prices down. Soon they offered a much better value, and they were selling us what WE wanted to buy, not what Madison Avenue wanted to sell us. In spite of all their efforts, easy credit, followed by a collapsing economy, destined General Motors and Chrysler to accept massive government bailouts to stay afloat.

No question about it, we are bombarded daily by advertisements crafted by experts in getting us to spend money. Delayed gratification is not easy, but here are a few suggestions that might help:

- Don't be tempted by TV commercials, even if you have to get a TiVo device or record programs on your VCR so that you can fast-forward through them.

- Skip the advertisements in magazines and newspapers by turning the pages to avoid them.

- Don't make going to the mall your recreational activity. Read a book, climb a hill, or take a walk in the woods instead.

- Avoid expensive restaurants. A BBQ in the back yard with friends and family can give you just as much enjoyment and cost a lot less.

- Make a game of walking through stores like Walmart and saying to yourself, "Look at all the stuff in here that I don't need!"

- Develop a habit of saving for big purchases. Feel the excitement and anticipation of watching your savings grow closer and closer to the amount you will need to pay cash for the purchases.

Delaying gratification is hard work at times, but if you make a hard-and-fast rule that you're not going to dip into your investment savings, no matter how strong the urge, you will be rewarded handsomely in the long run.

Notice how the line for the Special Purchases Account in Figure 5 goes up and down and up and down without having any effect on the Unearned Income line. Money accumulates in this account until there is enough to buy that boat you want, and then when the purchase is made, the account drops down. The same holds true for the car purchase and the vacation and will continue to do so with any other major expenditure. At least that's the way it works for people who are truly living the Lifestyle of Success.

Let's look at the role patience plays in building financial independence. Would you believe that you can drive a Chevrolet or a Cadillac for the same money? That's right! You read correctly! You can drive a Chevrolet or a Cadillac for the same amount of earned income. Want to know how? Well, look at the chart in Figure 6 below.

Chevrolet or Cadillac? The Power of Patience!

A $22,000 Chevrolet Financed for 60 Months at 10% Interest				The same payment invested at 8%		
Month	Payment	Principal	Interest	Balance	Investment	Interest	Balance
1.	$ 467.43	$ 284.10	$ 183.33	$21,715.90	$ 467.43	$ 3.12	$ 470.55
2.	$ 467.43	$ 286.46	$ 180.97	$21,429.44	$ 467.43	$ 6.25	$ 944.23
3.	$ 467.43	$ 288.85	$ 178.58	$21,140.59	$ 467.43	$ 9.41	$ 1,421.07
4.	$ 467.43	$ 291.26	$ 176.17	$20,849.33	$ 467.43	$ 12.59	$ 1,901.09
5.	$ 467.43	$ 293.69	$ 173.74	$20,555.64	$ 467.43	$ 15.79	$ 2,384.31
6.	$ 467.43	$ 296.13	$ 171.30	$20,259.51	$ 467.43	$ 19.01	$ 2,870.75
7.	$ 467.43	$ 298.60	$ 168.83	$19,960.91	$ 467.43	$ 22.25	$ 3,360.44
8.	$ 467.43	$ 301.09	$ 166.34	$19,659.82	$ 467.43	$ 25.52	$ 3,853.39
9.	$ 467.43	$ 303.60	$ 163.83	$19,356.22	$ 467.43	$ 28.81	$ 4,349.62
10.	$ 467.43	$ 306.13	$ 161.83	$19,050.09	$ 467.43	$ 32.11	$ 4,849.16
11.	$ 467.43	$ 308.68	$ 158.75	$18,741.41	$ 467.43	$ 35.44	$ 5,352.04
12.	$ 467.43	$ 311.25	$ 156.18	$18,430.16	$ 467.43	$ 38.80	$ 5,858.27
24.	$5,609.16	$3,943.65	$1,665.51	$14,486.51	$5,609.16	$ 735.34	$12,202.76
36.	$5,609.16	$4,356.61	$1,252.55	$10,129.90	$5,609.16	$1,261.93	$19,073.85
48.	$5,609.16	$4,812.82	$ 796.34	$ 1,252.55	$5,609.16	$1,832.24	$26,515.24
60.	$5,609.16	$5,317.08	$ 292.08	$ -0-	$5,609.16	$2,449.85	$34,574.26

Fig. 6

This chart is divided into two sections. I'll refer to the left side of the chart as Mr. Ordinary and the right side as Mr. Financial Independence. Mr. Ordinary buys a $22,000 Chevrolet and finances it at 10% annual interest for 60 months. (I know, you're thinking that you can finance a new car at 0% interest; but if that were really the case, why would car dealers offer you the option of 0% financing or a large "cash back bonus"? The reason is simple; the price of the vehicle is inflated to include the interest you aren't being charged when you finance at 0%, but if you pay cash, they will give it back to you.) Anyway, I'd prefer to be upfront about it and show you that Mr. Ordinary's payments are $467.43 per month for 60 months, which includes interest.

Mr. Ordinary's side of the chart shows the monthly breakdown of each payment during the first year, the portion that goes to reduce the loan balance (principal) and the amount that is interest. As you can see, the balance declines after each payment only by the amount of the principal portion of the payment. The amounts shown opposite 24, 36, 48, and 60 months are the cumulative totals at the end of years 2, 3, 4, and 5. Each year Mr. Ordinary has to take 12 x $467.43 or $5,609.16 from his earned income to make the payments.

The right side of the chart shows what Mr. Financial Independence does with his money. Like Mr. Ordinary, he takes the same $467.43 per month, $5,609.16 per year from his earned income, but rather than making payments on a car, he invests the money. In this example, he earns an 8% return on his investments and leaves the interest he earns in the account to compound and grow. This is the money that shows up in the Special Purchases Account on Figure 5.

So, here we have two people, both of whom have committed $467.43 per month of their earned income, but at the end of 60 months, what does each have? Mr. Ordinary has a five-year-old worn out Chevrolet and no money and will probably have to repeat the process over and over throughout his life. Mr. Financial Independence has $34,574.26 and could go pay cash for a new Cadillac if he so desired. Big difference! If you look at what each got for the effort it took to earn $467.43 per month for five years, the difference is staggering. Mr. Ordinary got a $22,000 automobile that started dropping in value the minute he drove it off the lot. Mr. Financial Independence started earning income from the very beginning and continued to do so for the entire five years. As a result, if he chose to buy a new car, he could get a $12,574.26 more expensive car than Mr. Ordinary for the same effort. That $12,574.26 difference is the price of impatience, a price that Mr. Ordinary rarely ever figures out, which is a big reason he remains ordinary. Think of it this way, the interest paid on a car loan is actually an increase in the price of the car. The interest earned while saving to buy a car becomes a discount on the price of the vehicle. Unfortunately, most ordinary Americans pay enough in interest and finance charges over their lifetimes to become millionaires if they had the discipline to save first and then spend, but that's not how they think. Sadly, the mantra in America, from the individual all the way up to the federal government, seems to be "BUY NOW; PAY LATER."

But, you say, "What did Mr. Financial Independence drive while he was investing his $467.43 per month?" The answer is simple; he bought as cheap a used car as he could get and drove it while he was putting himself in a position where he could drive a nice car for the rest of his life, without ever having to pay interest. Once he buys the new car and pays cash for it, all he has to do is keep making the same payment to his special purchases account and let it earn interest until he accumulates enough cash to trade cars and once again pay cash for the purchase. The interesting thing is, Mr. financial Independence doesn't have to wait nearly as long to get the next new car, because with the trade-in value of the car he owns debt-free, it doesn't take as much cash to make his next purchase as it did the first one. Because Mr. Ordinary chose to drive a nicer car in the beginning than Mr. Financial Independence, he unknowingly locked himself into a cycle of financing car after car for the rest of his life, a cycle he will probably repeat with every major purchase he will make during his lifetime.

Remember when I asked you in the beginning of Chapter 2 why you see neighbors living side-by-side, both earning the same income, yet one has a lovely well maintained home, nice clothing, new cars, and all the trappings of success, while the other lives in a house that needs painting, wears hand-me-down clothing, drives an old clunker, and is always broke? Could it be the price one is paying due to impatience? Think about it! The combination of interest paid for the use of a lender's money to finance large purchases, coupled with the lost income that could be earned by saving for them, is what makes the difference. I'm not saying that interest paid on consumer debt is the only difference between the Lifestyle of Success and the Lifestyle of Ordinary, because other factors, including lack of planning and impulse buying play big roles as well. But for Mr. Ordinary, there are few things that hinder his ability to achieve financial independence as much as interest on consumer debt, especially when it consumes large portions of his earnings without buying him anything.

Now that I've defined the different lifestyles that people follow, I want you to develop success thinking. The next step is to define *wealth* as I use the term. In the next chapter, I'll go into detail on this subject and share what I feel really constitutes wealth. I'll explain why so many people don't understand the concept of wealth and how this misunderstanding distorts their view of success.

Key points from this chapter:

- Ordinary people live well and pay their bills, but that doesn't mean they're building wealth or will ever be financially independent.

- Dipping into retirement savings to make major purchases is a sure way to lose the compounding effect that builds wealth and ultimate financial freedom.

- Segregate retirement investment funds from savings for large purchases, and have the discipline to keep them separate.

- Deferred gratification could allow you to drive a Cadillac for the same money ordinary people spend on a Chevrolet.

- Saving and paying cash for a new car puts you in position to earn interest instead of paying interest on car purchases for the rest of your life.

- Train yourself to resist temptation. A good way to start this training is by saying, "Look at all this stuff I don't need," when you browse through stores.

5

Wealth Defined

Ask 100 people to define wealth, and you'll probably get 100 different definitions. It seems that wealth means something different to everyone. To some, wealth is having good friends and being well liked; to others it is close family ties; to still others it is a loving relationship, good health, education, or the feeling of being appreciated. One might say that wealth is having an abundance of whatever is important to you. I won't argue or disagree with any of these definitions, but since this book deals with achieving financial independence, I feel I should define wealth as it relates to your financial condition.

One reason so many people think of wealth in subjective terms is because to most people, the idea of becoming a millionaire is so far beyond their imagination that it seems like a dream. Why? Could it be because they have been conditioned by society to think in terms of "earning" a living? When they sit down with a calculator and figure out that they would have to "earn" $12.50 per hour, 40 hours per week, 50 weeks per year, for 40 years just to "earn" one million dollars, they see the goal of becoming a millionaire as impossible. Unfortunately, many working people don't earn $12.50 per hour on their jobs, and that's before taxes. When they have to pay living expenses from what's left over after taxes, they struggle just to exist.

Even people who make $40–$50 per hour find that becoming a millionaire is a daunting task. Although this seems like a good wage, after it is reduced by taxes, they would still have to set aside more than 30 percent of their income to save $12.50 per hour. Practically no one is willing to do this, which is why so many people define wealth in subjective terms that have nothing to do with money. They simply don't believe it is possible for them to become wealthy financially, so they define wealth in other ways that can't be measured. But, for those who want to reach financial independence, wealth must be measured in terms of money or the monetary equivalent of assets that generate money, in other words, things that can sustain and improve your standard of living.

When I talk about wealth and money, a lot of people get nervous because they view money as the root of all evil. Perhaps that's based on biblical teachings. A few years back, I was in downtown Asheville, North Carolina, where I live, when I came upon a street preacher who had drawn a sizable crowd in a downtown park. The preacher was pounding his bible and shouting at the top of his lungs as he extolled the virtues of being poor. I stopped for a few minutes to listen to his sermon, which he closed with the quote, "It's easier for a camel to pass through the eye of a needle than it is for a rich man to enter the kingdom of heaven." With messages like this being delivered in the name of God, no wonder many people have negative thoughts about money. Money is not the problem; it's what some people do in pursuit of money or do with money after they get it that causes problems. Money is not the root of all evil; it is just a tool, a common means of exchange. For banks, money is their inventory, just as shoes are to a shoe store. They buy money wholesale (what they pay depositors) and sell it at retail (the interest they charge on loans). It is the greed, laziness, deceit, fraud, corruption, cheating, trickery, and other human flaws that lead to dishonest quests for money that causes problems.

Before the advent of money, the common means of exchange was barter. People would trade labor or something they could grow or produce directly with others who had what they needed. (They might trade vegetables they grew in their garden for milk, butter, and cheese produced by a dairy farmer.) The problem with barter was that people who had what you needed may not need what you had to trade, so eventually humans devised a monetary system whereby every product or service could have a value as measured in some form of currency. In more primitive times things like beads, feathers, precious metals, or stones were used as a common means of exchange. Today, this common means of exchange is money, which is generally defined as currencies issued by the various governing bodies of the world.

Building wealth is not about working for money; it's about money working for you. Wealth is not measured by what you own; it's measured by the degree at which what you own can enrich your life. In other words, wealth is an income stream, an income stream for which you don't have to work. You may think you want to be a millionaire, but being worth a million dollars is far less important than the income a million dollars can generate. Let me give you an example.

Suppose you have a million dollars' worth of gold locked in a safe deposit box at your bank. Technically you are a millionaire, but what is the gold doing to enrich your life? Suppose you took the gold out of the vault, turned it into money, and used the money to buy ten $100,000 homes that would rent for $1,000 per month each. Now you would still be worth a million dollars, but the million dollars would be generating $10,000 income per month, every month for the foreseeable future, an income that would grow as inflation pushed prices up. In this scenario, can you see how your invested money could enrich your life every month without depleting your million dollars? On the other hand, if you kept the gold locked in the vault, inflation would gradually erode its buying power, and other than the satisfaction of knowing you had it, the million dollars would not enrich your life at all.

When I speak to audiences, especially young people, the first thing I ask them is to define wealth. I get every answer imaginable, but I get almost unanimous agreement that people who have the visible trappings of wealth are perceived as being wealthy. Then I give my definition of wealth, which goes like this:

Wealth is not the big house in which you live.

Wealth is not the luxurious car you drive.

Wealth is not the expensive clothes you wear.

Wealth is not the exclusive country club to which you belong.

Wealth is not your boat or plane.

Many people have all of these, but that doesn't mean they're wealthy. It only means that they have a good income. The question is, is their income earned or unearned?

I define wealth as whether or not you can maintain your standard of living if you suddenly are no longer able to work and earn money. In other words, wealth is an income stream for which you don't have to work, income from your investments. Those living a modest lifestyle that the income from their investments will support are wealthier than those living a lavish lifestyle they can't sustain if they suddenly lose their job. I've known people who were flying high financially but crashed and burned in a couple of months after losing their income. Let me give you a couple of contrasting examples.

Early in my business career, I was in the sign business. One of my clients was a man named John who owned a popular restaurant. John drove a new Cadillac, lived in a beautiful home, and had a ranch where he raised show horses. His child attended an expensive private school. John owned a big motor home and had all the appearances of being wealthy. He rented signs from me to advertise his restaurant. He was one of my best customers and always paid his invoices promptly. Eventually, we developed a personal friendship that led to our taking hunting and fishing trips together.

John had been in business just a few short years longer than I had, yet he seemed to have everything he wanted, while I was struggling to keep my doors open. When we took trips together, John always had a big roll of cash in his pocket and made it a point to let me know how well he was doing financially. I always paid my share, but I didn't have money to spend frivolously the way John seemed to have. I liked spending time with John because I was very impressed, and, if the truth be known, was even somewhat envious of John's success. I hoped I could learn from John and that some of his good fortune would rub off on me.

Several years passed in which I struggled and pinched pennies in order to put money back into my business to make it grow. I never seemed to have any excess money to blow. All the while, John seemed to be on a roll. He bought a new Cadillac every couple of years, traded up to bigger and more elaborate motor homes, and even opened a second restaurant. It seemed he could do no wrong. He was obviously earning a very nice income.

Then one day I received a phone call. My friend John had been taken to the hospital, suffering dizziness and a headache. As soon as I received the call, I went to the hospital, but by the time I arrived, the doctors had already sent John to intensive care. He had suffered a massive brain aneurism and his outlook was doubtful. John was only 48 years old and had a wife and small child. Tragically, he failed to make it through that night, and his death set in motion a heartbreaking turn of events that had a lasting impact on me.

When news of John's passing broke, talk seemed to center around the fact that he had been so successful financially but had not lived long enough to enjoy his success. Some even commented that all he thought about was making money. Visitors at the funeral home and attendees at his funeral were united in their expression of sympathy to his family, and all commented that at least his financial success would ensure that they would be cared for after his death. But, as the days passed following his funeral, John's darkest secrets began to surface. He had spent everything he made as he went through life, and in death he left his family penniless and in debt.

His family ended up having to sell the restaurants, the ranch, the motor home, the Cadillac, and the family home. Even the life insurance they thought he had carried had been cancelled. For me this was not a lesson in greed, corruption, or any of the other human flaws that lead to unscrupulous quests for money. John was a man who earned his money honestly and paid his debts timely; he just failed to plan for the future. This is a characteristic that keeps average people average, and discovering it provided me with a lesson I never forgot and a lesson that played a big part in changing the way I thought about wealth.

Throughout our friendship, John always spent more than I did, but that was because he was spending everything he had. I just didn't know that at the time. On the other hand, I was more frugal and continued to invest part of my money into assets that would provide income for the future. That meant I did without some of the things John was buying, but my assets and income were steadily growing. In the beginning, I was investing in the construction of billboard signs to rent, but my accountant eventually advised me to diversify my investments, so I began to invest in rental real estate. I made it a point to reinvest at least 20 percent of my income into assets that would produce passive income, income for which I didn't have to work. John never enjoyed any passive income and was constantly under pressure to earn more to support his lifestyle.

The shock of learning that John had left his family in a desperate state of affairs strengthened my view of how important it is to plan for the future. Although I was still a young man, I believed that living well at the moment was important, but I also understood that unless I planned for the future, my family wouldn't be cared for if something should happen to me. Or, I might not be able to live comfortably if I should live to a ripe old age. I also wouldn't be able to enjoy the peace of mind I would need to be happy in life. This kept me investing 20 percent and more of my earned income into my business, plus investing a few hours each week of my spare time trying to find and structure real estate deals that would add to my passive income. Real estate soon became my investment of choice. While I know it quite well, it is only one of many ways to invest. There are many other investments that produce passive income as well.

Let me share one important step I learned. From the beginning, I set up a special bank account into which I deposited all of the income and paid all of the expenses from my rental properties. Starting out, this account contained very little money because the new purchases I was making had very little cash flow after expenses. Gradually, however, as rents increased and mortgages paid down, funds began to build up in this account. Instead of taking this money out and spending it, I reinvested it in the purchase of additional income-producing properties. Throughout the decade of the 1980s, I continued to look for more deals that I could purchase with little or no money down and continued to reinvest my positive cash flow. I never took any money out of the account while I was doing this. This was my way of building that unearned income line on the graphs in the previous chapters.

In the late 1970s, when I first started investing in real estate, I set an initial goal of having an extra $1,000 per month income. I reached that goal fairly quickly and then set a new goal of $10,000 per month income from my investments. This goal took longer, but it was also achieved within a few years. By now I was not only excited, but was also beginning to understand the power of real estate investing. Even though I was still working a full-time job, I set a new goal to have an extra $100,000 per month coming in. This was a huge goal, but I knew that if I could reach it, I would be able to retire from active work with a standard of living far beyond anything I ever imagined possible when I was a young man.

The decade of the 1990s opened very strongly, with me well on my way to reaching this latest goal, when fate dealt me an unexpected setback. Almost exactly a decade after the death of my friend John, and just days prior to my 44th birthday, I was flying home from Florida in a private plane, when I began experiencing severe pain in my lower abdomen. Fortunately I was not the only pilot onboard, so I insisted on continuing the flight all the way back to Asheville. When we landed, I was suffering such intense pain that my co-pilot friend helped me off the plane and rushed me to the emergency room at a local hospital.

Upon initial examination, the doctors thought I was suffering an attack of kidney stones, but tests proved this not to be the case. For days my condition continued to worsen. The doctors ran test after test and brought in various specialists to try to determine the cause of my problem, but I kept slipping further and further into a state of infirmity. Things were becoming critical as my condition worsened.

Eventually, one of the doctors decided to perform a heart catheterization to determine if my coronary arteries had suffered a blockage. This produced a very traumatic development for my wife. A few years earlier, her father had suffered a massive heart attack and died while having the same test. She became very distraught and refused to allow the test to be performed until she could bring our two young sons, ages five and seven, to visit their father. She felt she was bringing them to say goodbye, and it produced one of the most memorable moments of my life.

When my children arrived, my son Jason, who is known for verbalizing whatever is on his mind, quickly came to the side of my bed and took my forefinger in one little hand and my pinkie finger in the other. As he stood there squeezing my fingers, a big tear came into his eye and he said, "Daddy, are you going to die?" As sick as I was at the time, the sudden impact of this straightforward question from my son forced me to recall how my friend John had left his family in dire financial straits when he was suddenly taken from them.

I turned my head and looked into those innocent little blue eyes filled with tears and told him, "No Buddy, I'm going to be fine." When I said that, my resolve to get well skyrocketed, but I also had the satisfaction of knowing that if I didn't make it, my wife and children would not have to worry about the future. All those years in which I had spent less than I made and invested the difference suddenly became the most important thing I'd ever done. The peace of mind it gave me knowing my family would be financially secure confirmed the decisions I had made over the years. This allowed me to begin my recuperation knowing that they would be able to maintain their standard of living even if I could never work again.

Fortunately, the heart catheterization was uneventful and revealed no problems; however, subsequent tests discovered that I was suffering from a renal infarction. A clot was blocking the flow of blood to my left kidney, and the tissue was dying. With the problem diagnosed, the doctors immediately ordered intravenous anti-coagulation therapy. After several weeks in the hospital, I was finally able to go home and eventually made a full recovery.

The real lesson from this experience came several weeks after I had returned to work. I was in my office when the lead doctor who had cared for me during my nearly three-week hospitalization called. After making the obligatory inquiry as to how I was doing, the doctor asked me if he could take me to lunch one day. I thought this was very unusual, especially since our offices were several miles apart, but I agreed to go, and we scheduled a date.

On the appointed day, my doctor drove to my office, picked me up, and drove us to a nearby Mexican restaurant. As we ate and made small talk, my curiosity nearly got the best of me. I couldn't understand why my doctor wanted to treat me to lunch, but I held my tongue and waited as we talked. Finally, he got to the purpose of the luncheon when he looked up and said, "I'd really like to ask you a question, and if you don't feel comfortable with it, you don't have to answer, but I'm really curious; do you have a strong faith in God?"

Thinking this was somewhat of a bizarre question, I responded with, "Yes, I believe in God, but I'm really curious as to why you would ask."

"Well," replied the doctor, "I've been treating sick people for quite some time, but I've never seen anyone facing the possibility of death deal with it as calmly and self-assured as you did. I just wondered if it was because you had a strong faith and had put your life in God's hands."

As I pondered my doctor's comment, I closed my eyes, looked inward and did some soul-searching. Yes, I had been calm and self-assured throughout my illness, and, yes, I had been aware, especially in those first few days, that I might not pull through, but why? As I sat there searching for an answer, it suddenly hit me. I had no regrets about life up until that point. I opened my eyes, looked at my doctor and said, "I guess the reason I felt the way I did is that there is nothing I have wanted to do in life that I haven't done or was in the process of doing when I got sick. In other words, I feel like I have lived a full life up until this point in time. Sure, I've made mistakes, but I learned from them, and they made me a better person. I also didn't have to worry about my family because I knew they would be provided for if I didn't make it. I guess if I had to be perfectly honest about it, I wouldn't change anything, including getting sick. That tear in my little boy's eye when he asked if I was going to die made getting well mandatory. I didn't want that to be his last memory of me."

No doubt, God had a hand in the outcome, or I would not have been able to sacrifice the pleasures of the day in order to plan and prepare for the future as well as I had. I'd like to think that my full recovery from this serious illness was my reward for doing things right.

Now back to the lesson. Many people believe that wealth is having a good job and a high income. As you can see from these contrasting stories involving my friend John and me, there is big difference between earning a living and building wealth. Perhaps the stress and pressure of trying to maintain his high standard of living may have contributed to John's untimely death. Possibly, the tranquility I enjoyed helped me to recover from my illness and enabled me to watch my sons play sports, finish school, and become outstanding young men. What's not speculation is the fact that the small sacrifices I made by living a more modest standard of living while I was building wealth definitely contributed to the serenity I benefited from during this trying time and that it played a huge part in reassuring me that I was on the right track in life. As for my doctor's question about my faith in God, I think the best way to answer it would be to say that I believe God gave me a good mind and a strong body, but it was up to me to put them to use to the best of my ability.

Key points from this chapter:

- Wealth can be defined in many ways, but for the purposes of this book, I'm going to focus on wealth as measured financially.

- Don't shy away from the goal of becoming wealthy because it may seem like it is impossible to attain.

- Money is not the root of all evil. Evil comes from lowering your ethical and moral standards to get money.

- Wealth is not what you own or the size of your salary; wealth is a passive income stream that will ensure that you can maintain your standard of living if something unforeseen happens to you.

- Learning to live within your means and developing the habit of regularly investing will produce life-changing results.

- Making sacrifices today in order to save and invest for the future can give you the peace and serenity needed to face difficult times.

[6]

How Debt Impacts Your Journey

Has debt got you down? Are you struggling to make all those payments that come due each month? Do you sometimes get the feeling that no matter what you do, you just can't seem to get ahead? Do you hope for a raise so you can use the extra money to work your way out of debt? Or do you feel that the only way to improve your life is to change jobs, move, inherit money, hit the lottery, or find a get-rich-quick scheme that really works? If you responded positively to any of these questions, then you are experiencing the effects of destructive debt. For many people, the mounting pressure of debt creates problems with spouses, significant others, friends or co-workers, or simply drives them crazy.

Destructive debt is a terrible thing. It is debt to acquire items that are consumed prior to being paid for or that go down in value after their acquisition without generating income to service the debt. Examples of this are debt to pay for food, fuel, clothes, entertainment, gifts, recreation, personal-care items, telephone, electricity, water, cable television, and any similar items that people often charge to credit cards. Don't misunderstand me here; there's nothing wrong with using credit cards to pay for these items as long as you are able pay the bill in full when it comes due. As a matter of fact, I regularly use my credit cards for normal monthly expenses and enjoy the convenience of having to write only one check or make one automatic bank draft for the payment. It does not become destructive debt until it carries over to the next month.

Debt to acquire cars, boats, campers, motorcycles, furniture, or other large-ticket items that are not used to generate income are additional examples of destructive debt. As we saw in the example in Figure 6, Chapter 4, the cost of financing the purchase of these large-ticket items can be significant. In today's world, more people ask themselves, "Can I make the payments?" than ask, "Can I afford the purchase?" Why? Why do so many people succumb to impulsive buying urges? Could it be because we are continuously bombarded with advertising messages that make it seem like the "cool" or "in" thing to do? When the urge hits you, think of it this way, any debt that has to be paid from your wages, other than a house payment, is destructive debt.

As you travel on your journey to financial freedom, you will learn that overcoming these impulses will become much easier, and you will also discover that it allows you to make more informed buying decisions. Building wealth is more about managing money than it is about making money, but that's not what our educational system teaches. I once presented a program to a high school economics class in which I described the Lifestyles of Success, Failure, and Ordinary. After my presentation, the teacher asked if I would be willing to present the same program to another of her classes after lunch. I agreed, but at this second presentation, I noticed several adults had entered the classroom and were sitting along the back wall. Following my presentation, the teacher invited me out into the hallway, where she introduced one of them as her husband. She told me that part of the reason she wanted me to present the program again was so she could call and ask him to attend. I also learned that the other adults were faculty members who had heard about the program over their lunch break. I gave a similar presentation on a college campus at which the dean of the business department was in attendance. Following the program, he approached me and said that I had given the students more information in an hour about how the real world works than they would get from a full semester in the school's economics courses. It's situations like these that led me to title this work *The Financial Security Bible.* I hope you will keep it as a reference for those times when you are about to make financial decisions. I believe you will find the simple common-sense suggestions it contains are applicable to even large major decisions.

The dean's comment really hit home one day when I was asking my son Jason to proofread some of my writings. After reading several pages, he came to me and said, "Dad, I went all through high school, got a four-year degree from a major college, and this is the first time I've ever seen this. It's stuff everyone needs to know. Why don't the schools teach it?" Another of my sons, Matt, graduated from Furman University with a degree in political science and has since earned a Master of Business Administration from the University of South Carolina. One of the first courses he took was an accounting class. He did great in the course, but after completing it, he told me it was one of the hardest courses he had ever had. Then he went on to say that he had gotten more out of the course than any class he had ever taken. He said he finally understood why I had been so adamant that he learned how to balance his checking account, reconcile his credit card accounts, and track his spending. Today he is religious about keeping up with his finances.

Is there any wonder so many people get in financial trouble considering that most high school graduates leave school without knowing how to prepare a family budget, balance a checking account, understand credit, or fill out a financial statement? It should also come as no surprise that many college freshmen become addicted to destructive credit card debt before they complete their first year of higher learning. The sad part is they usually don't realize they are addicted until they are so far in debt it will take years and years of sacrifice to get out of the hole.

But all debt is not bad; you've heard it said that it takes money to make money. To most people, this means working harder and earning more, but to me it means getting money to work for you, and it doesn't have to be your money. That's where constructive debt enters the picture. If you could borrow money for 6 percent interest annually and invest the money in assets that would pay you 10 percent or more annually, how much would you want to borrow? Would you agree that this kind of debt could eventually make you wealthy?

Isn't this exactly what banks do? When you deposit money into a savings account or certificate of deposit, the bank is borrowing from you. Your account is debt for the bank and shows up as a liability on its financial statement. When the bank loans your money to another customer at a higher interest, this loan is an asset for the bank, an asset that is expected to pay the bank more than the bank is going to pay you for the use of your money. In this example, your deposit account is constructive debt for the bank.

Now, let's take this a step further. If you borrow money from the bank, the loan is a liability, but if you take that money and invest it into something that will pay you much more than you are paying the bank, whatever you invest in is an asset, and the bank loan becomes constructive debt. If, however, you borrow money from the bank by charging daily activities to your credit card, you have to go to work and earn the money to pay it back. The money you borrowed may have allowed you to have a little more fun or enjoy yourself a little more while you were doing it, but the burden it puts on you when it comes time to repay is what causes it to become destructive debt.

Following the Great Depression of the 1930s, most people developed a great fear of debt, any kind of debt. During this period, so many people lost everything they owned that wasn't paid for free and clear, that debt became something to fear. For decades following, debt was viewed by ordinary people as a tool of the devil, to be shied away from at all cost. They thought that only the foolish went into debt. Without going into the cause of the Great Depression and its overall effects, let's just agree that the generation of people who grew up during the 1930s and 1940s lived very frugally and focused more on saving than spending. If they did go into debt, it was rarely for something other than to purchase a home in which to live.

Following Franklin D. Roosevelt's New Deal and World War II, the country gradually began a period of recovery, and debt started to lose its stigma. Returning GIs, who had endured a time of great sacrifice, came home to a changed world. Modes of transportation were more advanced and travel became popular, new modern conveniences such as kitchen appliances and washing machines placed increasing pressures on family budgets, and buying things on credit that they couldn't afford to buy for cash became more accepted. During this time, retail stores frequently offered their customers the option to pay over time when they made large purchases.

Although metal cards giving deferred payment privileges to good customers date back as early as 1914, it wasn't until 1950 that Diners Club issued the first credit card as we think of it today. It was invented by Diners Club founder Frank McNamara and was set up to use for restaurant charges only. American Express followed suit in 1958, and during that same year Bank of America issued the first bank credit card, Bank Americard, which was the forerunner to today's Visa card. By 1966, the success of these credit cards prompted a group of US banks to form an association to exchange information on credit card transactions, and in 1967 they introduced Master Charge, the forerunner of today's MasterCard.

By this time, the baby boom generation was beginning to come of age, and it took to credit like ducks to water. Almost all of them wanted to give their children more than they had experienced growing up. Credit was a quick and convenient way of doing this. Merchants soon learned that people usually spent more when they purchased with credit cards than they did when they had to pay cash, and the banking industry discovered a huge new source of revenue from the much higher interest rates they could charge on credit card balances. The race to obtain new customers became so heated that banks were actually mass mailing active credit cards to people who had not even requested them. Fortunately, this was curbed by Congress in the mid 1970s, when it banned the practice.

As economists had learned, it was spending, not saving, that ultimately pulled the US economy out of the Great Depression. It was forced spending by the federal government in the form of hundreds of billions of dollars' worth of defense contracts with private companies during World War II, not the attempted reorganization of the economy with government jobs under the New Deal that built factories, boosted production, and put people back to work in meaningful jobs that set us on the road to prosperity.

The advent of the credit card and the ease of credit for consumer purchases kept the economy growing, but at a price. The payments consumers were making on this easy credit was coming from the cash they were earning on their jobs, where they were trading labor for money. What made this debt so destructive was the fact that a sizable portion of the payments was interest, which bought them nothing. That meant that part of the money they earned was merely being transferred to people who had money to loan, and the result was that the rich got richer and the poor got poorer.

To illustrate the effect of this destructive debt, back in 1929, at the start of the Great Depression, the top 20% of American society controlled just over 50% of the nation's wealth and the bottom 20% controlled about 5%. But, by 1997, things had changed dramatically; just the top 10% controlled over 72% of the wealth and the bottom 40% controlled less than 1%. Now can you see why I say that consumer debt is destructive debt? All working people in America who are making payments on consumer debt from the money they earn on their jobs is transferring wealth to the wealthy, not improving their own standard of living with all the new toys they are buying. Your true standard of living is determined by what you can purchase with your earned income plus the income produced by your investments. Financial independence, at whatever standard of living you want to live, does not occur until your investment income will fully support your lifestyle. Nothing more, nothing less!

So, if this is the case, how can debt, in any form, be used constructively? The answer is very simple! Don't borrow money unless you can put it to work and have it earn more than it costs you to borrow it. While that answer may be simple, the execution is not. You don't just run out and borrow money and then look for a place to invest it. You have to be patient, creative, determined, and committed. You need patience to sort through all the opportunities that present themselves in the marketplace if you expect to find the ones that have real potential. You have to use your creativity to develop opportunities with potential, into investment-quality possibilities. Then you must have determination in order to convert possibilities into probabilities and make a commitment if you expect to turn probabilities into performing investments. (See the connection to the three Ds of Success here?) This is a process you will learn as I take you on your journey toward developing financial independence, but first, let's discuss how debt can be used constructively.

In Chapter 2, I mentioned that I set a goal to become a millionaire by age 30 and retire by age 50. When I set this goal, I was a young man just 20 years old, married and living in an old rented house. I had just been laid off, or as we would say today, "downsized," from my $80-per-week factory job, and my total assets consisted of an old car on which I was making payments and $300 in severance pay my former employer had given me when I was terminated. It would be a stretch for even the most optimistic of people to have seen me as millionaire material.

But having this goal, and being committed to it, caused a transformation in me that started me down the road to financial independence. The first thing the goal did was help me understand that I would never become a millionaire by looking for another $80-per-week factory job. At $80 per week, it would take more than 240 years just to earn a million dollars, let alone be worth that much. If I was going to become a millionaire by age 30, I would have to build my net worth by an average of $100,000 a year for 10 years, a task that would seem impossible to the ordinary person; but I chose not to be ordinary, so I started asking myself, "How can I," instead of resigning myself to saying, "I can't."

When I was working my factory job, I had earned extra money by using my artistic talents to paint signs for the plant. Since I was now without a job, and had a huge goal, I decided I would start my own business painting signs for others. I used my $300 severance pay to buy an old van and a few supplies and started making calls on local businesses. I soon learned that there was much more to the sign business than I had experienced at the plant. With youthful naiveté, I visited a local sign shop that had been in business for several years, said I wanted to start a sign business, and asked the owner if he would tell me what kinds of materials to use and show me how to lay out the sign copy so it would be properly positioned. The shop owner Dave Cheadle, a fine Christian man who recently passed away in his 80s, generously shared his knowledge and expertise with me and allowed me to come back any time I had questions. Dave's kindness and generosity was never forgotten, and we remained friends the rest of his life. I still do business with his sons, who continue to operate the sign shop today. Dave meant a lot to me, and I'll mention him again in a future chapter where I discuss the sacrifices that come with starting a business, especially one that requires a lot of investment.

From this humble beginning, I started my business but soon learned that painting signs and selling them was not much different from working the factory job; all I was doing was trading labor for money. I was patient, and worked very hard, but after a full year in business, my total income was only $3,400, and I realized that either I didn't have enough time, or people weren't willing to pay enough for what I did, to reach my goal of becoming a millionaire by age 30. I knew there was potential in the sign business, but I would have to resort to creativity if I was going to turn it into an investment-quality possibility. As I pondered my options, one nagging thought kept entering my mind, "When I sell my work, where is my investment?"

Then I thought about the wealthy people I knew and saw that they all had one thing in common. They owned stuff, assets that made money for them. Although I had a sign business, I didn't own anything that generated income. The only income from my business came from the sale of signs that required my labor to create. Once the sign was sold, I had to make another one in order to earn more income. It wasn't much different from working at the plant.

One day I was having lunch with my friend John whom I discussed in the previous chapter. He was in the restaurant business and wanted a large roadside sign to promote his business. The problem was, he was just getting started too and didn't have the money to buy one. He asked me if I would build one and rent it to him. In my head, I quickly figured that it would cost more than $500 to buy the materials and another $500 worth of my labor to paint and erect a sign like he wanted, plus I would have to pay a landowner rent for permission to put the sign on his property. When I told John that I didn't have the money either, he offered to sign a contract to rent the sign for $50 per month for five years and suggested that with the contract, a bank would probably loan me the money based on the contract. This lunch conversation suddenly gave me an idea: a way to turn my business into a real investment possibility.

Little did I realize, but this would become my first experience with constructive debt; however, I was like most young people and didn't know the difference at the time. What I discovered when I went to my bank to get a loan was that my banker had never heard of financing a sign. He wanted to know where I planned to put it, did I own the property or have a lease on the land, how would the sign be constructed, how long would it last, what kind of maintenance would it require, how credit worthy was the customer, and what kind of contract did I have for the rental.

I hadn't thought of any of these things. When I went back to visit my banker, I had prepared a proposal showing how a loan for $1,200 would pay for the materials, pay for my labor, and pay the first 3 years' rental on the lease of the ground where the sign would be installed. I showed the banker that if the $1,200 was financed for 3 years at 10% interest, the payments would be $38.72 per month and my monthly lease rental of $50 per month would more than cover the payments. Then, I explained that after the first 3 years, the loan would be paid off and the entire $50 per month would be mine for the next 2 years. At the end of 5 years I would still own the sign and could either renew the advertising contract with John or rent it to another business. I thought this was a slam-dunk!

As it turned out, the banker agreed it was probably a good deal, but in spite of my enthusiasm, he had trouble determining how to make the loan. What was the collateral? Was it the ground lease, was it the advertising contract, or was it the sign structure itself that had the value. In the end, I assigned them all to the bank to obtain this first $1,200 loan, a process I would repeat frequently over the next several years.

As my business grew, if one bank wouldn't loan me any more money, I would go to another and another until I got what I wanted. Eventually I was able to borrow millions that I invested constructively in sign structures. It was this type determination and commitment that brought me the financial success that allowed me to attain the $1,000,000 net worth mark and reach the first part of my goal by age 28 instead of 30.

As my assets grew, so did my problems. In the early 1970s, Lady Bird Johnson, wife of former President Lyndon B. Johnson, successfully lobbied Congress for passage of the Highway Beautification Act, and numerous states, counties, and local municipalities jumped on the bandwagon and began regulating signs.

By the late 1970s, after listening to concerns from my bankers, lawyers, and others, my accountant, John Kledis of Asheville, North Carolina, suggested that I consider diversifying my investments. He suggested rental real estate as a possible alternative to signs. The problem was, all of my assets were already invested and I was constantly struggling to borrow additional money to keep my sign business growing. I didn't have any extra money to invest, but I took my accountant's advice and began exploring real estate anyway. I soon learned that renting houses was very similar to renting signs, but it was much easier to obtain the financing, and city and county governments weren't trying to eliminate housing.

I began spending a few hours of my spare time, mainly on the weekends, looking at properties and making offers. In the beginning, I had to make offers that would require little or no cash to complete. It took me nearly a year to make my first purchase, but with it I discovered a new way to use debt constructively. The next year, I purchased two houses. The third year I bought four, and the rest is history. It was the energy with which I tackled this new endeavor that ultimately led to extraordinary success and the accomplishment of my goal to retire by age 50. This success story is chronicled in the bestselling book co-authored with Roger Dawson titled *The Weekend Millionaire's Secrets to Investing in Real Estate: How to Become Wealthy in Your Spare Time* (McGraw-Hill 2003).

While I found success by borrowing money to constructively invest in billboards and real estate, other successful people discovered different avenues to wealth. One friend of mine invests in video games and vending machines. He has these located throughout the area, and even as he sleeps, people are filling them full of quarters. Another friend invests in coin laundry machines and actually has them located all over the area, including some in apartments I own. Yet another invests in automobiles that he leases to others, and another in private mortgages. These are all ordinary people who have found ways to invest borrowed money in assets that generate enough to pay back the loans plus make a profit. These are true investments, because these people do not have to work a job to earn the money to pay back the loans. Remember what I mentioned earlier, any debt that has to be paid from your earned income, other than the payment on a house where you live, is destructive debt. The home loan is okay because you have to have a place to live. If you didn't have a mortgage payment, you would have to pay rent.

Wherever you live, if you look around, you will see people who have found ways to constructively use debt to build wealth. This is probably where the statement, "It takes money to make money" originated. Borrowed money can be a great wealth-building tool, but as Henry C. Alexander, who effectively changed the way Morgan Guaranty Trust did business, said, "Increased borrowing must be matched with increased ability to repay. Otherwise we aren't expanding the economy; we're merely puffing it up." It doesn't matter whether that economy is the economy of an individual or the economy of a nation, when you borrow money to invest in income-producing assets, your wealth will grow and eventually your standard of living will improve. On the other hand, if you borrow money to live better today, your standard of living may improve for the moment, but it will surely suffer over time.

Once you learn the difference between destructive debt used for daily living and constructive debt to wisely invest, you will be well on your way to wealth. When statesman, lawyer, and orator Daniel Webster said, "Credit has done a thousand times more to enrich mankind than all the gold mines in the world," he definitely wasn't talking about making payments on credit cards. Although Webster died in 1852, prior to the advent of today's credit card, his comment is just as valid now as it was back then, but it applies only to constructive debt not destructive debt.

Let's hold that thought as we move to the next chapter and get you started on your journey to financial independence.

Key points from this chapter:

- Using credit cards to purchase items that you can't pay for when the monthly statement comes is the most common form of destructive debt.

- Building wealth and achieving financial independence is more about managing money than it is about making money.

- Don't sell yourself short. You may not be millionaire material today, but with patience and persistence, you can become millionaire material.

- Constructive debt is created when you borrow money to invest in assets that earn more income than it costs you to borrow the money.

- Learn to embrace constructive debt but fear destructive debt.

- Use constructive debt to build wealth and increase your income.

- Don't let obstacles deter your success; find a way over, under, around, or through them.

7

Defining Your Journey to Financial Independence

If you've read this far, you know that I've been discussing financial independence, but I haven't applied the term to everyday living. I've discussed how people who enjoy the Lifestyle of Success embarked on a course that led them to creating an ongoing stream of income that was enough to maintain their lifestyle without having to work. I've shown you that it takes patience, discipline, and delayed gratification in order to live better in the long run. I've also discussed the devastating effects of overspending and consumer debt. But, up until now, what I've done has just been to condition you to begin your journey toward financial independence.

As with all successful journeys, there has to be a starting point and destination to reach. The distance between your starting point and your ultimate goal determines the amount of time and course of action needed to get there. Where are you now in relation to your desired financial goal? If you are 25, college educated, have a great job, have already started accumulating some savings and investments, and your goal is to reach financial independence in 30 years at age 55, your course of action will be totally different from someone who is already 55, broke, out of work, and wondering how they are going to survive till the end of the month. But the one thing you both have in common is the fact that young, old, rich, or poor, everyone has 24 hours in a day and seven days in a week. It's what you do with your time that determines how quickly, if ever, you reach financial independence.

No matter what you have done in the past, you have already embarked on your own personal journey through life. Up until now it may have been a wandering journey with no more direction than trying to make it to the next paycheck. Whatever you've done in the past, it is only part of your journey through life; it isn't your whole life. Today is the first day of the rest of your life. If you don't like where you are or what you're currently doing, you can set new goals, change direction, take different actions, and become a new you. Yes, it takes courage and commitment, which is where I come in. I'm going to give you some new ideas and help you develop a different outlook on life. You may have never thought about it in the way I'm going to discuss here, so before I ask you to determine where you currently are on your journey, let's talk about the journey itself. The following chart illustrates a simple fact of life.

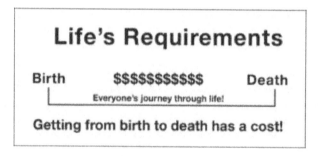

Fig. 7

As you can see in Figure 7, everyone's journey through life involves getting from birth to death, and the cost associated with doing so. How much is that cost? Who knows! It all depends on the length of the journey, how you conduct yourself on the trip, and when you pay for it. Some people live only for the moment and never worry about tomorrow. They take the approach that we have no guarantee of tomorrow; therefore, why not enjoy today to its fullest? If these people die young, but they've spent everything they've made having fun and enjoying themselves, so be it . . . they win. On the other hand, if they live to a ripe old age and end up spending the last half of their life in misery because they didn't plan for the future, they lose.

Some people spend their entire working lives living very frugally, saving, investing, and planning for retirement. They don't take vacations, live in fine houses, drive luxury cars, or enjoy any of the other pleasures money can bring, because they want to be sure they will be able to live well in retirement. Then, if they make it to retirement age, although they are very well off financially, they are often so accustomed to doing without or are in such poor health that they can't enjoy their wealth. If they happen to die before reaching retirement age, they leave behind a nice nest egg for their heirs to enjoy, but they didn't get much pleasure out of accumulating it. The odds are you will live into your 80s, so I'm going to help you plan for it but show you that you can enjoy life and be happy along the way too.

Unfortunately, some of our brightest and most energetic people end up as roadkill on life's economic highway. Granted, there are people born with problems such as physical defects or mental incapacities from birth that they can't do anything about. Some contract contagious diseases or have unfortunate accidents that limit their abilities, which may necessitate seeking help from others, but these aren't the people we're talking about. Those of us who enjoy good health, an education, and the ability to care for ourselves should find the generosity to help those less fortunate, but we should never lose sight of the fact that our primary goal is to take care of ourselves first so that we don't become a burden on society. If you want to help the poor, start out by determining not to become one of them. They certainly don't need the competition. The decisions we make day to day determine the amount of joy or pain we experience on life's economic journey.

Financial success means many things to many people, but financial independence is the same for everyone. Financial independence is the point at which you can continue to live your chosen lifestyle from the income generated by your investments. It's the "chosen lifestyle" that varies, not the definition of financial independence. Whether your chosen lifestyle requires $3,000, $30,000, $300,000, or $3,000,000 per month, you cannot be financially independent until you have an adequate stream of income from your investments to sustain whatever lifestyle makes you happy. Keeping this in mind, let's take another look at life's requirements.

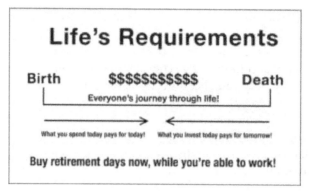

Fig. 8

As you can see from Figure 8, what you spend today pays for the days starting at birth and moving toward death. What you invest today pays for days moving from death back toward where you are now. With this in mind, can you see how life becomes a balancing act? Can you see that if you spend too much on today, you risk not having a good life tomorrow, but if you invest too much today preparing for tomorrow, you reduce the quality of your life today? That's the reason why developing the proper mindset is so important. As I said in Chapter 1, this mindset is rooted in little decisions, those small day-to-day decisions that position us to make better big decisions when the important times come.

To achieve the goal of financial independence, you have to start by determining the kind of lifestyle you want to live. In my case, when I set my goal in the 1960s to become a millionaire by age 30 and retire by age 50, I obviously knew that I wanted a higher standard of living than what I was living at the time. My dilemma was how to divide my earnings between improving my current standard of living and investing for the future. Isn't that a decision we all make consciously or unconsciously every day? Do we eat out tonight, or save money by cooking at home? Do we buy that new pair of sneakers, when we have a perfectly good pair, just because our friends have the newest style? Do we trade cars now and get that new one that smells and looks so good, or do we wait a year or two and invest the savings? Do we buy that Sea-Doo this summer and finance it, when we know our time at the lake will be limited, or do we wait until next year or the year after when we can save enough to pay cash for it and have more time to enjoy it? How many decisions like this, big and small, are you faced with every day? Do you realize that a day's income invested today could pay for several days 20, 30, 40 years from now? Do you have the three Ds?: the *Desire* to one day live your chosen lifestyle without having to worry about money, the *Discipline* to invest now, and the *Dedication* to keep it up long term so you can have that lifestyle in the future? If so, keep reading!

Look back at Figure 8. Notice how the lines with the arrows pointing from birth and death are about the same length. Don't be misled by this. The length of each arrow will be in direct relation to your standard of living. If you live the Lifestyle of Success we discussed in Chapter 2, start early enough in life, live an overall standard of living reasonably below your earned income, and invest wisely, your arrows may meet near the middle. If this is the case, you will be able to retire early, not have to reduce your standard of living, and be able to enjoy your retirement years, no matter how long they may last. By the same token, if you live the Lifestyle of Failure as we discussed in Chapter 3, you will have to keep earning all your life, suffer through dramatic swings in lifestyle, and probably have to settle for whatever standard of living you can manage on Social Security. And finally, those of you living the Lifestyle of Ordinary we described in Chapter 4 can look forward to a comfortable lifestyle, but one that will most likely have to be pared down when you retire because you will not have enough income to continue living the way you were accustomed to living while you were working.

Let's now begin to explore what you can do to start moving toward financial independence. As I mentioned in the beginning of this chapter, we all have 24 hours in a day, seven days in a week, so let's analyze this time and determine what we do with it.

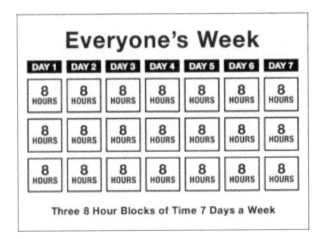

Fig. 9

Figure 9, above, is a graphic representation of what everyone's weeks look like. For ease of demonstration, I have divided each day into three blocks, each consisting of an eight-hour period of time. In this regard, everyone is equal. Time is a commodity of which we are all granted the exact same amount. You cannot save time, hoard time, bank time, or accumulate time. You cannot acquire time, purchase time, inventory, or collect time. You can only spend time. It's how you spend time that determines what you accomplish in life. There are many ways to spend time. You can spend it usefully, constructively, beneficially, creatively, efficiently, positively, productively, and wisely; or you can spend it wastefully, foolishly, frivolously, extravagantly, lavishly, carelessly, and inefficiently. If you think about it, you can come up with hundreds of other ways you can spend time, but not a single way to get more of it.

So, if you can only spend time, what can you do to become more financially successful? The answer is simple: you improve yourself. Through education and practice, you learn how to produce more in the same amount of time. For example, if you are a typist and you type 40 words a minute accurately, you can become twice as valuable by increasing your typing speed to 80 words per minute with the same accuracy. This is done with practice. If you take a medical first responder course, you may be able to get a job with an ambulance crew, but if you are willing to dedicate years to intense study, you can become the doctor who treats the patients the ambulance crews bring to you. I don't need to tell you how much difference there is between the compensation of a doctor and that of an ambulance-crew member. This is due to education. In both of these examples, I'm talking about ways to make the time you spend more valuable, not have more of it. Unfortunately, most people try to get ahead by spending more time rather than by improving the output of time spent. Let's look at a typical workweek.

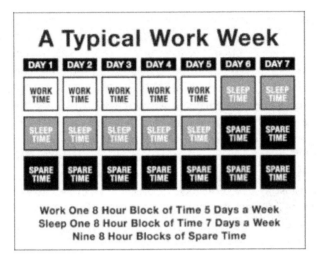

Fig. 10

The chart in Figure 10 shows how ordinary people spend their time. They typically spend five of their eight-hour blocks of time working, seven of them sleeping, and have nine left over as discretionary time, which I call spare time in the chart because "discretionary" won't fit in the box. But, seriously, work and sleep are mandatory for most people, but what you do with your discretionary, or spare, time is up to you . . . or is it? What you earn with your work time has everything to do with what you can do with your spare time. If your knowledge and skills during work hours enable you to earn $2,000 per week, you will be able to enjoy your spare time much more than if you only earn $200 per week during these hours, which brings me to the biggest secret to achieving financial independence. There is something else you can do with time other than spend it. You can invest it!

If your typical workweek is like most people's, you have 72 hours of discretionary time. Let's analyze how you might spend this time. You might spend two hours per day—some people spend more—getting up, getting dressed, and getting to and from work; based on a five-day workweek that uses up 10 hours, but leaves you with 62. You may not do it, but a lot of people spend another couple of hours per day, every day, just lying in bed sleeping or just doing nothing. Whether or not you do this, let's allocate the time anyway, which takes up another 14 hours per week, but that still leaves you with 48. Throw in another couple of hours per day for eating, bathing, grooming, and now you're down to 34, but, everyone has other things they need or want to do, so let's allocate another three hours per day, every day, to doing things like watching television, playing video games, golf, tennis, jogging, housework, laundry, or other chores around the house, and suddenly you only have 13 hours remaining. Of this time, let's assume you give eight hours to your church, civic, or charitable activities, which leaves you with just five hours per week. Granted, in this description, I've painted you as spending a good portion of your spare time doing nonproductive things. I realize that you have the discretion to change how you use many of these hours, but indulge me for the benefit of this example, because even if you live just as I've described, I'm going to show you how you can "invest" these few remaining hours and become financially independent.

Before you start thinking thoughts like, "I don't lie around in bed doing nothing" or "I only sleep six hours a day" or "It only takes me 30 minutes a day to get ready and get to and from work" or "I have a two-hour commute each way to work, plus the time it takes me to get ready" or any of a hundred other examples of why my example doesn't apply to you, stop and think about what you do. If you don't need as long to get ready and get to work, great, but what else are you doing with the time? Suppose you have a two-hour commute each way, isn't that your choice? But the key point here is how you invest that time. You can spend it listening to a shock-jock on the radio or listening to country and western music. Or you can slip in an educational CD and invest the time learning knowledge and skills that can raise your earning power. You might also consider that something as simple as listening to educational CDs during your commute may give you the additional knowledge you need to find and acquire profitable investments. Isn't this entire example just a series of little discretionary things that people choose to do with their time? But this isn't a time-management course; it's a book to encourage you to manage your time, your money, and your life in ways that will lead you to financial independence.

The amazing thing is that it doesn't require you to live like a pauper while you're waiting for your ship to come in. It won't make you feel like you have to devote all your spare time to building wealth and sacrifice the fun times in life that everyone needs. What it will do is help you identify your strengths and weaknesses, show you how to rely on your strengths, assist you in strengthening your weaknesses, and help you to become a well-rounded, confident, and financially secure person.

You have already completed part of your journey through life; the following sections of this book will help you determine where you are on this journey and how much further you need to go. Now let's move on and position you to continue your journey to financial independence.

Key points from this chapter:

- Financial independence is reached when you have an ongoing stream of income that is enough to maintain your lifestyle without having to work.

- The decisions you make day to day determine the amount of joy or pain you experience as you travel down life's economic highway.

- What you invest today while you still have strong earning power determines how well you will be able to live in retirement when you aren't earning as much.

- Time is the same for everyone. What you do with it determines the kind of future you will have.

- Investing part of your spare time in education is a great way to increase the earning power of your work time.

- Investing part of your spare time in acquiring income-producing assets will set you squarely on the road to financial independence.

PART II

Life Lessons from Your Formative Years

Everyone's life is a series of experiences, some good, some bad, and some that come and go with little thought one way or another. The interesting point about these experiences is the number of them that contain important life lessons, but we let them pass unnoticed. In this section and the two that follow, I will be describing a number of events from my life that implanted strong life lessons in my subconscious mind, even though I failed to recognize it at the time. It was not until years later when I found myself unconsciously applying some to these lessons that I was able to look back, analyze the events, and understand the impact they had on my future. I understand that my life experiences may be completely different from yours, but I use events from my life to illustrate certain behaviors, because I know the lessons derived from them are the same for everyone. Think of it as traveling different roads to reach the same destination.

As you read this section, I want you to think about your own life. Look back to incidents from your childhood and try to recall events that changed the way you act or react today. Keep in mind that all of these changes may not be positive; in fact some of them may have produced strong negative reactions. It's the events that left lasting impressions, both good and bad, on which I want you to focus. As you read my stories, if one of them prompts you to recall an incident from your past, stop and jot down a note to help you remember it later. Be sure to write down any events that come to mind, no matter how insignificant they may seem at the time. Don't try to look for the lessons in your life experiences at this point; just make notes for future reference. I'll ask you later to refer to these notes after you have read about how I discovered the lessons embedded in some of my seemingly insignificant experiences.

I will be sharing my stories to help you see how I used these life experiences to guide my growth and development, but it will be the events from your life that you will use to plot your course to financial independence. I will not be getting heavily into psychoanalysis by trying to convince you that you aren't where you want to be in life because someone stole your doll or football when you were four years old. What I will be doing is teaching you how to examine your cumulative life experiences and helping you find valuable life lessons that may have been embedded in them. If so, it will help you learn how to discover and implement these lessons in ways that can improve your life going forward and guide you to financial freedom.

Developing a new way of thinking is a journey, not a destination. Change doesn't usually come easy. It is a personal journey you have to take, because everyone's experiences are different. Opportunities abound, but if you aren't ready and aren't prepared, you will often fail to recognize them when they arise. You'll join the ranks of those who whine and complain about how other people have all the luck. When an opportunity comes your way and you aren't prepared, someone else will grab it and you will be telling everyone what you would have done if you had that kind of luck.

The formative years are those years when you are like a sponge: young, innocent, and willing to soak up everything that comes your way. The problem is that during these years, it's just as easy to soak up bad information and develop bad habits as it is good. If you soak up too much bad information, it can turn you from a sponge soaking up knowledge into a rock that resists all change. But even if you've already become somewhat of a rock, I encourage you to take a second look at those times when you soaked up bad information, because I'm going to teach you how to get rid of the negative from your mind and become a sponge once again. Greed, jealousy, hate, envy, bitterness, mistrust, and suspicion are all negative thoughts and emotions that come from bad experiences. Hurt, anger, and resentment can devour you like a cancer if you don't get rid of these emotions.

You'll see from the stories in this section that I didn't always react well when things didn't go my way, but it was up to me to choose whether I let disappointment and failures get me down or teach me a lesson. Some of the best lessons life taught me were what not to do. It's the choices we make when things happen, good or bad, that affect the way we think. Yes, there is a cause and effect to almost everything. Life deals two people a lemon; one complains about the sour deal he got, while the other makes lemonade. Why? Why do people have such differing reactions to the same event? Why do some people let negative emotions destroy them, while others use the same emotions to get stronger? These are all part of what I will be exploring in this section and the two that follow it.

Before you turn to Chapter 8, get a pad and pencil so you that can make notes as you read. I know that the stories and events that follow will trigger some memories from your past that you will be able to use to build a better tomorrow. I also know that if you don't jot these down as soon as they come to mind, by the time you finish reading this book, many of them will be forgotten. You must understand that it is your stories, not mine, that are the building blocks you will need to change your thinking. You'll see what I'm talking about as I share stories from my life, describe the life lessons embedded in them, explain how I was able to extract these life lessons and put them to work to change my life. Don't just dismiss this suggestion and keep reading, because you will find that the more of your stories you have to work with, the easier it will be to reroute your journey to financial success.

8

Character Is Formed in the Crucible of Hard Times

As a young man, I grew up poor, but I didn't know it at the time. Other than memories of fishing with my grandfather when I was a toddler, my first memories of growing up involved the hard-luck town of War, West Virginia, and a stepfather I thought was physically abusive. My move from the loving, nurturing surroundings of my grandparents' home to the hostile and foul environment of the coalfields of Southern West Virginia left an impression that would impact my life forever.

Psychologists say that most of our view of the world is well developed by the time we're seven years old. By that age, we have developed a paradigm or a mental map of the way the world operates. As you read this story from my early years, be thinking about how your early life may have affected your view of the world.

Shortly after I was born, and for reasons that were never discussed with me until after I was an adult, my mother left my father and returned home to live with her parents in Abingdon, Virginia. My grandparents' home was a loving and safe setting surrounded by relatives and friends. My grandfather, whom I fondly called Pop, was a railroad conductor who worked with Norfolk & Southern Railway and was also an avid outdoorsman. He was gone most of the week, but when he came home for the weekend, he would often take me on fishing trips to South Holston Lake or to nearby rivers, where, with incredible patience, he would sit by the water's edge as I ran around, making noise, throwing rocks in the water and doing almost everything imaginable to scare the fish. In spite of my rambunctious behavior, we always managed to catch fish.

When we would return home, I would run in first and start yelling for everyone to come and look at our catch of bluegill, bass, trout, or other fish. Pop would always say that I caught them all, which everyone knew wasn't the whole truth, but I would swell out my little chest and feel great when everyone bragged about what a good fisherman I was becoming. Pop and I would then take the fish to the basement and dump them in an old cast-iron laundry sink, where we would clean them and get them ready to be cooked. Pop taught me how to scrape the scales from the fish, but for safety's sake, he would handle the knife and do the cutting while I watched and learned. When it came time to eat the fish, my grandmother would prepare a great meal of cornbread, beans, potatoes, and other vegetables. The big table in the dining room would be set and the whole family, including aunts and uncles, would gather round for a wonderful fish dinner.

After the food was blessed, my grandmother would make it a point to let everyone know that their meal centered round the fish that I had caught, and she would ask me to tell everyone how I caught them. As you can imagine, the tales coming from me as a three- to four-year-old could be quite colorful at times, and, naturally, there was always that big one that got away. I became quite a storyteller. Those were the good times.

I looked forward to Fridays when Pop would be returning home from work. I would be the first to greet him, and before he could even get into the house, I was asking if we could go fishing. This was like a marriage made in heaven, because Pop liked to fish about as much, maybe even more, than I did. I was a great excuse for him to go, because how could anyone in the family begrudge him taking his grandson fishing?

Week after week we would make trips to the nearby lake and rivers. I soon learned that by calming down a bit and being more patient, I could usually catch more fish. Pop always seemed to find a place on the lake or a pool in the river where the fishing was good. I would sit on the bank for hours watching the float bob on the water, waiting for it to go under so I could give my pole a big jerk and hook another fish. Little did I realize that this joyous time was about to come to an abrupt end.

In June of 1950, my mother remarried and moved with her new husband to the small coal-mining town of War, West Virginia, and took me to live with them. Nestled in the heart of the Appalachian Mountains, War is the southernmost town in West Virginia. I think it must have been the place Johnny Cash sang about in his song *A Boy Named Sue*, when he told his son that the reason he gave him that name was because he knew "he would have to get tough or die." Back then, War was a place where differences were settled with your fists, and I can recall the Ku Klux Klan burning crosses at night. It was an inhospitable place, where the drinking water smelled like rotten eggs from the sulfur it contained. There was no sewer system in the area, and when those with indoor plumbing flushed their toilets, the waste was straight piped directly into the rivers. Several times a day, steam locomotives would roll through town belching black smoke and stirring up jet-black dust from the coal that spilled from the rail cars hauling bituminous coal from the numerous mines throughout the area. War was a filthy place.

During the heyday of the coal boom, jobs were plentiful in the dark, cold underground mines, but many workers breathed in the coal dust that would later develop into deadly black lung disease. For most young men, the future held little promise other than following in their father's footsteps and taking jobs working in the mines. That was the world I was suddenly introduced to when my mother remarried.

Eventually, the mines began to close, jobs were lost, and today, War is a place lost in time. It is home to about 2,000 people, the majority of whom receive some form of public assistance. Most of the stores have closed, people still live in houses with cracks in the walls and leaks in the roofs, and children still wake up hungry with no hope for the future.

Homer Hickam's book *Rocket Boys* (Delta, January 2000), which inspired the movie *October Sky,* describes what life was like in War in the 1950s. Homer grew up in Coalwood, another small mining town just a few miles away, but he attended Big Creek High School in War, where his rocket-building science project led to his winning the West Virginia State Science Fair. His determination eventually pulled him out of this dismal area, and he later became a scientist with NASA. Although he was a couple of years older than I was, his accomplishments in the 1950s were an inspiration and helped me to realize there was more to life than a job in a coal mine. Today, Homer's writings about life in the coalfields of Southern West Virginia bring back many memories of what it was like going to War.

My earliest memories of War consist of trying to adjust to life with a new stepfather, Paul, who was a strict disciplinarian who believed in the old adage "spare the rod and spoil the child." He was the oldest of 12 children. His father had died just after the youngest was born, and he was left to assume the role of helping his mother raise his younger siblings. This experience is probably what made him such a strong believer that children should earn their keep around the house.

Paul was 40, ten years older than my mother, when they married. His whole life, with the exception of military service during WWII, was centered in War. When he took my mother and me to live there, it was a far cry from those wonderful days of loving grandparents and sitting on the bank of the lake with Pop catching fish. Suddenly I went from being nurtured and pampered to this hostile place where I always seemed to be in the way. Today we'd call that a traumatic experience. It was then too!

There were always chores to do before I could play and the "thank you" I got was the privilege of staying there and having something to eat. Getting paid was unheard of, and allowances were out of the question. Little did I realize at the time, but this experience started me on my journey to developing a tenacious desire to excel. Today I am convinced that the experiences that followed this traumatic occurrence are what molded my character and propelled me to success. As the chapter heading notes, character is built in the crucible of hard times.

I wanted to share this and other early experiences to help you understand that I started out in life like many others, just below the first rung on the ladder of success. As you will learn, I didn't let this keep me from wanting to climb the ladder. Throughout the chapters that follow in this section, I will describe some of the experiences that demonstrate how I learned valuable life lessons even when I didn't realize I was learning at the time. So read on, and remember that if any of my stories trigger recollections of memorable events from your past, make notes about them. These notes are what you will use to alter your thinking and begin mapping your journey to financial independence.

Key points from this chapter:

- Life can hand you difficult situations, but these don't have to ruin your life.
- Childhood memories, both good and bad can be used to build character.
- Start preparing to change your life by altering your behavior.

9

If You Want It Enough, You'll Find a Way to Get It

In his book *All I Really Need to Know I Learned in Kindergarten*, Robert Fulghum writes that wisdom was not at the top of the graduate-school mountain, but there in the sand pile at kindergarten. After outlining the things he learned, he continues by saying, "Think what a better world it would be if all—the whole world—had cookies and milk about three o'clock every afternoon and then lay down with our blankies for a nap." That's a nice thought, but unfortunately, that's not the way it works in the real world.

People don't always share everything, nor do they always play fair. They do occasionally hit each other and don't say they're sorry. They often take things that aren't theirs and fail to put them back where they found them or clean up their own messes. In fact, people sporadically violate each and every one of the things Fulghum says he learned that would make the world a better place; and of course, they violate most of the Ten Commandments too.

What I want you to learn from this book is how to get along in the real world, a place where people don't always live by playground rules or follow God's laws. We come into this world as innocent children with eyes wide open and filled with wonder. We're like sponges that soak up what we see and hear and allow these experiences to shape our lives. Isn't it amazing how children playing on a playground make up rules and settle differences without missing a beat until the adults show up? Have you ever noticed that when parents arrive and start giving advice, problems that seemed insignificant before suddenly become major arguments?

Moms and dads have their own ideas about what's fair and what the rules should be, based on their own life experiences. When they inject these ideas into their children, it often results in them losing their innocence and seeing things in a different light. When left alone, it's amazing how children seem to know who is best and who struggles at a particular sport. Watch them make allowances for these differences. They have a unique ability to handicap the players in ways that evens the competition.

I remember playing games where everyone agreed on the best two players and then let them alternate choosing from the rest to make up teams that were fairly even. We would agree upon the length of a game, and if the sides seemed too unbalanced after the first game, we would trade a player or two to balance the sides. Sometimes, we would let the two worst players be the captains and pick the teams. The bottom line is, we had great fun, played hard, and everyone went home happy. As we grew older, however, priorities changed, and our individual wants and needs took us down different paths. The games we played became more serious, and the consequences of losing were more dramatic.

By far, the most important game we will ever play is the game of life. How we deal with the defining moments with which we are presented is what determines our success or failure in the game of life. I lived in War, West Virginia, from age four until age 12, and as you will see from the story that follows, I am a testimony to the saying in the last chapter, "Character is formed in the crucible of hard times." At age eight, I faced a situation that provided me with several defining moments, and the life lessons I learned from this incident are the subjects of the next several chapters.

The story unfolds with my best friend receiving a new bicycle from his parents for his birthday. In the years that followed my mother's remarriage and the move to War, I developed a close friendship with a neighbor boy named John Allen. I was a year older, but the two of us became practically inseparable. John's parents owned the Western Auto, one of the few stores in town, and they were constantly bringing home new toys for John to play with. I felt that John's parents must be rich because they owned a store, but this never presented a problem with our friendship because I was John's best friend and he always shared everything with me.

When his family got the first television in town, he would invite me over to watch Saturday morning cartoons and Western movies. We would roam the neighborhood together and usually wherever you would find one of us, the other would not be far away. John's parents even let him use a big section of their yard to do with as he pleased, and he and I would dig holes, build roads, and play with toy trucks and bulldozers for hours. I was somewhat envious of the fact that we could dig in John's yard because I had to keep mine mowed with an old push-type mower, but this never came between our friendships. It was not until John got the new bicycle that I experienced my first memorable life lesson.

Suddenly, John was able to ride all over the neighborhood, but I still had to walk. This was the reality of life; John's parents could afford things that mine couldn't. No matter how hard I tried, I couldn't talk my mother and stepfather into buying me a bicycle. It would have been so easy to have wallowed in self-pity and let jealousy eat at me while my best friend rode his new bicycle, but that was not my nature. Although my family struggled to get by financially, my mother never complained. Looking back today, I realize that my mother is the most positive person I have ever known. She lacked many of the things other women enjoyed, but she never let it affect her happiness. Although I didn't realize it at the time, the way she reacted to my wanting a new bicycle taught me my first life lesson: **Everyone is not equal, but opportunities are.**

She took me aside and said, "Honey, I'm sorry we can't afford to get you a bicycle, but if you really want one, I'll bet you can find a way to get it." Of all the compliments I could pay my mother, probably the greatest is the fact that she never discouraged me. Throughout my life, each time I sought her advice or guidance about some new idea or about whether or not to try something I had never done, she would just say, "If you think you can do it, I'll bet you can." This was basically what she did when she told me that if I wanted a bicycle she'd bet I could find a way to get one.

I realize that many children don't have nurturing and supportive parents, and even after they reach adulthood, they use this as an excuse for their failures. Yes, I was blessed with a supportive mother, but her support was easily offset by my stepfather's criticism. I could easily have used his treatment as an excuse to whine and complain, but I chose not to. Looking back with today's knowledge, I can see how the choice I made back then about the bicycle was so different from the choices so many young people make today.

Throughout my years in War, I was always a very industrious child. Since I received no allowance, my choice was to do without or do something about it. I soon learned that I could scour the riverbanks and roadways to find discarded soft-drink bottles or scrap metal that I could sell to earn spending money. I learned that I could walk the railroad tracks and pick up coal that fell from the trains, which I could put in sacks and sell for a few cents. It was always exciting when I could earn a quarter because this was enough to get in to see a movie, buy popcorn and a soft drink, and still have a nickel in change. Money bought a lot more back then!

When my mother told me that if I really wanted a bicycle, I'd find a way to get one, I doubt if she realized just how much she was empowering me to achieve success later in life. It wasn't until I reached adulthood and began reflecting on this experience that I realized that what she had given me was an opportunity instead of a handout; however, it was up to me to take advantage of it. I could easily have just given up, but I really wanted that bicycle. I thought that since I had always been able to make a few cents when I wanted to buy an occasional toy or a candy bar or go to a movie, why couldn't I earn enough to get a new bike? While John and I were not equal in the things our parents could buy us, I was blessed with a mother who gave me something that money couldn't buy. She gave me confidence and taught me that opportunity, like being able to pick up bottles, scrap metals, and coal to earn spending money was equal for everyone.

While the opportunity was equal, our level of desire was not. John had his bike; why should he have to scrounge around trying to earn money? I didn't have a bike, but I wanted one very badly. The result was that I was willing to do things John wouldn't in order to get one. In the process, I learned the power of Desire, the first of the three "Ds" of success. Without even realizing it, my intense desire for a bicycle like John's started me down the road to the financial security I enjoy today. As you will see in the chapters that follow, this road was filled with potholes, bumps, curves, and obstacles, but it was a journey filled with life lessons that contributed to my success.

Had I made different choices and succumbed to jealousy and envy along the way like so many people do, there's no way I'd be writing this book. I can't stress enough how people's success or failure in life is the direct result of the choices they make. Think of times in your life when you have had to make choices. Oh, by the way, whether they were good choices or bad, don't forget to make a note of them. You'll use these notes later to learn from the bad ones and build on the good ones as you change your life for the better.

Key points from this chapter:

- Life isn't always fair—bad things do happen occasionally.
- When life isn't fair, you can either complain about it or do something about it.

- Everyone is not equal, but opportunities are.

- A key step in attaining financial security is learning to create strong desire. A desire so strong you'd overcome almost any obstacle to reach your goal.

- Don't be afraid to do things others aren't willing to do, as long as they are legal, to achieve your goals.

- Success is directly related to the choices you make.

10

Success Doesn't Just Happen; It Requires a Plan

If it's going to be, it's up to me! That must have been the thought running through my head when I left home that morning in 1954 without telling my mother or anyone else where I was going and I headed into town. I was on a mission. I wanted that new bicycle and I thought I had come up with a way to get it, so I was on my way to see John's mother at the Western Auto store. She knew me very well, since I was at her home about as much as I was at my own. I just knew she would go along with my idea.

When I arrived at the store, Mrs. Allen, who was a generous woman, saw me walk in and she promptly asked, "What are you doing here by yourself?"

"I came to talk with you about buying a bicycle like the one you got John," I said.

Mrs. Allen, who had always been kind to me, leaned down and said, "Honey," that's what she called me, "does your mother know where you are? You know she wouldn't let me sell you a bike without her permission, besides where did you get the money to buy a bicycle?"

"No, Mom doesn't know I'm here, but she told me that if I wanted a bicycle I would find a way to get one. Since she told me that, I've been thinking about it, and here's what I've come up with. If you will let me have a bicycle, I'll pay you a dollar a week until I get it paid for."

"Honey, where are you going to get a dollar a week, every week?" she responded.

I hadn't thought about that! I knew that I had been able to collect soft-drink bottles, scrap metal, and coal to make a little spending money, but I'd never made even close to a dollar in a week. That was a lot of money for an eight-year-old to think about earning in 1954 in War, West Virginia. I didn't have an answer to Mrs. Allen's question.

When she saw my head drop and my shoulders slump, Mrs. Allen pulled me to her and said, "I know you would like a bike, Honey, but you don't always get everything you want. I'll talk to John and see if he will let you ride his when he's not using it."

"But, you don't understand," I said with tears in my eyes. "I want to ride with John so we can do things together. I don't want to ride by myself."

I'll tell you what," Mrs. Allen replied. "You show me how you can earn a dollar a week and I'll sell you a bicycle just like John's as long as it's okay with your mother."

With this statement, she taught me my second memorable life lesson: **It takes planning to be successful.** I had gone to her with an idea that met my desire, but it lacked a reason for her to accept it. I had approached her with an intense desire to have a new bike, but with no plan for how I would make the needed dollar a week. Although I didn't comprehend it as such at the time, this experience taught me that people do things for their reasons, not yours. As much as Mrs. Allen empathized with me, I was not her child, and it was not her responsibility to see that I got a bike.

It would have been very easy for me to have left the store that day feeling defeated, but Mrs. Allen's comments encouraged me. When I returned home, I told my mother about the encounter and asked her if she had any ideas about how I could earn the dollar per week. Her advice was the same as before, "If you really want the bike, you'll find a way to make the money."

Since the only way I had made money in the past was collecting bottles, scrap metal, and coal, I went to work immediately. I scoured the town looking for the usual items I could turn into cash. I didn't go to the extremes of ripping up railroad rails to sell to the scrap-iron dealer that Homer Hickam and the Rocket Boys were portrayed as doing in the movie *October Sky*, but I did work at it diligently. I wanted to see if I could find enough stuff in a week to earn a dollar. Sadly, my valiant effort led to earning only about 45 cents, and although it was more than I had ever earned in a week before, it fell far short of the dollar I was hoping to earn.

Discouraged, but not defeated, I talked with my neighbors, my school teachers, my friends, and anyone else who would listen to me, but no one had any suggestions as to how an eight-year-old could earn a dollar a week. I even took a stack of old magazines my mother had saved and went around the neighborhood trying to sell them for a nickel each.

A few people who probably felt sorry for me bought one, but it was what I discovered while alone in my room one night that changed my fortune. I was lying on my bed feeling a bit sorry for myself and flipping through one of the old magazines, when I saw an ad with the headline "Kids—Earn Extra Spending Money." It was an advertisement for people to sell a weekly newspaper called *Grit*. The ad explained that it was a large nationally circulated newspaper that offered young people an excellent opportunity (there's that word again) to earn money. The ad explained that the papers sold for a nickel, they cost three cents, and the other two cents was profit. Bingo! Here was the answer I had been looking for.

I ran in and showed the ad to my mother and told her that I was going to sell newspapers to make the money to get my new bike. She read the ad and finally looked up and said, "See, I told you that if you really wanted it, you would find a way to get it."

I was so excited I could hardly sleep that night. I couldn't wait to go see Mrs. Allen the next day to get my new bike. Promptly at 9:00 a.m. when the doors opened, I was the first person in the store. I ran up to Mrs. Allen waving the ad in my hand, and with a big smile and youthful enthusiasm, I exclaimed, "Look, Mrs. Allen, I found a way to make the dollar a week to buy my bicycle." I handed her the ad and continued, "I'm going to sell *Grit* newspapers. They sell for a nickel each, and I get to keep two cents from each one. All I have to do is sell 50 papers each week and that will give me the dollar a week I need to pay you. Can I get my bike today . . . pleeeease?"

Since it had been a few weeks since I had first approached her, Mrs. Allen was caught a bit off guard by my enthusiasm. She vaguely recalled telling me to show her how I could earn a dollar a week and she would sell me a bike, but she had no idea that I would follow through and come up with a plan to do so. Not wanting to dampen my enthusiasm, but looking for a way to buy some time, she asked me, "What makes you think you can sell 50 newspapers a week? That's a lot of papers."

As when she asked me before where was I going to get a dollar a week, I hadn't thought about this either. Again, I couldn't answer her question. Thump! I had just hit another pothole on the road to success. I had been so focused on how many papers I would need to sell to earn a dollar a week that I completely failed to consider how I could do it. Although I'm sure she had no intention of bursting my bubble, Mrs. Allen had just hit me squarely between the eyes with a dose of reality. Making a plan involves more than just talk. Was this another opportunity to quit? Absolutely! Did I let it get me down? Absolutely not!

This experience exposed me to another of the three Ds of success, which is Dedication. I really wanted that new bike; I had demonstrated my desire by continuing to look for ways to make the money I would need to get it, now I was faced with having to find the dedication to keep moving toward my desire. Let's continue this story in the next chapter, where I will discuss how I overcame this obstacle and kept moving forward. I'm splitting this experience into several chapters so I can show you how each step in the process produced another life lesson.

But before we move on, I want to remind you once again to reflect on your past. Think about similar experiences you may have had in your life. Have you ever wanted something very badly, but you hit an obstacle that kept you from getting it? If so, did you learn from the experience? Have you put what you learned to work? If not, don't worry; we all face problems, and this book is going to teach you how to look back at the decisions you've made, learn from them, and use that knowledge to start developing a plan of action that will set you squarely on the path to financial independence. That's why I keep reminding you to make notes. Don't let these recalled experiences slip back into the depths of your mind and be buried once again without extracting the lessons from them.

Key point from this chapter:

- Being successful takes more than positive thinking; it takes planning to be successful.

- People do things for their reasons, not yours.

- When facing an obstacle, immediately start looking for ways to get over, under, around, or through it.

- Another key step to success is being determined. Determination is what keeps you going even when obstacles get in your way.

11

A Plan Is More Than Just Having Good Intentions

We've all heard it said that good ideas are a dime a dozen, but implemented ideas are priceless. My plan to sell 50 papers a week was a good idea, but Mrs. Allen's question about how would I sell them exposed a fundamental flaw in the plan. I had an idea, but I hadn't thought about how to implement it. Isn't that what happens time and again to people who come up with great ideas, only to keep them to themselves until they see someone else implement them? Then they will say something like, "I thought of that three years ago; why didn't I follow through on it?"

As an eight-year-old growing up in the coal fields of Southern West Virginia in the mid-1950s, I didn't have a clue about how this high-powered psychology stuff was supposed to work, but what I have learned since is that I had at least two of the three Ds of success, which were Desire and Dedication. It was these two characteristics that kept me looking for a way to get that bicycle.

As you can imagine, when I left the Western Auto that day, once again I was extremely disappointed. I had gone to the store expecting to ride home on a shiny new bicycle, but instead I found myself walking back feeling very dejected, but having learned a third memorable life lesson: **Ideas must be implemented to be valuable.** I thought I had a great idea about selling papers to earn the money to buy a bicycle, but I hadn't thought about how to put it into practice. Later, in my adult years, I found a quote by William Benton, a former senator from Connecticut that fits this situation perfectly, one that still guides me in business today. "The rewards in business go to the man who does something with an idea." The same could be said about life in general. Wow! So simple, but so true!

I really wanted that new bicycle, and I wasn't about to let this new obstacle stop me from getting it. Once again, I talked with my mother and my friends, but it was my favorite teacher who pointed me in the right direction. Ora Ann Hash had taught me in the second grade. I had been a rowdy and rambunctious student who started the year full of mischief. By year's end, however, I was her favorite student and she was my favorite teacher. A particular incident early in the school year endeared us to each other in a very unusual way and provided her with a story she was still telling long after she retired. Even in her 80s, she was describing it as her most memorable incident as a teacher.

This story has nothing to do with my getting the bicycle, but it makes a great sidebar because it was so humorous and it gave me some insight into the type of child I was in my formative years. It will also help you understand the special relationship I formed with Ms. Hash. I hope you'll find it worth the few extra lines it takes to include in this text.

Ora Ann Hash was an excellent teacher and a kind and generous young woman, but very gullible. Early in the school year I discovered that I could put a thumbtack in her seat and she would sit down on it without ever looking. I could make obscene noises, and she was never able to tell where they were coming from. Once, I even put a big water snake in the pencil drawer of her desk, and when she opened it, she nearly fell over backwards trying to get out of its way. But the most memorable incident occurred when she had finally had enough of my antics and she made me go to the blackboard, which was directly behind her, draw a circle on it with a piece of chalk and then stand there on my tiptoes with my nose in the circle.

For me, all of my tricks and clowning around were done in fun, but having to stand in front of the class with my nose in a circle was just too embarrassing. I wanted to get even with her, so I started to peek around to either side when she was standing at her desk with her back to me instructing the other students. On one of my peeks, I noticed that she merely stood up from her chair to talk and then sat back down again when she finished. I also noticed there was a trash barrel right next to me and directly behind her chair. What an opportunity!

I want you to picture this trash barrel; it was one of those squatty containers made of heavy pasteboard with a smooth metal ring around the top that had been used at one time to secure a lid. It had once contained a floor-sweeping compound and was considerably wider than a normal wastebasket. Mrs. Hash was a rather large woman, with a healthy derriere just about the same size as the trash barrel.

You guessed it; the next time she stood up, I quietly switched her chair with the trash barrel. True to form, she spoke for a couple of minutes and then sat back down . . . right smack into the barrel. Now picture this, she initially caught herself near the top, but with each movement her plump bottom slipped farther and farther into the barrel until it eventually wedged all the way to the bottom. Her knees were pulled directly up under her chin, and her lower legs and arms hung over the sides of the rim, which fit neatly up under her knees and armpits. This left her in quite a predicament . . . especially since she was wearing a dress.

Completely stuck in the barrel and unable to move, she screamed at me to go get the principal. Scared nearly to death, I ran down the hall to the principal's office, knowing I was going to get the paddling of my life. I returned minutes later with the principal in tow. Poor Mrs. Hash; she was wedged tightly into the barrel totally unable to move. All of the students were huddled around with worried looks on their faces. As soon as the principal saw her, not knowing at the time that I was responsible for her predicament, he lost all restraint and burst out laughing. "Ora Ann, what on earth are you doing in that barrel?" he howled. By now she had determined that she wasn't hurt, just stuck so tightly in the barrel that she couldn't move. When the principal laughed, it dawned on her what the scene must look like to him, and she started laughing too. Now you need to understand that she was notorious for having a loud high-pitched laugh that could be heard all over the small school. When she started laughing, it started all the children laughing too. This raucous noise brought other teachers running, and the instant they saw the situation, they too began to howl with laughter. It would be near impossible for the best screenwriters to produce a more hilarious scene.

Eventually, with the help of the principal, the custodian, and two other teachers, Mrs. Hash was extricated from the barrel. One got her by the legs and another by the arms, and they lifted her up while the other two stood on opposite sides of the barrel and pulled down on it. When she was finally out, she told the principal what I had done. He grabbed me by the arm and started hauling me toward the office, but she stopped him. "This laugh has been too good to paddle a child over; let me deal with him," she said.

She told me to stay after school to meet with her. Although the incident occurred in the morning, I was so scared I could hardly breathe all afternoon. I didn't know what was going to happen to me. I was afraid she would tell my mother, and then I would have to deal with her and my stepfather when I got home.

Once the other students left, she sat me down next to her desk and we began to talk. The first thing she asked me why I was being so mean to her. I told her I was mad about her making me stand up in front of the class with my nose in a circle and I just wanted to get back at her for doing it. "Well, at least you're honest about it," she said.

We continued to talk, and she finally got around to what I was the most afraid about. She said, "You know what will happen if I tell your mother what you did, don't you?"

"Yes," I replied. "She will tell my stepfather, and he will kill me!"

"Can we make a deal?" she asked. "If I don't tell your mom, will you promise me that you will behave the rest of the year, do your work, and stop with all the pranks and things that disrupt the class?"

"Oh yes," I promised. "I won't ever do anything like that again." I knew I would be getting a reprieve, and I didn't want to blow it.

"Okay," she said. "Here's the deal; you keep your end of the bargain, we'll let this be just between us and I won't say anything; however, if you start up with the pranks again, I'll call her in for a conference and let her know what you did to me."

Following that act of kindness on her part, I vowed to never pull a prank in Ms. Hash's class again, and I didn't. If fact I ended up becoming a model student. She called me her favorite student and even let me occasionally spend time at her home helping her with chores. The loving relationship that developed between us was what led me to seek her advice in finding a way to convince Mrs. Allen that I could sell 50 papers a week.

The next day after meeting with Mrs. Allen, I stopped by Ms. Hash's room to talk with her about it. I told her about John getting the new bicycle and about how badly I wanted one too. I explained how my mother had told me that if I really wanted one, I would find a way to get it. I told her about my trips to see Mrs. Allen and how she wouldn't let me have a bike until I could prove to her that I could earn a dollar a week to pay for it. I showed her the advertisement I had taken to Mrs. Allen and explained what Mrs. Allen had said.

Mrs. Hash opened her desk drawer and pulled out a small notebook. As she held it in her hands, she said, "I'm going to give you an idea, but it will require a lot of work and discipline on your part to make it work. I'm going to give you this notebook, and I'm going to put my name in it first, saying that I will agree to buy a paper from you each week. All you have to do now is find 49 more people who will agree to do the same thing and get them to sign up under my name, but don't get just 49; get a few more in case something happens and some of them end up not taking the paper. If you can do this, it will give you something to take back to

Mrs. Allen to show her how you are going to make the money to pay for the bicycle."

With this statement, she introduced me to the third of the three Ds of success, which is Discipline. Throughout life I would come to realize that these three Ds, Desire, Discipline, and Dedication are like the legs of stool. With all three you have stability and almost anything is possible, but if you're lacking any one of them, it's difficult to maintain balance, and success is much harder, if not impossible, to achieve. The question was did I have the discipline to go out and find 49 or more people who would agree to buy the *Grit* paper each week?

Filled with enthusiasm, I immediately paid a visit to the other teachers in the school and got six of them to sign up. Then each day after school, I called on nearby neighbors, where I got another 12 to sign up. Gradually I started working my way farther and farther out from home, and after nearly two weeks of calling on anyone who would talk with me, I had more than 60 people signed up to buy. Now it was time to go back to see Mrs. Allen.

When I walked through the doors of the Western Auto this time, nearly three months had passed since my first visit. While many people would have given up long before, maybe even after the first disappointment, my desire for a new bicycle, my dedication to finding a way to get one, and the discipline I demonstrated by sticking with it until I found more than 60 people willing to buy a paper from me each week proved I was committed.

This time, when I sat down with Mrs. Allen, she was impressed. "I can't believe you have put all this work into getting a bicycle," she told me. "Now that you've shown me how you are going to pay for it, I guess I don't have any choice except to sell you a bicycle." I was bursting with excitement when she took me to the back area of the store where there were several bikes to choose from.

"Pick out the one you want, and we'll work out a payment arrangement," she said. "I talked with your mother a couple of weeks ago, and she said you were out signing up people to buy the paper, so I've been expecting to see you."

"You mean I can pick out any one I want?" I asked.

"Yep," she said, "with all the work you've done to prove to me how you are going to pay for it, I'll let you have any one you want, even one that's more expensive than John's."

"No," I said. "I want one just like his, the only thing different I want is a basket on the front to carry the papers in when I deliver them."

That day, I concluded my first entrepreneurial transaction and learned that my mother was right: if I wanted something badly enough, I would find a way to get it. What would have happened if my mother and stepfather, knowing how much I wanted a bicycle, had simply given me one? No gift could have taken the place of the life lessons I learned from this experience. Imagine the problem-solving skills, feeling of accomplishment, growth in confidence and self-esteem I would have been denied.

As I pedaled home on that shiny new bicycle, my chest swelling with pride, little did I realize that I had just completed my first leg on the journey to financial independence. Everyone has experienced situations in life like these; the problem is that only a few have the Desire, Discipline, and Dedication to see the problems through to a successful conclusion. It's always easier to find fault, complain, and commiserate about the tough times life hands us than it is to stand up and do something about it. As I continue with this section, I will analyze more stories like this and point out the life lessons that were embedded within them.

When my friend Roger Dawson was president of one of California's largest independent real estate companies, he learned that there was a question that he could ask job applicants that, if answered correctly, could virtually assure them of success as real estate agents. The question was, "How old were you when you first started earning money outside of your family?" You'd be amazed at how the answers to that question would vary. Some, like me, would say, "When I was eight, I started my own business delivering newspapers." Some would say, "When I graduated from college when I was 22." It turns out that there is a remarkable correlation between a person's level of initiative and the age at which they started earning money outside of the family. I found the same reaction when I joined Roger to write about investing in real estate in our book *The Weekend Millionaire's Secrets to Investing in Real Estate*. Readers who had started making money early in life had a high degree of initiative and were almost certain to do better than those who had been given everything in youth.

I hope you are following my earlier suggestion to make notes about your memorable life experiences that these stories trigger. Whether you realize it or not, you have learned from these experiences even if what you have learned has been more negative than positive. I don't mean to be redundant, but reflecting on the choices you made, and the results you received from these choices, is how you will be able to improve your decision making and start improving your financial situation.

Key points from this chapter:

- Ideas don't make you rich; the implementation of them does.

- Good ideas are a dime a dozen; implemented ideas are priceless.

- A good sense of humor, even in difficult situations, makes life more enjoyable.

- You never know when a seemingly small incident might have a lasting impression.

- Having a plan of action makes your ideas easier for others to accept.

- The three Ds of success, Desire, Discipline, and Dedication, are equally important to achieving success. It takes all three, not just one or two of them.

- The age at which you first started earning money outside of your family can be a good indicator of your degree of personal initiative.

12

Opportunity Finds Dedicated, Responsible People

When I pedaled away from the Western Auto store, the proud owner of a beautiful new red Western Flyer bicycle, I left knowing that I had committed to pay Mrs. Allen one dollar a week for 34 weeks. The sense of pride I felt knowing that she trusted me to fulfill this responsibility was enormous. My mother had to sign for me to place my first order, since the company needed a responsible adult to guarantee payment for the papers. Mrs. Allen graciously agreed to wait three weeks before my first payment would be due in order to allow me time to place my order for papers, have them shipped to me, and then give me time to get them sold.

It turns out that I was about to face another defining moment in my life. Like most kids my age, all I was interested in back then was riding the new bike home to show to my mother and my friends. The last thing on my mind was the thought that I had just been given an opportunity that would teach me one of the most important lessons of my young life.

I had a new bicycle and was bursting with the pride of accomplishment that came with having successfully met a challenge, but I had something even more important: I had a big responsibility. Now that I had the bike, I had the responsibility of paying for it. While Mrs. Allen had given me three weeks before the first payment would be due, I was still committed to paying her one dollar a week for 34 weeks. That might not seem like much today, but in 1954 in War, West Virginia, a dollar a week was a lot of money. For a child about to turn nine, it was a huge undertaking, considering that some adults in the community were working for just 25 cents an hour.

With the help from my mother, I immediately placed an order for my first 60 papers. When they arrived at the post office, rolled in two bundles, I opened the packages, put a load in the basket, and mounted my new bike to head out to deliver them. I was in business for myself. With each stop, I handed over a paper and collected a nickel. Several of the people who had signed up to buy a paper told me that they didn't really think I would follow through and actually deliver to them. It made me feel good when people complimented me on my determination and commitment. As the nickels in my pocket grew, so did my feeling of accomplishment. It still works that way today.

By the time the final paper was delivered that first week, two more people had signed up for delivery starting with the second week. I increased my order to 62 papers and repeated the process the following week. As word began to spread about how I was working to pay for my new bicycle, more and more people signed on for delivery. Within six weeks, my paper route had grown to 73 customers and I had religiously paid Mrs. Allen a dollar each Saturday.

People all over the small town were talking about me. They couldn't believe that a young boy like me would spend his spare time working to pay for a bicycle he had purchased on credit. This investment of my spare time may well have been the first evidence that one day I would learn how to convert spare time into financial independence. It also taught me something very important about credit. I learned that credit, when used to purchase something that earns money or can be used to earn money, is not bad. I was using the bicycle, purchased on credit, to deliver papers to earn the money to pay for the purchase. This was a criterion I would maintain into adulthood, one that has served me well to this day.

After a few weeks in which more people bought the paper each week, I again visited Ms. Hash, who had given me the original idea of signing up people for regular weekly delivery. I wanted to tell her about my success. As I explained that I was now earning enough to pay Mrs. Allen the dollar a week I had promised plus earning an extra 35 to 40 cents per week, she asked me what I was doing with the extra money. I said I was putting it in a jar in my bedroom.

Then she gave me some additional advice that would end up playing a big role in my success later in life. She advised me to accumulate two or three dollars and put them away to have in case something happened that I couldn't earn a full dollar one week. She explained that if I would do that, I would always be able to meet my obligation even if I had an unexpected problem. Little did I know back then that what she was doing was advising me to set aside reserve funds to use in case of an emergency. But in spite of these wonderful lessons I learned from buying my bicycle, the biggest lesson was yet to come.

One of my customers was the manager of the Western Union telegraph office in War. After he had observed my commitment to delivering the papers over a several-week period, one day when I went by his office with the current week's issue, the manager asked me to come in and talk with him. He directed me to a chair next to his desk and asked me to have a seat. My first thought was that he was going to tell me that he had decided to stop buying the paper, but to my surprise, the manager started out by saying, "I've got a problem that I'll bet you could help me solve if you're interested."

"What kind of problem?" I asked.

The manager began, "I've been observing your commitment to delivering the papers each week, and I've talked with Mrs. Allen, who tells me that you haven't missed a payment on your bike since you got it. That's remarkable for a youngster of your age—in fact it's not a bad record for any age—but it shows me that you are a responsible young man. For that reason, I have a proposition for you. We get several telegrams each week that have to be delivered. I've been doing this myself, but it's a real headache because I need to be here at the office most of the time. Since you know nearly everyone in town because of your paper route, if you're interested, I'll pay you 25 cents each to deliver the ones here in town. What do you think?"

"Wow!" I said, "How many are there each week?"

"Some weeks there are three or four; others there may be 10 to 15," the manager replied.

Now this really excited me. "What would I have to do?" I asked.

"Just come by my office each day after school. If any come in that day, I'll let you deliver them. When you give the telegram to the person to whom it is addressed, you will need to have that person sign a receipt for it. Bring back the signed receipt, and I'll pay you. That's all there is to it."

With that, I began a new job and learned one of the most important lessons of my young life: **People help those willing to help themselves.** The Western Union manager saw me as a responsible young person and gave me an opportunity he had never given a youngster before. I didn't ask for the opportunity; it was just offered. Some people would say, "Oh, that was just luck," but a careful analysis of the situation would reveal that this was merely an example of preparation meeting opportunity. As I mentioned in the preface to this section, if you aren't prepared for an opportunity that comes your way, you may not even notice it, and then when someone else grabs it, you will be talking about how lucky they were.

In this case, I was prepared. I knew the town, I knew the people, and I had the bicycle. As a result, I got the extra job and was able to pay off my bicycle in just over three months instead of the eight months I was expecting it to take. I also had extra spending money to do other things. Throughout my life I would find that the better prepared I was, the bigger the opportunities were that were presented to me. I guess you could say I was pretty lucky.

But back in War, my paper route kept growing, and I continued delivering telegrams. This continued until 1958, when I moved with my family to the big city (or at least it seemed like a big city compared to War) of Bluefield, Virginia, where I would continue my formative years, but I'll continue the story in the next chapter.

Key points from this chapter:

- The more you demonstrate responsibility, the more opportunities you will be given.
- People help those willing to help themselves.
- Borrowing to purchase something that makes you money can be good debt.
- Create an emergency fund to see you through difficult times.
- People notice people who are industrious and are trying to help themselves.
- The better prepared you are, the luckier you get.

13

Learning the Value of Patience and Persistence

My move to Bluefield, Virginia, in June of 1958 was like a breath of fresh air after living with the black coal dust, open sewers, and putrid-smelling drinking water of War, West Virginia, but it also brought additional challenges and life lessons. While in War, the family had grown from three to six with the birth of my two half-brothers and a half-sister. The home we moved to in Bluefield was like a palace compared with the one in War. It was a new three-bedroom one-bath home on a large two-acre parcel in a subdivision. I still had to share a bedroom with my two half-brothers, but I didn't mind.

During our years in War, my stepfather Paul had sold insurance. He was employed by People's Life Insurance Company, for which he worked a weekly route called a debit, covering several small coal-mining towns, including War. He would leave home each morning to sell life and accident policies to miners who hoped the insurance would provide for their families if they were injured or killed in the mines. He kept a route book in which he posted the weekly premiums he would collect in person by visiting the miners' homes. Each day when he returned from work, he would put away the money he collected that day, and each Thursday night he would prepare a report that he delivered to the company's offices in Bluefield, West Virginia (the town straddled the Virginia/West Virginia state line), on Fridays. Paul was a man of impeccable honesty and strong work ethic, and it had paid off for him. When the sales manager position became available, the company promoted him and moved us all to Bluefield to work out of the district office.

During our years in War, my relationship with Paul gradually deteriorated. Whether this deterioration came from me feeling slighted after the birth of Paul's natural children or from the frustration I felt because I was unable to learn anything about my real father is hard to say. I became more withdrawn and resentful of the busywork that Paul always seemed to find for me to do. I resented the fact that I never received an allowance or was paid for any of the things I did around the house, because most of my friends got allowances. Paul always said, "You live here so you have to earn your keep."

The only work for which I can remember getting paid occurred during the winter prior to our move to Bluefield. The old house where we lived in War had a coal-fired furnace for heat. One day Paul had a large truckload of coal delivered to the house. The truck backed up and dumped its load in the yard beside a small window that opened to a coal chute that went into a coal bin in the basement. When Paul came home that evening, he informed me that my job was to shovel the coal into the coal bin. He explained that I would need to shovel the coal into the chute until the center of the bin filled up, and then I would have to go inside the bin and shovel it to each side to make room for the rest of the load.

When I came home from school the next day, I changed into old clothes, found a shovel, and went out to the side of the house where the pile of coal awaited. I was very small for my age, so as I stood beside the pile that towered over my head, I knew it would take days to complete the job. Because I was so small, I was only able to lift the shovel when it was about half full. With each partial shovel of coal, my resentment toward Paul grew. It took two days to fill the center of the coal bin, then another day inside working in a cloud of black dust to shovel the coal to each side. When breathing became difficult, I would blow my nose and fill the tissues with jet-black mucus, stained that way by the coal dust. With each shovel of coal, I would ask myself, "Why me? Why can't I go play like all the rest of the kids my age? Why do I always have to work?"

It took days, but I finally completed the job. When I had all of the coal in the coal bin and the yard cleaned up, my animosity toward Paul had reached an all-time high. He must have sensed this, because he took me aside, put his arm around me and said, "You did a good job. Here!" and with that he handed me a dime. A dime! I couldn't believe my stepfather was being that cruel to me! I had been earning 25 cents per delivery from the telegraph office and over a dollar a week from my newspaper route. A dime! It seemed more like an insult than a reward, but that was the only money I can ever remember receiving from Paul.

I tell this story to give you a better understanding of the feelings that existed between Paul and me just prior to the family's move. To say it graciously, the pent-up emotion I felt was a seething hostility lying just beneath the surface, waiting to erupt. What transpired after the move did nothing to ease the tensions.

The new home we moved into was located on top of a rolling hill in a new subdivision that was just getting started. There were very few homes in the area; in fact, hunters regularly hunted rabbits and quail in the undeveloped fields throughout the subdivision. Only the main road through the subdivision was paved. The rest of them were dirt, with some even being single-lane dirt roads. The road that accessed our new home was one of these single-lane tracks that had been cut into the side of the hill in front of the house. The driveway branched off it and went up and around the hill to the back of the house, where it ended with a turnaround at a basement garage door.

The house was located on the very top of the hill. It had a full basement that included a single-car garage that opened to the turnaround at the top of the driveway. The yard consisted of a small level area that extended away from the house for a few feet, but most of it sloped sharply away down the hill in all directions. There were six lots with the new house, which gave it a total of about two acres of yard. Guess whose job it became to keep it mowed? You got it! I had to keep the yard mowed in the summer and the snow shoveled off the driveway in the winter, but the event that brought things to a head with me was an earthmoving project.

With very little level land around the house and just a single-lane dirt road leading up to it, Paul came up with a brilliant idea. Why not have me dig into the bank along the road in front of the house and haul the dirt up the hill in a wheelbarrow to build a terrace so my mother could have a level place to put a clothesline. This would also widen the road. It was a brilliant idea for everyone except me, who would have to do the work.

Each day Paul would assign me a number of loads of dirt to haul up the hill and dump. I was not allowed to spread the dirt out until he came home so he could count the loads to see if I had hauled enough that day. Each day it wasn't raining or snowing, I would have to haul my assigned loads of dirt before I could play with my friends. Can you imagine how this made me feel? While the other neighborhood kids rode bikes or played ball, I was hauling dirt. Often they would come by and make fun of me, calling me names like "dirt digger," "wheelbarrow jockey," and other names as I worked beside the road.

For two years I continued this routine of digging into that bank with a pick and mattock, shoveling the dirt into a wheelbarrow and hauling it up the hill to build the terrace. The days I didn't haul enough loads,

Paul would send me back out after dark to finish my assigned work. It was not a fun time, but it was a huge learning experience. Gradually, I grew stronger and improved my techniques for digging and shoveling dirt. I learned that by striking the same spot repeatedly with the pick or mattock, I could drive the blade deeper into the bank, thereby loosening larger amounts of dirt with less effort. I found out that a pointed shovel could be pushed into the dirt easier than a flat shovel. I learned to use my feet and legs to push the shovel into the dirt instead of my back. I tried several different ways to push the wheelbarrow up the hill and in time learned that by keeping my body erect, moving up between the handles and letting the weight rest on my fully extended arms I could get up the hill with larger and larger loads without hurting my back.

These dirt-digging and hauling techniques may not seem important, but like so many other experiences in my young life, I learned valuable lessons from them. First, I discovered how practice, with a focus on improvement, could make me better at whatever I was doing even if it was simply digging and hauling dirt. During the two years I worked on this earthmoving project, I constantly focused on ways to haul the required number of loads with less effort and in less time. By the time the project was finished, I was able to do the same amount of daily work I was doing in the beginning but do it in less than half the time and with much less feeling of exhaustion. By seeking out better and more productive ways to do the work, I learned that it gave me additional time and energy to do other things I wanted to do for myself.

Throughout this project, I didn't haul a single load of dirt up that hill without my resentment toward Paul growing. The name-calling I experienced from the kids in my neighborhood gradually made its way to the high school I attended. One day I was seen working in a light rain, and for the next month, I became known as "Mud Dauber" at school. All these things took their toll on my psyche, and by the start of my junior year of high school I began to contemplate leaving home, but something else was happening at the same time.

As the road widened and the terrace grew and I began to see the results of my efforts, I discovered the real-life lesson from this experience. **Patience and persistence are unstoppable.** Slowly, with just a few loads of dirt a day, spread out over time, I had changed the landscape around my house. The road was now wide enough for two cars to pass, and my mother had a new clothesline on the wide terrace I had built in the back of the house. The work was hard, but it hadn't killed me. My resentment toward Paul was at an all-time high, but at the same time the pride of accomplishment I felt was even higher. It was not until later in life when I was reflecting on this experience that I realized it was the event that taught me that patience and persistence could literally move mountains, or as the old saying goes, "A mouse can eat an elephant if you give him long enough."

As I have mentioned several times already, I am sharing these stories and experiences from my life to stimulate your thinking and help you recall events from your past. Your path to financial independence will be forged by the lessons embedded in your life's experiences, not mine. Hopefully your notepad is filling up with reminders of these experiences as you read this text. When preparing this manuscript, the more stories I wrote about, the more that were recalled. To include them all would take several volumes, and since this book is not meant to be an autobiography, I have distilled them down to just the ones that taught me significant life lessons and helped me develop traits that have led me to much success.

In this Section I have been sharing experiences from which I learned life lessons as a younger child in my Formative Years. In Section III I will continue with learning experiences I encountered as a teenager and young adult. I call these times the Learning Years.

Key points from this chapter:

- With change comes challenges, but these can make you stronger.
- Harboring resentment and hard feelings only makes work more difficult.
- Practice, with a focus on improvement, improves performance even if you are simply digging dirt.
- Tasks that may otherwise seem daunting become very doable when you break them down into small pieces; think one shovelful at a time.
- The combined forces of patience and persistence are unstoppable.

PART III

Lessons from the Transition/Learning Years

While all the years from birth until death are learning years, I consider the Transition Years between childhood and adulthood as the real Learning Years. These are the years when many life lessons, especially those regarding finances, are learned, or not learned. They are the years between the time when you first start making decisions for yourself and the point in life where you become established on a steady career path. I realize that some people have more of these years than others; in fact, it could be said that there are people who never get beyond the Learning Years, because they never get established on a steady career path. These are also the years when lessons learned during the Formative Years can subconsciously cause people to run into trouble. I call these the Learning Years because they are the years in which you discover that you don't know everything after all.

I'm sure you've known young people who dropped out of school with great career aspirations only to run head-on into the reality that life doesn't always deal the hand you expected. Even those with high school diplomas or college degrees often face unforeseen setbacks that change their direction in life and set them on different courses than they thought they would take. Whether you want to admit it or not, money and the need to earn a living alter the lives of nearly everyone in some way or another.

Unfortunately, our public education system concentrates so much on preparing students to get a "job" that it inadvertently diminishes or kills the entrepreneurial spirit in many young people. Guidance counselors and other academic advisers present students with charts and graphs that show the average difference in income between high school dropouts, high school graduates, college graduates, and those holding advanced degrees as a way to encourage them to advance their education. Don't get me wrong; I certainly don't mean to imply that education is not important. What I want you to understand is that an education merely puts tools in your toolbox. The more tools you have the better . . . most of the time, but tools aren't worth much unless you put them to work.

Where I feel public education falters is by not focusing more on the application of the tools. High school students are taught math and science, English and foreign languages, but very few graduate with the ability to balance a checking account, understand the proper use of credit, or prepare a family budget. They aren't taught how critical these skills are to financial success, no matter what field one chooses to pursue. I once hired a man for a manual labor job who was in his mid-30s and held a doctorate degree in some exotic field of geology. When I questioned him as to why he was applying for such a menial job, he said, "Because I can't find a job in my field and I need to work." I soon discovered the man's problem; he had a great education but didn't have a clue how apply it. He was what I call an educated idiot!

The Learning Years begin when you start trying to apply what you've learned in school and from your childhood experiences to situations in the workplace. During these years, many people become frustrated because they find that what they learned as theory doesn't always work when applied to practical situations. It's like a person who takes a sales job, goes through the company's training program, and learns to make a great sales presentation only to call on prospects who didn't attend the same training program. Unless they come to the realization that it's not how good the presentation is, but whether or not the sale is made, they just become more and more frustrated. Unless they look for the reasons why customers aren't buying and make changes to meet the customers' expectations, they end up leaving that job, and move on to "try" something else. Success isn't the result of how hard you work; success comes from what you are able to accomplish.

The stories in this section, like the ones in the previous section, are designed to help you understand the role common sense plays in financial success. Once again, I urge you to keep that notepad handy and jot down any situations from your life that my stories may trigger as you read these chapters. I know you're probably getting annoyed with me for saying it over and over, but it's your experiences that you will need to delve into and examine to find the building blocks of your success. It's from your life experiences that you will be able to discover the successes and failures that have brought you to the present. It's by analyzing your own mistakes and what you could have done to correct them that will allow you to change your direction in life in the future. My stories are being told solely for the purpose of letting you know that, like you, I had many obstacles to overcome as well. I want to encourage you to examine your own life experiences with an open mind, looking for the life lessons embedded in them that you may have missed. Believe me, they are there! I feel that by explaining mine, it may help you look at yours in a different light and be able to see things you might have overlooked.

You may be thinking, "I don't have any experiences like yours," but you do! No, they won't be the same experiences I've had, because everyone is different, but you've had experiences that contain hidden life lessons just as I have, and this book is all about helping you learn how to find them and extract the lessons they contain. I share my experiences to help you see how I distilled the key learning points out of my experiences, even the ones that weren't always pleasant or comfortable. What's important is that you keep making notes as you read and recall events from your life. In time you will begin discovering things you missed at the time, things that will help you make better decisions in the future. You will also see that the decisions you make are what determine your success or failure in life. Wherever you are in life today is a direct result of the decisions you have made up until now.

Now, let's move on to discuss the Learning Years in greater detail.

14

How Positive Thinking Enables You to Grow

I closed the last section by mentioning that my building animosity toward my stepfather as I started my junior year of high school had me dreaming of leaving home. Throughout that school year our mutual hostility grew, and by spring we had actually exchanged physical blows. I was headstrong, stubborn, and toughened from growing up in the crucible of hard times. Paul was just as determined to have things his way. By late spring the situation reached a point where I refused to listen to any more criticism or be given any more orders by him. One day Paul was in a bad mood, and I caught the brunt of it. "You're so stupid; you don't have the sense God gave a dumb goose," he yelled at me.

"Oh yeah, we'll see about that," I yelled back as I swung a fist at Paul. My defiance was met with a sharp slap across the face that knocked me into a corner, where Paul stomped and kicked me until I apologized and agreed to succumb to his demands.

With rage boiling inside, I crawled to my room and made the decision that enough was enough. I would leave home, but with no money and nowhere to go, I knew I would have to bide my time and wait for the right moment to leave. That moment came in June 1962 shortly after the school year ended. We were paying a weekend visit to my grandmother's home in Abingdon, Virginia. The afternoon as we were getting ready to depart for the return trip to Bluefield, I slipped out the back door and ran. I didn't know where I was going, but I knew I wasn't going back to Bluefield. I ran until I reached a nearby swamp where thick brush and cattails would hide me from view. As I hid crouched in the muck and mud of the swamp, I knew I had made a decision from which there would be no turning back.

This would become the first life-altering decision of my Learning Years, and with it came a rapid series of life lessons. Knowing there would be no turning back, I was forced to learn the importance of making a decision and then making it work. I had to find a way, not make an excuse. This was an attitude that would stick with me for the rest of my life. When I walked out that back door and ran, I did so with the total commitment that I would never return to the life I had known up to that time. Was I scared? Absolutely! Did I know what the next day would bring? No! What I did know was that I had made a decision, I was committed to it, and I would find a way to make it work . . . no matter what.

The rest of that afternoon was an intense time. In an area of rolling hills with little ground cover, the swamp upstream from the dam at an old grist mill was the only thick cover for miles around. I knew that Paul would be looking for me, so concealment became my first order of business. Sure enough, within an hour, he was driving up and down the road next to the swamp yelling as he passed by, "I know you're in there somewhere; either get out here now or you'll wish you had."

I had worked my way deep into the swamp to ensure that Paul would not be able to see me. But as the car drove up and down the road, and I heard him calling out to me, the fear that the color of my clothes would stand out too much in the brush and cattails and give me away caused me to slip into the water up to my neck so I would be completely concealed. Despite the water snakes, muskrats, turtles, and other swamp creatures that I saw swimming around me, I remained submerged in the water until nightfall gave me the cover I needed to feel safe to move.

When I crawled out of the swamp, my skin was wrinkled like a prune from being in the water so long, and I was covered in thick smelly swamp mud. I had no other clothes, so all I wanted to do was get the mud off me and try to clean up a bit. I made my way along the opposite edge of the swamp from the road until I reached the dam that backed up the stream. I carefully made my way down to the bottom of the dam, where I stripped naked, stepped under the edge of the spillway, and let the water rushing over the dam wash me off. I stood there for several minutes letting the water rinse the mud from my body. Once I got somewhat cleaned off, I spent the next several minutes washing my clothes in the spray until they were relatively clean too. Then, shivering from the cold water, I wrung out my clothes, put them back on, and sat down on a rock to contemplate my next move.

There was an old mill next to the lake created by the dam. As I sat there, I thought, "What have I done?" I was wet, cold, tired, and hungry and didn't have a clue what to do next, but I knew I had made the right decision. I decided to look around the old mill, which was still in operation back then, but has long since been torn down, to see if I could find something to eat and maybe a place to rest. It was Sunday night, and the mill was closed; there were no houses around, so I felt comfortable exploring the grounds. When I came around the building to the parking lot, I noticed a truck backed up next to a loading dock, and upon closer examination, I discovered that the truck contained vegetables that were probably bound for market. I lifted a couple of tomatoes, a cucumber, and two potatoes from the truck, went back to the river, washed them, and sat back down on a rock to eat.

After eating the raw vegetables, which curbed my hunger, I began looking for a place to rest until morning. On the uphill side of the mill, near the dam, there were several corncribs and other small storage buildings. I tried a number of them that were locked before finding a crib with the door open. It contained several feet of dried corn, still on the cob, and scattered around the crib were a number of empty burlap sacks that had probably held corn at one time. I gathered up several of the sacks, pitched them into the crib, and then crawled in with them to create a makeshift bed in the corn. By this time, my clothes were nearly dry, and I curled up on the sacks and immediately fell asleep. I didn't wake up until the following morning when the sun began to rise and I heard birds chirping.

At first, I didn't realize where I was, but when I opened my eyes and looked around, it dawned on me that this would be the first day of a new life for me. I sat up, stretched, and let my mind sort through thoughts of what I should do next. I knew the mill would open for business soon, so I wanted to be gone before the employees started to arrive. I also knew I would be welcome at my grandmother's home, but I was concerned that Paul may have stayed overnight and would be waiting for me to show up. Daylight was just beginning to break, so I decided to make my way back to my grandmother's to see if his car was still in her driveway. I wanted to get there before people in the house woke up and started stirring.

I left the mill and cut through the fields away from the road until I arrived at the edge of the neighborhood where my grandmother lived. I made my way through people's yards and quickly crossed streets until I was close enough to see her house. I approached from the back along a high hemlock hedge that surrounded the next-door neighbor's lot until I could see her driveway around the corner of the hedge. To my relief, it was empty. Paul's car was not there. I eased into the edge of the hemlocks and sat down where I could keep my eye on the driveway, yet still be concealed from view. I wanted to be sure Paul wasn't just out looking for me again in order to try to force me to return to Bluefield.

One hour passed, then two, then three! The sun climbed higher in the sky, the dew evaporated, and as the temperature began to climb, the reality of the situation began to settle in. I had no money, no clothes other than what I was wearing, and no idea what to do next. The only thing I was sure about was that I was not going back to Bluefield. As I sat there pondering my next move, I recalled the time when I lived in War and really wanted that bicycle. I recalled my mother saying, "If you really want one, I'll bet you can find a way to get it." When I thought about the obstacles I had encountered and the things I had done to overcome them in order to get the bicycle, it dawned on me that this was just another challenge. Although I had no idea at the moment how I would survive, I knew I would find a way. I was anxious and maybe a bit nervous, but I wasn't afraid. Although I couldn't define it as such back then, this was a learning experience and one of many that would teach me that **growing requires stretching, getting out of your comfort zone.** I was definitely not in my comfort zone.

My decision not to return to Bluefield was a leap of faith . . . a stretch. Spending time submerged in a smelly swamp, showering with cold river water pouring down from a spillway, eating raw vegetables, and sleeping in a corncrib, all in less than 24 hours, definitely took me out of any comfort zone I might have had. These were short-term inconveniences though that I was willing to endure to possibly build a better life. As I sat there huddled in the hemlock hedge facing life with no shelter, no money, no job, no transportation, no education, and none of the necessities even an abusive home could provide, it was scary and quite a stretch. I kept staring at the empty driveway and getting hungrier and hungrier. Finally I got up the courage to go to my grandmother's house to see if I could get something to eat and talk with her about my future.

I came in the back door and found her sitting at the kitchen table having a cup of coffee and staring out the window. When she saw me, she jumped up, ran over, and threw her arms around me, and with tears in her eyes said, "Oh, I'm so glad to see you. I've been up all night worrying. Where have you been?"

"Where's Paul?" I asked.

"He and your mother and the other children went home last night," she replied. "He was so mad at you; I hope he didn't take his anger out on your mother or the children. Why did you run off like that?"

"I just couldn't take it anymore. Nothing I did pleased him. He called me stupid and dumb; he said I didn't have the sense God gave a dumb goose and stuff like that. It made me so mad I just finally had enough of it. I made up my mind before we came over here that I would not go back to Bluefield and live like that anymore. When they were getting ready to go home yesterday, I knew that the only way I could keep him from forcing me to go back was to run away and hide, so that's why I left."

"I understand how you feel," she said, "but what are you going to do? You haven't even finished high school."

"I don't know," I replied. "I don't know what I'm going to do; I was hoping I could talk with you about that and make some decisions. The only thing I know for sure is that I'm not going back to Bluefield. I've been thinking about it for hours, and I was hoping you'd let me stay here and finish my last year of high school, and after that I'll get a job and take care of myself. If you'll let me stay here, I promise, I'll earn my keep. I'll mow the lawn, trim the shrubs, and do anything else you want; I just need a place to stay for a year until I can finish high school."

"Honey, you know you're welcome here anytime, but your mother is worried sick about you. She called last night when they got home and has already called this morning to see if I've heard from you. Let's give her a call so we can at least put her mind at ease, okay?"

"You can call her, but I'm not going back," I said. "Yesterday was one of the most miserable days of my life. I spent the afternoon up to my neck in swamp water and mud, washed myself and my clothes in a cold creek, ate raw vegetables for dinner, and slept in damp clothes in one of the corncribs down at the mill, but as bad as that was, it was better than going back to Bluefield."

That exchange began a yearlong roller coaster ride that transitioned me out of my Formative Years and into my Learning Years. It was a year that would solidify my ability to make decisions and then make them work, to focus on the future without looking back or second-guessing myself. It would become an unbelievably difficult year of growing and stretching.

My grandmother called my mother and relayed my feelings about returning to Bluefield. She told her that I would be staying with her for my senior year of high school. Mom made arrangements to have my clothes packed and put on a bus to Abingdon, where they arrived the next day.

During that summer, I mowed and trimmed my grandmother's property just as I promised I would. I also did numerous other odd jobs to earn some spending money to help pay my way. I caught small painted turtles in the swamp and sold them to a local pet shop for 25 cents each; I cut cattails and sold them to flower shops for a dollar a dozen; I mowed lawns, trimmed shrubbery, cleaned gutters, painted, and did any other odd jobs I could find.

Toward the end of summer, I enrolled at Abingdon High School for my senior year. The first day of school, I didn't know a soul, and, even worse, no one seemed to be interested in meeting me. I tried to make friends, but with little success. I soon became labeled as a pest by the students and a disruptive student by the teachers. By Christmas I had been sent to the principal's office numerous times, and the guidance counselors began to realize there was more to my disruptive behavior than showed on the surface. The first week after the holiday break, my guidance counselor called me in to discuss my behavior and try to help me get the second half of the year started on a better footing. As we talked, I told her that I realized I had a chip on my shoulder that was causing me problems, but I didn't know what to do about it. She told me that she knew a good psychiatrist and asked if I would consider meeting with him to see if he had any suggestions that may be helpful. At this point, I was willing to try almost anything, so I agreed to go.

The guidance counselor took me to Bristol, Virginia, for the meeting. I only attended one session, but what I learned during that session resulted in some enormous personality changes and started me on the road to changing my life for the better. I opened up to the psychiatrist very quickly and revealed my feelings about my childhood, my life with Paul, my resentment and bitterness toward him, and the emptiness I felt about never having met my real father. As my emotions poured out, I broke down into tears and cried, "Why can't I just have a life like everyone else? Why does everything have to be so hard?"

The psychiatrist allowed me to regain my composure and then gave me some advice that has stuck with me for the rest of my life. He gently laid his hand on my arm and said, "Son, nearly all the problems you've described are your fault. Now before you get upset with me, let me explain. Whenever something happens to you, whether it is good or bad, you have a choice as to how you react to it. When something good happens, it's easy to react in a positive way, but when bad things happen, it's much more difficult to feel or act positively. Let me explain. Have you ever noticed how when you react negatively to something someone does that it always seems to make matters worse? You end up saying things you shouldn't say, doing things you shouldn't do, and acting in ways that bring negative responses from other people. Once you perform a negative act or utter hurtful words, they can't be taken back, and this causes people not to like you."

As I sat there listening, I was mentally playing back my responses to criticism, directives, and other actions I hadn't liked. The longer the psychiatrist spoke, the more I realized the guy was right on target. I couldn't think of a single time when I hadn't reacted negatively when things didn't go my way. Suddenly it became clear that I had brought much of my anger and disappointment upon myself.

As the session neared its end, the psychiatrist said, "Let me give you a challenge. When you go to school tomorrow, the first time someone says or does something that bothers you, stop and mentally say 'positive, positive, positive' to yourself three times before you make a comment. While you're doing this, think of something good to say, or don't say anything at all. Remember that how you react is your choice, no matter what other people say or do. If you can't think of something good to say, then just choose not to say anything. Try this for one week, and see if it doesn't make a big difference."

This was all new information. Like so many young people, at this stage of my life, the only way I knew to react to negative words or actions was to retaliate in kind. When people would pick on me or make fun of me, I wanted to get even. This "get even" attitude was especially damaging because my small stature made me an easy target to be picked upon. As late as my junior year of high school, I was the smallest student in class, standing less than five feet tall and weighing less than a hundred pounds. Even the girls were all bigger than me.

I experienced a huge growth spurt after leaving home, and by the start of the school year, I was no longer one of the smallest students in school, but I still had a chip on my shoulder about being picked on. When the psychiatrist explained that I was probably bringing on most of the treatment I disliked by the way I reacted, I listened. I left that counseling session determined to accept the psychiatrist's challenge and agreed that if I faced adversity during the coming week, I would either respond positively or not at all. At least, it was worth a try.

My first opportunity to try out this new commitment came very quickly. When I got on the school bus the next morning, the first thing that happened was my biggest nemesis tried to trip me going down the aisle. I stumbled but didn't fall, and several of the other kids laughed, but I just continued to an empty seat near the back of the bus and sat down. The trip to school was otherwise uneventful, but as I got off the bus, the boy who had tried to trip me was waiting.

"Didn't you see my foot when you were getting on?" he asked in a cocky tone of voice. "What were you trying to do, step on my foot on purpose?"

"Positive, positive, positive," I thought before answering. Then I responded, "No, I wasn't trying to step on your foot. I saw that shirt you're wearing, and I really like it. I guess I was looking at it and didn't see your foot. I'm sorry."

This was such a change for me, because before the counseling session, I would probably have responded with something like, if you hadn't stuck your damned foot in the aisle trying to trip me, you wouldn't have gotten it stepped on. All that would have accomplished would have been to start an altercation that probably would have landed both of us in the principal's office. But to my amazement, this boy who had picked on me all year, simply said, "You really like the shirt? Thanks! My girlfriend gave it to me for Christmas and today is the first time I've worn it."

"It's really a neat shirt," I replied. "I wish I had one that nice."

And with that, a grin came on the boy's face, and he again said, "Thanks!" as he headed off to class. I just stood there kind of stunned for a moment. "Wow, maybe this positive stuff really does work," I thought as I also headed to class. I couldn't help but think about the kind of altercation the incident could have turned into if I had responded in my usual way. Without even realizing it at the time, this incident became a defining moment on my road to success.

It's very difficult to make dramatic behavior changes, but in spite of the fact that I never made a return visit to the psychiatrist, the more I practiced what he had told me, the more surprised I was at how differently both students and teachers were treating me. By the end of that trial week, I could see some real benefits from thinking positively. By the end of January, I was feeling much better about myself. By the end of February, in spite of experiencing a few minor slipups, my confidence was growing, my spirits had lifted, and I was beginning to look forward to the future. I felt better about myself than I could ever recall.

Although I was experiencing positive effects from my changed behavior, nothing could have reinforced the power of thinking and acting positively more than what happened the following month. It was mid-March and I was in the attic helping my grandmother with some spring cleaning. All winter she had been telling me that she wanted to get in the attic as soon as the weather improved and throw away a bunch of old stuff that had been stored there for years. For several hours we had been going through boxes of old clothes, shoes, toys, and other similar things that get stored away in most homes. I was going up and down the stairs carrying boxes to be thrown away, when on one trip back to the attic I noticed an old cigar box lying off to one side. I picked it up, opened it, and my life changed forever. Inside the box was a single envelope addressed to my mother, and the return address on it was from Leroy Summey, my biological father.

I sat there holding the letter; my hands were trembling, my heart was racing, and an overwhelming feeling of anxiety swept over me. Because of all the problems I had experienced with my stepfather Paul, the anger, the hurt, the animosity and disruptions in my life had created an intense longing to learn about my real father, and yet I had no idea where he was or even if he was still alive. This was the first evidence I had ever found that might help me locate him. My mother's breakup with my father had been such a bitter one that no one in the family would talk with me about it or give me any information as to his whereabouts. I wasn't sure if I should tell my grandmother about it or hide it to look at later. She must have realized what I'd found, because she said, "Honey, I saved that letter to give to you when you were old enough to understand. It was a letter that came to your mother when they were in the process of getting divorced. I forgot about it being up here with all this junk."

My grandmother was always the one person I could turn to for support. She was a small woman who insisted on all her grandchildren, nieces, and nephews calling her by her first name, Sallie. She would stand up for me when she was around Paul, and I felt that she was the only one who really understood my plight. My one big problem with both my mother and Sallie was that they would never tell me anything about my father. Now I had a letter with an address, albeit 16 years old, that I could write to and maybe get a response. That's just what I did. That very night I sat down and wrote a letter that would alter my entire direction in life. The following exhibit, Figure 11, is a copy of the front of that letter:

Fig. 11

I found this old letter in 2004 while cleaning out my dad's house after he passed away. You can see the note I put on the front of the envelope that reads, "Address 16 years old Foreward [sic] if possible."

Several days passed after I mailed the letter, and deep down inside, I doubted if I would ever receive a response, but Tuesday, March 26, 1963, as I stepped off the school bus a little after 3:00 p.m., I saw Sallie standing on the front porch waiting for me. In her hand was a letter, and when I got to the end of the walk and started up the steps, she reached out and handed it to me. She didn't say a word; she just gave it to me. When I looked down and saw it was from my dad, the first thing I noticed was that the handwriting looked very much like mine. I dropped my schoolbooks on the porch and sat down on the steps with the letter. This was one of the most emotional moments of my life. Sallie must have sensed that, because she sat down beside me and put her arm around me.

"Go on, open it," she said.

But I was afraid. "What if he's remarried? What if he has other children? What if he doesn't want to see me? What if he does?" These and a dozen more similar thoughts ran through my mind as I sat there holding the letter. I wanted to open it, but I didn't. The anticipation about what it contained was so great it almost overwhelmed me. I sat there looking at the envelope for what seemed an eternity before I took out my pocketknife and slit it open. I took out the single sheet and unfolded it. The letter was brief, but it contained everything I hoped it would.

"I've thought about you many times over the years and wondered how you were doing, but due to the circumstances under which your mother and I separated, I didn't feel like I could contact you," my dad wrote. "I'm not much for letter writing, but I'd love to talk with you. Please call me collect after 5:00 p.m. at . . . ," and he listed the telephone number. I had just turned 17 in January, and for all those years I had longed to have a dad like the other kids around me. Now, I was less than two hours from talking with my father for the first time in my life. What would I say? What would my dad say? What would he sound like? What kind of job would he have? Would he want to see me? My head was spinning. A thousand thoughts rushed through my mind in a blur of mixed-up feelings and emotion.

If **growing requires stretching, getting out of your comfort zone,** this was one huge growing experience. As I waited for five o'clock to arrive, I paced the floor. I wanted to scream at the top of my lungs with excitement and at the same time wanted to sit down and cry. I couldn't tell you why I felt either way; I just did. The closer it got to the time, the more nervous I became, and Sallie sensed my discomfort. She tried to comfort me and assure me that everything would be all right, but the wait was gut wrenching. Finally at 5:02 I picked up the phone and dialed the operator.

I gave her the phone number and told her I wanted to place the call collect from Mike Summey. On the second ring, a man's voice answered, "Hello!"

"Sir, I have a collect call from Mike Summey. Will you accept the charges?"

"Yes, absolutely," the male voice answered.

"Go ahead, sir, your party is on the line," the operator said.

"Dad, is that you?" I asked.

"Yes, it's me, boy. It's sure good to hear your voice," my dad replied. "How are you doing?"

And this started a phone conversation that lasted over an hour. I learned that my dad, Lee, was remarried to a nice lady named Madge. I even spoke to her on the phone and learned that they did not have any other children and she would love for me to come for a visit. She also informed me that it was my dad's 44th birthday and this was the best present he could ever have gotten. We all agreed that we wanted to meet each other, and the sooner the better. The problem was we were several hours apart over twisting mountain roads. I was in Abingdon, Virginia, and my dad was in Asheville, North Carolina. Dad suggested that I hang up and call the bus depot to find out when bus service was available between the towns and then call him back with the information.

I made the call and learned that the only service available left Abingdon at 8:30 in the evening and arrived in Asheville at two in the morning. The next bus was less than two hours from leaving. I immediately called back and advised my dad of the schedule.

"Can I come tonight?" I asked with great anticipation. "I don't think I can wait another day."

"Sure," my dad replied. "If you can catch the bus, Madge and I will meet you at the bus station."

"I'll catch the bus, one way or another," I replied.

"What will you be wearing, so we will be able to recognize you?"

"I'll be in blue jeans and a plaid shirt, but I have a red baseball cap. I'll wear it so you can spot me easier," I said.

With that, I threw a change of clothes in an old grocery bag, grabbed the few dollars I had been able to save, and ran nearly three miles to the bus station. I had just enough money to buy a one-way ticket and hoped my dad would cover the cost of the return ticket. That began a larger journey that would take me from the hills of southwestern Virginia to the mountains of western North Carolina, where I still live today. The trip was a leap of faith, because when I stepped off that bus, I had little more than the clothes on my back and two dollars in my pocket. I had come alone to meet a father I had never known. Talk about getting out of your comfort zone!

My visit lasted from early Wednesday morning until I reluctantly returned the following Sunday afternoon. During that trip, I learned that I had a whole family in Asheville, aunts, uncles, cousins, and a grandmother who was definitely the matriarch of the entire clan. My dad wanted me to go back and finish high school but also wanted me to come to Asheville to live with Madge and him following graduation. This was what I had hoped for, and I couldn't wait. Finally, good things were coming my way and coming in bunches. On the bus trip home, I closed my eyes and wondered if all my good fortune could be the result of the positive attitude I had developed after seeing the psychiatrist.

When I returned to school on Monday, I had some explaining to do about the days I had missed the previous week, but everyone in the office could sense my enthusiasm and see the excitement on my face as I told them where I'd been. I was granted excused absences for the days and allowed to make up my missed work. As each new day dawned, I faced it with renewed vigor and growing self-assurance. I could sense that I was turning my life around and doing it on my own. There really did seem to be something to this positive thinking stuff after all, but I still wanted to put it to the test.

Throughout the school year, I had kept my eye on what I considered to be the prettiest girl in the school. Donna Woodward was a gorgeous little girl in the junior class who was just under five feet tall and weighed less than a hundred pounds, but she had the voice of an angel. She would sing the National Anthem at school events and always got the singing parts in school plays. I had been infatuated with her from the time I first laid eyes on her, but so were most of the boys in the school. With my newfound courage, I decided it was time to really put this positive thinking to the test. I decided to ask Donna to be my date for the Junior/Senior Prom, another stretch in the growing process, especially since I had never had a date before.

It took me several days to find the opportunity to get her aside so I could ask her, but when I did, she readily accepted. I couldn't believe it. Now what was I going to do? I had no car, no nice clothes, and no one I could turn to for help. Once again my mother's words came back to me, "If you really want it badly enough, you'll find a way to get it." Taking Donna to the prom was something I really wanted to do.

With only a few weeks to go before the big dance, I was nearly in a panic. There was no way I was going to tell her I couldn't go after she had accepted my invitation. I would find a way! For the next month I did anything and everything I could to make money. I trimmed shrubbery, I cleaned gutters, washed and waxed cars, anything to earn a dollar or two. Finally I had enough to buy a new suit to wear to the prom, but I still had to get there. That was going to be the challenge. I kept working and saving, and by the time the big day arrived, I had saved enough to afford a taxi to take us to the prom.

I had never mentioned to Donna how we would get there, and she probably assumed that I would have a car, so when I showed up at her house in a taxi, her mother was nearly in shock. She wasn't about to let her daughter go to the prom in a taxi. She was so gracious when she took me aside and told me to send the taxi on its way. She would let us drive her car. June Woodward is to this day one of the kindest, most understanding people I have ever known, and I will be eternally grateful to her for making it possible for me to have a wonderful prom to cap off an otherwise tumultuous roller coaster year in my life.

I have only touched upon a few of them, but from June 1962 until June 1963, I faced enough emotional problems and obstacles to rip most people apart. The first half of the year was a dismal downhill slide that focused on negative thoughts and deeds, while the second half focused on the power of positive thoughts and actions. Everyone faces problems, but as I learned, it's not the problems; it's how you respond to them that determines your success or failure in life. Reflecting back on that year, the biggest lesson I learned was that you don't become successful with a head full of anger, resentment, and negative thoughts. Positive, positive, positive is the way to go.

This has been a difficult chapter to write, but hopefully it has allowed you to see why I say that **growing requires stretching, getting out of your comfort zone.** Now let's move on to the next chapter, where I will pick up with additional life lessons I learned following my move to North Carolina.

Key points from this chapter:

- It takes commitment to change your life, the kind of strong commitment that I had when I wanted to change my life so badly that I ran away from home.

- Life gets better when you get better; learn to take charge of your actions.

- You can't control what happens to you, but you can control the way you react to what happens to you.

- When bad things happen, think positive, positive, positive before you respond.

- When you experience difficulties, think of them as growing pains.

- Remember, growing requires stretching, getting out of your comfort zone.

15

The Grass May Look Greener, But It Has to Be Mowed Too

The day after graduating from high school, I packed my few possessions into a cardboard box and boarded a bus for Asheville, North Carolina, to live with my father. Although I had learned how thinking and acting positively could improve my situation, I still had deep-seated emotional wounds that needed to heal. I carried with me high hopes and dreams for a better life. The move represented a fresh start in a new town with a new family and a chance to establish a promising future. I was thinking positive, positive, positive.

I very quickly learned that my dad was not a man of means, but he liked to play the part. He was a bookkeeper for a small coal and oil company and lived in a modest three-bedroom, one-bath cinder-block house that had been built by two of his brothers who were in the building business. He drove a new Buick and always wore a suit and tie . . . even when mowing the lawn. He dabbled in the stock market and owned a few utility stocks, but he loved to give the impression he was a heavy hitter. This all seemed strange to me, because I had grown up in a family where discussions of money centered more on what we didn't have than what we did have.

From the day we first met, Dad seemed to want to impress me with how smart he was and how much he was worth. He had learned from my first visit that I hadn't grown up in an affluent family, and it seemed that he wanted to be sure he appeared better off financially than his ex-wife. He was now married to a wonderful Polish lady from Texas named Madge, whose family owned a farm with several oil wells on it. She was one of several children, and her parents had arranged for the oil royalties to be split between themselves and all the children. Although the monthly checks were only a few hundred dollars, Dad never missed an opportunity to talk about the oil wells he had in Texas.

As soon as I arrived in Asheville, I went to work with my dad's brothers building houses. For the first time in my life, I had extra spending money from the $40 I made each week. Over the next few months, I borrowed my dad's car and used part of my newfound money to have a few dates and buy some new clothes. I also purchased three $25 US savings bonds as a way of setting aside some money for the future. Eventually, my dad helped me buy a 1959 Studebaker Lark for $300, and I moved on to a new job as a lab technician in a textile factory where one of his brothers worked. I mixed and matched dye colors at the big salary of $60 a week.

The longer I lived with my dad, the more I came to realize that there was a vast difference between the two of us. Dad was an ultra-conservative person who was extremely reluctant to try new things or take any risks in his life. The salary he made at his boring bookkeeping job at the small coal and oil company, coupled with the monthly oil royalty check they received from Madge's family's oil wells, provided them with a comfortable, but modest living. They were comfortable, but not wealthy, and when I would ask why he didn't look for a better job, Dad would go into a long dissertation about how well he was doing financially and how comfortable he and Madge were going to be when he retired because they would have the oil checks to go along with his Social Security income.

On the other hand, I had spent my entire life facing one challenge after another. Taking risks was nothing new or frightening to me. Dad believed that I should get a job and stick with it and not dream about whether or not it provided me with the things I wanted from life. I was different. I believed that if I wanted something badly enough, I could find a way to get it. I thank my mother for instilling that trait in me. These differing beliefs soon began to cause problems between us. Furthermore, when I said I was thinking of quitting my factory job to go to work with an encyclopedia company making door-to-door calls, it caused a real problem between us.

I had seen a help-wanted ad in the classified section of the local newspaper offering $80 a week for individuals to make calls on people to place sets of encyclopedias in their homes. I answered the ad and arranged to come in for an interview after work. During the interview, the manager explained that they needed people to make calls in the evening on families with children who would be willing to let the company place a free set of encyclopedias in their home. In exchange they would have to agree to write an endorsement the company could use in its marketing efforts. All the recipient family would need to do was subscribe to the company's research services. There was no mention that this was a sales job. The manager explained that the job paid $80 per week during the training period, and then as long as I placed one set per week, the pay would continue to be $80 a week. Then he told me that if I was doing well, I could switch to a pay plan that would pay me $80 for each set I placed. This was very enticing. I asked him to let me consider it for a few days and told him I would get back with him. I wanted to talk with my dad about it.

When I tried to discuss this job with Dad, it precipitated a series of lengthy discussions and heated arguments over several days. Dad viewed the job as having lots of risks and no guarantees beyond the training period. I viewed it as an opportunity to make more money and had the self-confidence to know that I could do it. The more we talked about it, the more our difference came to the surface. Finally, our discussion escalated into a heated argument, during which my dad told me, "If you're foolish enough to give up a secure factory job to go sell encyclopedias, then just find yourself another place to live too because you're not going to hang out here and live off me."

This lack of support surprised me and hurt my feelings as well. If I had confidence in myself, why couldn't my dad have confidence in me too? What had seemed like such a rosy future with my dad a few months before had turned into a shouting match and an uncomfortable coexistence. The more I tried to get my dad to understand my feelings, the madder he became. At one point, he even picked up an ashtray and threw it at me.

As the ashtray shattered against the wall, I learned another valuable lesson. **The grass may look greener on the other side of the fence, but it has to be mowed too.** What had seemed like an entirely new life of love and happiness in Asheville had turned into a nightmare. I could not believe that the relationship with my dad that had promised so much just a few months ago could have deteriorated so far in such a short time. All I wanted to do was find a job in which I could make more money, one where I wasn't just paid for my time, but where I could be rewarded based on what I accomplished. I never dreamed that such a job would be so intimidating to my father that he would order me out of the house if I accepted it.

I was faced with a difficult decision. Did I follow my heart and pursue something I was sure I could do, or did I allow my dad to dictate my future? Each time I tried to bring up the subject, it only made matters worse. I finally decided that if my dad wouldn't support me in this endeavor, he probably wouldn't support me in others, so I began looking for a place to live that I could afford. I eventually located a two-room furnished apartment in the attic of an old house in downtown Asheville that I could rent for $50 a month. All of the utilities were furnished, so all I would have to pay was rent. The problem was, the landlord wanted a $50 security deposit plus the first month's rent before I could move in, and I didn't have that much money.

I had money for the rent, but not the deposit. I had the three $25 savings bonds I had purchased, but when I tried to cash them in, I found out that I had not owned them long enough for them to be redeemed. Since I had decided to take the new job with the encyclopedia company and my dad had told me I would have to move out if I did, I went to him and asked to borrow the money for the deposit. Dad refused! I never knew if he was trying to discourage me from moving out or just trying to dissuade me from changing jobs.

My request for a loan led to another heated argument in which I yelled, "Whether you loan me the money or not, I will find a way to get it, and I will move."

Dad retorted, "You're moving out to take a crap job like that and you want me to loan you money? What do you think I am, stupid? All you're going to do is make a fool of yourself and then come crawling back here wanting to move in again, plus I doubt if you'd ever pay me back even if I did loan you the money."

That comment cemented my determination, and I assumed an "I'll-show-you attitude." I looked Dad directly in the eye and said, "I know you don't think I can do the job, but I know I can, and it pays a lot more than what I'm making now. I'm going to get my own place, and I'm going to take the job. I wish you would support me, but if you won't, so be it; I'll do it on my own. I wouldn't have asked to borrow the money if the bank would have let me cash in my savings bonds, but don't worry about it; I'll find a way."

"What savings bonds are you talking about?" Dad asked.

"These," I said as I held out the three savings bonds.

"Where'd you get those?"

"I bought them with some of the money I've earned over the last few months," I told him.

"I'll tell you what," Dad said. "I'll loan you the money, if you will sign a note and let me hold those bonds as security until you pay me back."

"That's a deal," I said, "but you have to promise that you will give them back when I repay the loan."

"You pay me back, and you'll get the bonds back."

That was my first experience with borrowing cash money. I viewed it differently than financing a bicycle. Dad sat down at the kitchen table and wrote out a loan agreement. When I saw it, I questioned the 6 percent interest the note contained. I was able to negotiate a zero percent loan (something I would do many times and on a much larger scale later in life), as evidenced by the correction shown on the note in Figure 12 below. I signed the agreement and Dad then slid the paper across the table to Madge to have her witness my signature. Once the papers were signed and I gave him the savings bonds to hold, he gave me the $50 I needed for the deposit on the apartment.

This transaction took place on Thursday, April 2, 1964. On Friday, I paid the deposit and first month's rent and moved into my own place that weekend. This was another turning point in my life, because from that day forward, I would never rely on anyone else to provide me a place to live, food to eat, clothes to wear, or anything else. With this move, I assumed total responsibility for myself. It had so shocked me that my own father would make me sign a note and put up security for a $50 loan, that I knew I would never be able to rely on him in the future. As much as I regretted the break with my father, I knew that if I was going to accomplish anything beyond mere existence in life, it was going to be up to me, not someone else.

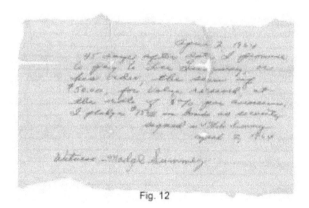

Fig. 12

I tell this story, because of its significance later in my life. I'll jump ahead a bit and explain that, later in life, after I had achieved much success, a number of people, who didn't know me during these early years, would assume that I had been born with a silver spoon in my mouth. This misperception was probably caused in part by my dad. For several years prior to his death, I heard reports from people that he had told everyone he had provided the money to help me get started. Out of respect, I never revealed the truth until after my father's death, but a big part of developing my tenacity and drive is depicted in Figure 12. You'll have to admit, it doesn't have much resemblance to a silver spoon.

The move into the attic apartment and acceptance of the job with the encyclopedia company were some of my first steps into the Learning Years. Throughout the next several chapters, I'll share other events that left lasting impressions and further helped me learn the skills I needed to achieve financial independence.

Key points from this chapter:

- Building wealth involves believing in yourself and taking calculated risks, risks that even your closest friends and family may not support at times.

- Lessons learned in early childhood can stick with you throughout your life. Positive lessons like the one my mother taught me that if you want something badly enough, you will find a way to get it can guide you throughout the rest of your life.

- Changing your surroundings and meeting new people may give you good feelings initially, but it's your performance once you get there that determines what you get out of life.

- When you believe in yourself, don't let others, even family members, keep you from pursuing your dreams.

- The grass may look greener on the other side of the fence, but don't be lured into thinking greener grass means an easier time. Life, like green grass, is just what you make it.

16

Winners Perform, While Losers Make Excuses and Quit

I moved from the security of my father's home into the small attic apartment and promptly gave a two-week notice to my employer that I would be leaving to take another job. Thoughts of starting a new job brought anxious feelings and caused me to have butterflies in my stomach, but that was nothing new for me. Could I have made a big mistake? Could my dad have been correct; would this be nothing but a crap job? These and other similar feelings ran through my mind, but not once did I doubt that I could do the job.

After working my notice, I arrived at my new place of employment at 8:00 a.m. Monday morning to begin the training period. I was surprised at how bare bones basic the furnishings in the office were. There was a secretary's office, a manager's office, and a training room. I was ushered into the training room, which was filled with writing desks that reminded me of the ones I had in school. I was given several forms to complete so the company would have my personal information and tax status. I soon noticed that several other people were arriving and being asked to fill out the same forms.

Shortly after eight o'clock, before anyone had completed the forms, the well-dressed gentleman who had interviewed everyone walked in and introduced himself as the company's regional manager. After welcoming each employee individually, he explained that he was there to set up a new office to serve western North Carolina and upper South Carolina. He went on to inform the group that they were the company's first recruits from the area and would form the nucleus of the new office. He asked all of us to take our time completing the forms and to give them to the secretary when we were finished. He pointed to soft drinks, coffee, and a tray of pastries on a table in the back of the room and told us to feel free to help ourselves to the refreshments. He said he would give us a few minutes to get to know each other and would return at nine o'clock to begin our initial orientation.

Promptly at nine, he stepped into the training room, reintroduced himself, and asked the 12 people in the room to tell everyone their name and give the group a little information about themselves. At this point, he handed out adhesive-backed labels and asked us to write our name on one and stick it to our shirt. He said we would use name tags for the first couple of days until everyone got to know each other better. Once the introductions were made and the name tags applied, he pulled up a stool at the front of the room and began to tell the group about our new jobs.

He began by explaining that the company was planning a major sales effort in the area within several months, and the first phase of this campaign involved placing free sets of encyclopedias in a number of homes with children. All the families would need to do to receive the free books was sign up for a fantastic research program the company offered owners of their encyclopedias and be willing to write a letter of recommendation that it could use in future sales drives. Most of the rest of the morning was consumed with a discussion of how the research program worked and how fortunate it would be for a family with children to be able to subscribe to it without having to spend several hundred dollars to buy the encyclopedias first. The catch, if there was one, was that the subscription to the research program was several hundred dollars.

When the group broke for lunch, the new recruits went to a nearby fast-food restaurant to eat. During the lunch, two of the recruits began talking about the morning session.

"That guy must think we're stupid," one said.

"Yeah, what does he take us for, a bunch of fools? All he wants us to do is go out and sell encyclopedias and tell people they're getting them for free if they will sign up for their big fancy research program," the other added.

"You guys can go back and listen to more of that bull if you want, but I didn't take this job to be a door-to-door encyclopedia salesman," the first one remarked. "I'm going home and look for a real job."

"Yeah, me too," the second one replied. "I'm not going back either."

"Don't you think you should at least give it a chance? I asked. "We've only been there half a day, and even if it is selling encyclopedias, what's wrong with that as long as we get paid?"

"Well, it's just not for us," they responded in unison.

From this I learned another lesson that has served me well in future years. Losers always move in the direction of doing nothing. Winners always move in the direction of doing something. Losers make excuses. Winners get results. Losers fear making mistakes. Winners understand that making mistakes, learning from them, and then applying what they learn is the secret to accomplishment. It didn't matter to me whether we would be giving away free encyclopedias or selling them. What was important to me was the opportunity to make more money than I'd ever made.

Back at the encyclopedia company, the group had returned from lunch, minus the two who quit. When the regional manager entered the room, it was instantly apparent that something had happened. The level of enthusiasm that had been there during the morning session was gone. Looking around the room, it looked more like a funeral wake than the first day of a new job.

"Okay, what's up?" the manager asked.

Everyone just sat there with long faces until I spoke up, "We were talking at lunch, and two of the guys said that this was nothing but a door-to-door encyclopedia sales job and it wasn't for them. They aren't coming back."

"Yeah, it looks that way to me too," said one of the other recruits.

"I can understand your concerns," the regional manager began. "When I first came to work with the company, I felt the same way, but once I learned more about it, I had a better understanding of the company's program. You see, hardly anyone wants to buy a set of encyclopedias, but they will buy a research program that helps their children in school. So from that standpoint, yes, you will be selling, but it won't be encyclopedias. When you make a placement, you will legitimately be giving families a new set of encyclopedias and asking them to purchase the research program.

"Now here's the kicker; you aren't stupid and neither was I. We all know the company can't stay in business giving away its product. What we're banking on is that children will be able to find so much of what they need in the encyclopedias that they won't use the research program that much. And for every family that enjoys the books and sends us a nice testimonial letter, it gives us more credibility when we talk with new people.

"I didn't mean to get into this so soon, but let me show you something," and with that he brought out a big notebook filled with letters from satisfied customers and passed it around to the group.

"So, our jobs will be to make as many placements as possible, correct?"

I asked. I was so determined (there's one of those three Ds again) that I wasn't interested in the overall marketing strategy; I just wanted to get started making money.

"That is true," the manager replied, "and as long as you make at least one placement per week, we will pay you $80 per week. Eventually, when you learn our system better, you will be given an opportunity to earn even more based on your performance."

"That sounds good to me," I said. "Let's get started. I want to learn how to do it."

The following day, two more of the recruits called in and quit, but I didn't let this deter me. I threw myself wholeheartedly into learning the way the company operated and how they wanted me to present myself and their products to prospective customers. There were classes on how to dress, how to greet people when they came to the door, how to introduce myself, how to invite myself into their homes, how to build rapport, how to introduce the encyclopedias, how to present the research program, how children in school could use it, how parents could use it to help with homework, the importance of building the benefits of the program before discussing the cost, how to explain the various payment options, and how to write the agreement.

By the end of the two-week training program, two more of the recruits had left, but I had taken the training seriously. I had worked at home memorizing the materials and had practiced over and over what I would say and how I would act. At the end of the training, I was eager to get out in the field and go to work. Most of the remaining recruits were enthusiastic, but cautiously hesitant at the same time. As for the quitters, they had passed up an opportunity without even giving it a try. That wasn't in my nature.

On the afternoon of the final training day, the regional manager asked, "How many of you are sure you will be able to make at least one placement a week?"

All hands went up.

He continued, "As you recall from the first afternoon you were here, I said you would have an opportunity to be rewarded for performance if you wanted it. You've completed your training and are now ready to go to work. You've all raised your hands indicating that you are sure you will be able to make at least one placement per week. As you know, that's the minimum requirement for the company to be able to guarantee your $80 a week salary.

"If you would like to be **rewarded for performance, not promises,** here's the deal I'm going to offer you. You can choose to accept the $80 per week salary and have it paid to you regularly with the understanding that each six-week period you will be evaluated to see if you have made an average of one placement per week, or you can forgo the guaranteed salary and we will pay you $80 for each placement you make with no guaranteed salary. In other words, if you make two placements per week, you will make $160, but if you don't make any you won't get paid that week. This is totally your choice, so I'm going to leave the room for a few minutes and let you think about it before you make your decisions. Whichever choice you make, you will be able to change it later, but not until your first six-week review comes up."

With that, he left the room, and we newly trained recruits began to talk among ourselves.

"I'm going to take the fixed salary option for the first six weeks," one said.

"Me too," commented another. "This all sounds good, but I want to wait and see how hard it is before running the risk of not getting paid some weeks."

"Well, I'm sure I can do it, so I'm going for the performance-based plan," I said. "If I can't make at least one placement a week, I don't need to be working here."

When the manager returned with forms for each recruit to complete indicating their choice of pay plans, I was the only one who chose performance over promise. The following Tuesday would be our first day in the field. That weekend, I spent every available hour practicing and rehearsing what I would say and do when I started making calls.

Since it was required that both husband and wife be in attendance when a presentation was made, our actual "in the field" hours would be from six until nine o'clock in the evenings and all day on Saturdays. Sunday and Monday would be our off days. The regional manager brought in two sales managers from a different district to supervise us new recruits.

With only six of the original 12 new hires remaining, each sales manager was only responsible for three people. Tuesday afternoon, the sales managers held a meeting prior to going into the field. They explained that each person would be dropped off in a neighborhood between five-thirty and six and then be picked back up at the drop-off point between nine and nine-thirty. Everyone should be at his or her pickup point no later than nine-thirty.

I was raring to go, so I was the first one to be dropped off, and as it turned out, I ended up being the last one to be picked up. I didn't make it back to the pickup point until almost 10 o'clock, and the sales manager was furious.

"I told you to be here by nine-thirty," he said. "You've kept us all waiting nearly a half hour. I hope you've got a good excuse."

"What did you want me to do, walk out on someone who wanted the program without getting their order, just so I could get back here on time?" I replied.

"You mean you made a placement?" one of the new recruits asked.

"Of course," I said. "Didn't you?"

"No," he answered. "I must have knocked on 50 doors, and I didn't even get to talk with anyone, not even one presentation."

"Same here," the other new recruit added.

"Well, don't worry about it," the sales manager said. "This was just your first night, and it's always tough. Mike, let me see the contract you got for your placement."

"Which one?" I asked.

"You mean you made more than one?"

"Yeah, I only got to call on seven houses, but I made placements in three of them."

"What!" the sales manager exclaimed. "Let me see."

I pulled the contracts from my briefcase and handed them to him.

"How did you do it?" the new hires asked.

"It was simple," I said. "I just did exactly what we were trained to do."

"But didn't you have people slam doors in you face?" one of them asked.

"Only one," I said. "But I think he was having a fight with his wife. I could hear them yelling at each other when I rang the doorbell."

"Mike, this is unbelievable," the sales manager said. "I don't think I've ever heard of anyone making three placements on their first night in the field. Tomorrow, in our meeting, you're going to have to tell everyone how you did it."

I wasn't impressed with the fact that I may have pulled off a first, what impressed me was the fact that I'd earned $240 in a single night. That was as much as I'd made in four weeks at the job I left at the textile factory.

The next day I learned that of the five other new people, only one had made a placement. The other four talked about how many doors they had knocked on and how difficult it had been to get to talk with anyone. They seemed contented that they had worked hard, but they didn't have anything to show for it. Only two of them had even gotten to make presentations, and in both cases, it was just a single presentation. They all wanted to know what I'd done. Again, I emphasized the fact that I had done exactly what the company had trained me to do.

My second night, I only made one placement. My third night, I made two. By the end of the week I had made eight and earned $640. By the time my six-week evaluation arrived, I had made the list of the top 10 performers in the nation and had earned nearly as much as I would have earned in a whole year at the textile company. Three of the remaining people who started the same day I did had quit, two of them without making a single placement. It was obvious to me that they didn't believe in what they were doing, or they would have had more success.

I was ecstatic. I had never made so much money, yet during the same six-week period, I noticed that all the other reps seemed to do was complain and make excuses. At my six-week evaluation, the company offered me a promotion to sales manager and asked me to help train new recruits. They explained that in this position, I would make $100 for each placement I made personally, plus I would get $20 for each placement the reps under me made. Naturally, I jumped at the opportunity.

This promotion propelled me to another experience, one that was not as pleasant as this one, but one that one that reinforced the fact that in life **you are rewarded for performance, not promises.**

During that first six weeks, I continued to rehearse and practice in my spare time. Each time I made a call that was not successful, I would make notes and try to determine where I had gone wrong. My delivery and success rate continued to improve, but with the promotion came problems, which is another whole story and produced another learning experience. Let's move now to the next chapter, where I will describe what happened following my promotion and analyze how I learned another valuable lesson from being promoted.

Key points from this chapter:

- Losers always move in the direction of doing nothing; winners move in the direction of doing something and making it work.

- Once you commit to a project, stick with it. You may hear a thousand excuses for why other people aren't successful, but if you stay committed and look for ways to make it work, you won't have time to make excuses.

- Negativism is contagious, as was proved by the number of people who quit without experiencing success.

- Don't sell yourself short by making other people's goals your goals. While the other recruits had a goal of one sale a week, my goal was to make as many placements as possible.

- You get rewarded for performance, not promises.

17

Why Climbing the Ladder of Success Takes More Knowledge

I tackled my new sales manager position with the same enthusiasm, drive, and determination that I demonstrated as a field representative. As a sales manager, I would supervise four people. My first day on the new job, I called the representatives that would be working under me together for an initial meeting. I expressed great enthusiasm over my promotion and assured them I would do everything in my power to help them achieve the kind of success I had enjoyed.

Although I had only been with the company for eight short weeks, including the first two-week training period, everyone in the office was aware of my success. Prior to my promotion, the other representatives were constantly asking me how I did it. At the daily briefings, everyone would be waiting for me to tell how I had done the day before. They were envious of my ability to make placements nearly every day I was in the field, and those assigned to work under me were looking forward to learning from me.

At this initial meeting, I told my charges that I would be working closely with them to ensure their success. I explained that in addition to conducting training classes, each day I would select one of them and make at least one call with that person that evening. I explained that by doing this, I could evaluate their presentations in actual real-life scenarios, which would enable me to determine how best to help them. Almost instantly, I sensed a feeling of uneasiness in the room.

One of the representatives finally spoke up, "You mean we're going to have to make a presentation in front of you?"

"Sure," I replied. "There's a reason I want to do this. When we meet in the office and practice our presentations, it's not the same as giving them in front of real-live prospects. Each of us, me included, makes mistakes or has weaknesses. Otherwise, we'd all be making two or three placements a day. The reason for wanting to go with each of you is because we are all different. What may be a strength for one of you is a weakness for another and vice versa. By going with you, it will help me hone in on the specific areas where I will need to work with each of you."

"Okay, I understand," one said. "I think we were all afraid you just wanted to go along to criticize us."

"Not at all," I added. "My job is to help you make more placements, not make you nervous. You have to realize that I make money when you make money. I just want to help you get better and become more productive."

Over the next six-week period, my work with the people paid off handsomely. I encouraged each one and helped them improve their areas of weakness, and as a result, my group preformed remarkably well. Although my personal production fell off a bit because I was spending part of my time going on calls with my reps, my group's production was nearly three times that of the next-closest group in the office. Both my income and my stature with the company grew tremendously. I had made more money in a 14-week period than I would have made in an entire year at the factory job I left. I waved a few of my checks in front of my dad just to rub things in a bit, but what happened next surprised even me.

At my next six-week evaluation, I was shocked to find both the regional manager and one of the company's vice presidents at the meeting. I had expected my review to be conducted by the manager of the Asheville office to whom I directly reported, but here was the company brass sitting in on my review. My first thought was, "What have I done wrong?"

The meeting began with a glowing review of my accomplishments, both as a field representative and then as a sales manager, but then the vice president dropped a bombshell on me.

"Mike, we have offered the office manager here a transfer to a larger market, and he has accepted. That leaves his position in this market open. Based on your outstanding performance, we want to talk with you about the office manager's job."

"I appreciate your vote of confidence," I responded, "but what all does the job entail?"

"As you know, we are expanding here," the VP replied. "We now have five teams with four field reps and a sales manager in each team; that's 25 people. We would like to double that within the next year. The job would be to interview and hire the new recruits, supervise and assist a full time trainer, and supervise the sales managers. It would also involve being responsible for all the paperwork and reports from this office and making sure they are prepared accurately and timely, and we will provide a secretary to handle the telephones and help with the paperwork. Of course, if you accept the job, we will be available to guide you while you are getting a grasp on the way things work and will always be available if you run into problems. We realize that you have only been with the company a short time, but you have done such a great job that we want to offer you this opportunity to grow with us and move into management."

"Well, I'm pretty happy as a sales manager, and I'm making more money than I've ever made," I said. "What kind of opportunities will I have if I accept the job?"

At this point, the regional manager spoke up, "As office manager, you won't have to make calls in the evenings like you do as a rep or sales manager. You'll be hiring people, training them, working with your sales managers, and in general making sure everything in the office runs smoothly. You won't have to go out in the field unless you need to fill in for a sales manager occasionally. The way you will be compensated is by getting overrides on what everyone under you produces; that includes all the reps and the sales managers too. If you do as well as office manager as you have as a rep and sales manager, you could easily double what you're making now."

I accepted the position and arrived at the office to begin my new job with the same enthusiasm and energy that had served me so well in the past, but this time I quickly discovered that **the ability to do and the skill to manage are very different.** The first morning, two of my sales managers quit with no notice. They were apparently upset by the fact that they had been with the company longer than me and had been overlooked for promotion. The office secretary turned in her resignation, but at least agreed to work a two-week notice. She had found another job paying more and had agreed to take it.

Before I could sit down behind my new desk for the first time, I had a handful of problems and the sudden realization that I knew nothing about managing. I was in over my head and sinking fast. Although I tried everything I could think of, the situation only got worse. My limited education did not include organizational skills, people skills, communication skills, or management techniques. Sure, I was great at persuading people to let me place a set of encyclopedias in their home and getting them to sign up for the research program, but trying to get 25 people to work together was an entirely different task.

Instead of growing the office from 25 to 50 employees, within a month

I was down to just 14 people. Morale was at an all-time low, and many of them were on the verge of quitting. I had been able to hire a new secretary who was answering the phones, but my ad in the help-wanted section of the newspaper was only producing an occasional call. After two weeks of interviews, I had only been able to hire six new recruits to begin the next training class. That was the smallest number of recruits in a class since I started with the company. New placements from the Asheville office had fallen to less than half what they were when I took the job. No matter what I did, things just kept getting worse.

Eventually, I started going out in the field at nights myself in an effort to make placements to improve the office's performance. This only created more dissatisfaction among the field reps, because they thought I was taking opportunities away from them. As I neared my next six-week evaluation, I knew I had failed. I also knew that I didn't have the skills to repair the damage I had done. I couldn't believe how difficult it was to supervise an entire office, especially after doing so well with the four people I supervised as a sales manager.

I think it's important to point out here that, although I didn't realize it at the time, I had taken over the district manager's job with a huge impediment hanging over my head. My hire had left the district without its best sales manager when the company had moved me into management. The leadership of the company had evidently not thought this through, which tells you that even smart, successful people sometimes make dumb mistakes. I have since learned that this is a mistake that is made quite frequently in companies. They have a top producer and then feel that just because he or she performs well when dealing with customers, the person will do the same when moved to management. As I mentioned earlier, **the ability to do and the skill to manage are very different.**

When I was a sales manager, although I had "manager" in my title, I wasn't really in management. I was more like an extremely productive co-worker than a manager. My willingness to make calls with my reps and work individually with each one endeared me to them and gave them the feeling that I was one of them. When I took on the role of office manager, I was suddenly placed in a different role. I could no longer make calls with everyone and didn't know how to communicate this fact in a way that gained me respect. Instead of teaching my sales managers how to do the things that had made me successful in that position, I held classes with everyone, reps and manager alike. I didn't realize that this was undermining my sales managers with their reps. It left them feeling as if their position wasn't important. If I was going to do the training, why did I need them?

Although I didn't know it at the time, I was learning some valuable lessons. Management is getting things done through other people. Leadership is not jumping in front of a crowd and yelling, "Follow me"; it's being the kind of person others want to follow. My limited education prevented me from understanding these basic principles of management, and in total frustration, I tendered my resignation from the company.

Suddenly I found myself down in the dumps, with that sinking feeling of failure. I was embarrassed, insecure, and without a job. As I sat in my apartment on my first day of unemployment, I knew it was only a matter of time until my dad found out and would gloat when telling me, "See, I told you so!" Fortunately, I had saved a little money when I was doing well, so I wasn't broke, but I would need to find a job soon. I had a nice landlord, but one that insisted on the rent being paid on time. I had enough to make it about two months before I would run out of money. I swallowed what little pride I had left and walked down the street to pick up a newspaper.

I returned to my apartment and sat down with the newspaper. There were several listings under the help-wanted heading, but the only one that interested me was a listing for a lab technician at a defense plant. Since I had worked as a lab technician (that's a fancy title for a gofer) at the textile plant before going to the encyclopedia company, I decided to call on the job. My call was taken by a receptionist who gave me little information on the phone. When I told her I had worked in a lab before, she asked me to stop by and fill out an application.

I endured a little over a month of unemployment before I received a call from the defense plant offering me the job. When I accepted it, I viewed it as a step backward and had no idea that it would lead me to a transition from plant worker to financial security. Let's move on to the next chapter, where I will describe the series of events that changed my entire outlook on life and started me down the road to financial independence.

Key points from this chapter:

- The ability to do things yourself and the skill to get others to do them is very different.
- Even intelligent, successful people sometimes do stupid things. Act on well-thought-out judgment, not on the convictions of others.
- Learn to identify your strengths and your weaknesses.

- Accepting promotions may make you feel important in the beginning, but if you lack the skills needed to do the job, it may lead to an embarrassing failure.

18

Opportunity Knocks; It Doesn't Kick the Door Down

Stung by failure in my recent management position, I began my new job at Northrop Carolina Incorporated with doubts about my abilities for the first time in my life. I had never before failed at anything I had set my mind to doing. When I reported to work that first day, it was with serious reservations. Did I have enough education? What would be expected of me? With the Vietnam War raging and the company a defense contractor, everything was so secretive. My first stop was the personnel office, where I spent the entire morning filling out forms with information that would be checked and rechecked during the process of obtaining "Secret" security clearance.

After lunch, I was introduced to Dr. John Godfrey, a brilliant PhD chemist under whom I would be working. Jack, as he was called by his co-workers, was a heavyset balding gentleman with a pleasant demeanor and a hearty laugh. He welcomed me to the company and then spent the rest of the afternoon showing me around those areas of the plant and lab I could visit without the security clearance and discussing the job I would be doing. By the end of the day, I felt much more comfortable about my new position.

I was still stinging from my failure at management, but the thought that kept running through my mind was, "positive, positive, positive!" How could I make something positive out of such a dismal failure? The job paid $80 per week, which was $20 more than I had been making at the textile plant, but it was still far below what I had earned as a field representative and sales manager with the encyclopedia company. At first, the only positive thing I could think of was the fact that I was making more than before I left the textile plant, but then it dawned on me; the most positive part of my failure was that it taught me the importance of learning.

When I talk about learning, I'm not talking about formal education. Education gives you tools; learning comes from the application of those tools. Many highly educated people are functionally illiterate in everyday life. They have vast stores of knowledge but seem to lack the ability to put it to work in ways that produce meaningful results.

As I mentioned in the introduction to this section, I once hired a man for a manual labor job who was in his mid-thirties and held a doctorate degree in some weird field of geology. With all that education, I couldn't understand why he was applying for such a menial job. We talked about it, and he said, "I can't find a job in my field, and I need to work." I'm not so sure that was the real reason. The more we talked, the more I realized that while he was technically brilliant, he had virtually no common sense. He could barely hold a conversation unless it centered on his exotic field of study. He had a vast store of knowledge, but little ability to apply it. I have since found this to be true with many highly educated professionals. The focus required to earn very high academic degrees often leaves people with huge learning gaps on how to deal with basic daily activities or to interact with other individuals not versed in the same fields.

On the other hand, there are people with little formal education, but with extraordinary abilities to apply what they have. Many highly educated people often suffer from the paralysis of analysis; they make few mistakes but accomplish very little. Conversely, those with less education, but with the ability to apply what they have, aren't nearly as fearful of making mistakes, so they learn when they make them, make corrections, and accomplish much. Financial success occurs when you combine study and analysis with action and accomplishment. This combination produces the frame of mind that allows you to succeed.

After receiving some of the large paychecks from the encyclopedia company, I knew that my new job would only be a steppingstone, not a career. I would use my meager income to pay the bills while I improved my knowledge. From the very beginning, I noticed something the PhD chemists were doing that intrigued me. Every week, each of them would bring in a new word, give its definition, and then challenge the others to use it in conversation as often as possible. I asked if I could participate in their game.

To illustrate the power of applying what you learn, I still remember the first word I learned in this game. It was *vitiate*, which means to make imperfect, faulty, or impure; to spoil or corrupt. Although it has been more than 45 years, I also remember the first sentence in which I used the word.

"I'm going to vitiate that smile on your face if you don't get off my back," I said to another lab technician who was making fun of me for playing the bosses' game.

"Whatever," my co-worker replied, obviously having no clue what I was talking about and too embarrassed to ask.

This exchange taught me a very valuable lesson about the difference between education and learning. Although I knew the meaning of the word *vitiate*, my co-worker didn't, and it was obvious that no communication had occurred. Sure, I may have momentarily impressed my co-worker with my vocabulary, after all, I was just playing a game, but I later learned that my co-worker perceived it as a self-serving insult and a put-down.

This exchange became a defining moment on my road to financial success. It also helped me understand why I had failed so miserably in my management position. The lesson is so simple that most people completely overlook it. **THE BURDEN OF COMMUNICATION IS ON THE PERSON DOING THE TALKING.** However, the communicator who is unaware of this knowledge often blames the listener for not paying attention or understanding. As the great American philosopher Archie Bunker would say, "The problem, Edith, is that I'm talking to you in English and you're listening to me in Dingbat."

It makes no difference how well educated you are, how great your vocabulary is, or how well you can perform a task yourself, if you can't communicate with others in a way they can understand, you are handicapped. From that day forward, I vowed to practice speaking and writing at a level equal to or just below that of the person to whom I was addressing.

Another observation that left a lasting impression on me was the way experiments were conducted. Since my job was in a research laboratory, there was a constant search for new products and improvements to old ones. What impressed me the most was how experiment after experiment would fail before finally arriving at the right combination to produce the desired results. I was amazed at Dr. Godfrey's patience when we were working on a new project. If an experiment failed, he would merely sit down at his desk, fully document everything about the experiment, and then give me another assignment to try.

As I observed this calculated approach to developing new products, subconsciously it worked its way into my thought process and began to direct my actions. I found myself applying this approach to life in general, and rather than viewing failures like the one at the encyclopedia company as permanent, I started looking at them as simply obstacles that I had to get over, under, around, or through if I wanted to succeed. What I learned from conducting these experiments was not the old "If at first you don't succeed; try and try again," but rather **"If at first you don't succeed, don't keep doing it the same way; try it a different way."**

Although I had no background other than one high school course in basic chemistry, the longer we worked together, the more I learned from Dr. Godfrey and the more curious I became. Unlike the other lab technicians who came to work, did their jobs, and went home, I was constantly questioning the chemist and asking him to explain the results of each experiment I performed. I wasn't content to just pour some chemicals together, watch them bubble, time the reaction, and then tell Dr. Godfrey how much if any precipitate was produced; I wanted to know what caused the reactions, what they produced, and why.

Eventually, my barrage of questions led to Dr. Godfrey's calling me into his office for a consultation. He began by praising the work I was doing and my interest in learning. He complimented me on the precision of my work and the confidence he had developed in my ability to carry out tasks correctly; then he got to the real point of the meeting. He pointed out that each time he had to stop and explain something; it pulled him away from his work and lessened his performance. He explained that it had taken him many years of undergraduate and postgraduate studies to earn his doctorate in chemistry and that no matter how long we worked together, I would never understand all of the chemical reactions without going back to school and studying chemistry.

He must have seen the disappointment on my face, because he quickly shifted gears and assured me that I didn't have to learn all about the chemical reactions, because that was his job. He assured me that I was performing well above expectations in my job and he would be willing to help me learn as much as time would permit, but that we couldn't stop after every experiment for a chemistry lesson. Then he gave me what is still the best advice I have ever received.

He said, **"If you will read an hour a day about something you know nothing about, within five years you will be amazed at the impact it will have on your life."**

I was young and impressionable, and I had tremendous respect for Dr. Godfrey. As a result, I left the meeting with a commitment to myself that I would do just that. It was difficult in the beginning. I found it hard to find that hour a day, but I finally settled into a routine of reading about 30 minutes before going to sleep each night and about 30 minutes after I awoke each morning, a routine that I still maintain to this day. This method is very mentally stimulating because it gives me something new to think about as I go to sleep each night and something new to think about and discuss with others each day.

I read everything from *The Enquirer* to the Bible, from *Playboy* to Plato; nothing is off limits. Some of my reading is technical, some is instructive, some is just pure pleasure; but I try to learn something new from each thing I read. It may be what's happening in Iraq or Afghanistan, a new medicine being tested, how to design and build a birdhouse, how to deal with difficult people, the differences in men and women, the plight of minorities, new law-enforcement techniques, financial journals, a love story, a murder mystery, or thousands of other seemingly unrelated bits of information. This has been a major factor contributing to my success, which I am proud to say includes a PhD in life from the University of Hard Knocks.

If you were to visit my home, you would find a library containing many thousands of books, most of which I have read. I have books on the floor, books all the way up to the ceiling, books on the nightstand, and books in the kitchen. I once thought, "Wouldn't it be amazing if every thought man or woman has ever had were written and made available to the rest of the world? Wouldn't that be something?" Then I realized that that it has already happened. Every worthwhile thought (and a few not so worthwhile, frankly) is already recorded. All you have to do is pick up the right publication.

Throughout the next several months after this meeting with Dr. Godfrey, I became extremely resourceful and gradually gained his confidence that I could accomplish virtually any task I was given. Whether it was finding the source for a particular piece of equipment, conducting specialized tests, or locating resources within other parts of the plant, I was very successful. It was during this phase of my development that I learned another valuable lesson. **OPPORTUNITY KNOCKS; IT DOESN'T KICK THE DOOR DOWN!**

One Monday morning Dr. Godfrey called me into his office and told me he needed to have three "Danger— Keep Out" signs made that he could put up at a test area he would be using. I called all of the sign companies listed in the phone directory, but none of them could meet the two-day turnaround time Dr. Godfrey needed. Rather than having to report that I was unable to get the signs, I used the opportunity to exploit one of my other talents. I had always been artistically inclined, and although I had never used this talent to paint signs, I was confident I could do an acceptable job. That afternoon, I met with Dr. Godfrey and explained the situation.

"I've called every sign company listed in the phone book," I began, "but none of them can get the signs done by day after tomorrow. The best I've been able to do is get them promised in a week."

"Well, I've got several tests I need to run on Thursday, and I have to have the area sealed off and signs up before I can run them," Dr. Godfrey said. "Could you look around the plant and see if you can find any that aren't being used?"

"I have another idea," I replied. "We have plywood and paint in the company's store. If you would approve it, I'd be willing to work overtime and make the signs myself. I could go get the plywood and paint now, and then after work I could get it cut to the size you need and get one coat of paint on it; it would dry overnight. I could go by a paint store after that, pick up a small brush to letter with, and then I could come in early tomorrow morning and put on a second coat. It would dry throughout the day, and then I could stay over tomorrow after work to get them lettered. That way they would be ready when you need them, and what I would make in overtime probably would be less than what it would cost to have a sign company make them."

"Do you think you could make them look professional?" Dr. Godfrey asked.

"If you aren't satisfied, you don't have to pay me for my time," I said. "How's that?"

"Well, go ahead and get started," Dr. Godfrey replied. "These experiments are time critical and I can't do them without putting up the signs at the test area."

This was another opportunity that knocked, and I took advantage of it. Not only did I get to pick up some extra income, but it also gave me an opportunity to show that I could produce a nice-looking sign. When I undertook the project, I had no idea that it would ultimately lead me down a life-changing path.

Dr. Godfrey was so impressed with the signs that he brought them up in a management staff meeting a few days later. Within days, I started receiving requests from other departments throughout the plant to make signs for them. It seemed that the ones I made, while not perfect, filled the needs of the plant and cost the departments considerably less than having them made at one of the local sign shops. Before I knew it, I was working several hours overtime each week and bringing in a considerable amount of extra money. Within a few months, what started as a small opportunity had turned into an extra income stream; it was allowing me to save a little money for the first time since I had worked for the encyclopedia company.

Then, as often happens, I was dealt another blow. After more than two years of loyal service, Dr. Godfrey called me into his office and dropped another bombshell in my life. The employees in the plant were aware that with the Vietnam War winding down, the plant was struggling to obtain new defense contracts. This had already caused some layoffs (or as we would say in today's politically correct world, some downsizing), and more were expected, but no one thought it would affect the research lab. Wrong! Dr. Godfrey praised me for the fine job I had been doing but explained that the lab's budget had been cut and they were going to have to lay off some lab workers. Since I had the least seniority, he had no choice but to lay me off first. He offered his regrets but told me that he had no control over the situation. The only good part was that I could work for two more weeks, and then I would receive $300 in severance pay with my final paycheck.

I was stunned! I had heard about layoffs in other parts of the plant but never dreamed that I would be affected. What was most troubling to me was the fact that of my last two jobs, I lost one because I wasn't performing and now I was losing the other in spite of the fact that I was performing exceptionally well. These are the kinds of life-changing experiences that provide the impetus that propels some people to greatness and relegates others to failure. As my friend W. Mitchell, a great motivational speaker, says, "It's not what happens to you; it's what you do about it."

In this case, I was dealt an unfortunate and unexpected blow, but it recalled the advice I had been given by the psychiatrist when I was in high school, "You always have a choice. Just think positive, positive, positive." But, what could be positive about losing my job, my livelihood? It is at low points in life like this one that many people take on an "Oh, woe is me" attitude and never recover from it. They fail to realize that just as a chain is no stronger than its weakest link, a life is no better than one's ability to handle the difficult times. One of my favorite sayings is, "It's not how you handle the good times, but how you handle the bad ones that make you or break you in life." Anyone can do well when everything is going right. Even a dead fish can swim downstream. I had a choice, I could let the experience drag me down and make matters worse, or I could look for a positive way to learn from the experience and get on with my life. In the next chapter, I'll share how I dealt with this adversity and how I used it to propel me to greater success than I could ever have imagined at the time.

Key points from this chapter:

- Increase your ability to communicate by learning to use words and phrases that your listeners can understand.

- Learn from scientific research methods. If what you're doing isn't working, don't give up; just keep making adjustments until you find a way that does.

- Daily reading on a wide variety of subjects will not only expand your knowledge, but will also help you to become more well-rounded and will have an amazing impact on your life.

- Opportunities don't always jump out at you; the best ones are often embedded in what appear to be problems.

- View problems as opportunities to expand your knowledge and your skills and improve your life.

- It's not what happens to you. It's the way you react to what happens to you that determines whether you succeed or fail.

19

If You Don't Have Goals, You Don't Have Direction

Most people when dealt a blow like the loss of a job or some other unexpected event seek out others who are going through similar adversities because they think these people will better understand their plight. Although they tell themselves they are looking for advice, what they really want is sympathy. The problem is, sympathy doesn't solve problems; in fact, more often than not, it exacerbates the problems.

When I first received word of my pending layoff, or my downsizing, as we would say today, I felt the same way most people in that situation would feel. My first action was to contact a couple of former employees of the plant who had been laid off to see what they were doing. As expected, what I got were tales of disappointment and woe. They had been unable to find jobs; their severance pay was running out and so were their savings. Bills were piling up, and they were at a loss as to what they would do. None of my conversations with these people gave me any encouragement or positive suggestions; in fact, they were downright depressing.

I remembered the advice Dr. Godfrey had given me months before, when I was only 19 years old, about reading an hour a day. Since receiving that advice, one of the books I had read was on goal setting. At the time I was reading it, it was dull and boring and wasn't of great interest to me. Now I was about to experience the first major impact the suggestion of reading an hour a day would have on my life. Facing the loss of my job and an unknown future, I recalled the message I had distilled from the book, which was: **IF YOU DON'T HAVE GOALS, YOU**

DON'T HAVE DIRECTION. When I asked myself, "What do I want out of life?" I realized that I had no idea!

This revelation was a turning point in my life. Rather than thinking about where I could find another job, my mind was consumed with thoughts about what I really wanted out of life. Based on my rather limited work experience, I couldn't see working a job as doing anything more than providing me with a living. I wanted more out of life than just a mere existence. I had dreams of living in a nice home, driving nice cars, taking exciting vacations, having a boat and any number of other things people associate with wealth. The problem was, I couldn't see myself ever having these things if I kept doing what I had been doing.

Then I remembered I had read that goals, to be meaningful, must be specific and doable and have a time frame for completion. That's when I began to comprehend that **wishes are not goals; goals are what make wishes come true.** I needed inspiring goals, something that could guide me in life, goals that if I accomplished them, would provide the things for which I wished. The more I thought about it, the more aware I became that what I really longed for more than anything else was financial security. I had already learned that I couldn't depend on a job working for others to provide this. Although I was still very young, I was already tired of worrying about where I would get the money for even the basic needs. I recalled the struggle I had gone through to get my first bicycle when I was just a child. I recalled many other times when people around me were able to purchase things I would have loved to have had or were doing things I would have liked to do, but couldn't afford it. Now I was facing the loss of my job and the real prospect of having to count my money before I could go through the checkout line at the grocery store. I didn't want to live that way.

During this time, I was lying in bed one night, when I awakened in the middle of the night and began pondering the impending financial difficulties I was facing. I worried and agonized over the problem until suddenly I sat bolt upright and yelled, "Why can't I be rich?" As I sat there in bed, with the words still echoing off the bare walls, my wife did what a lot of wives would do in the same situation: she rolled over and said, "Because you ain't doing anything to become rich; now go back to sleep!"

That's when it dawned on me: she was right. I didn't have a goal to become rich; in fact, the more I thought about it, I realized I didn't have a goal to be anything. How could I expect to achieve a goal I didn't have? How would I even know if I made it if I had never defined rich? I lay awake for hours pondering the future, when a simple thought passed through my mind. I got up and picked up the notepad I kept by the bed and wrote it down: **I WILL BECOME A MILLIONAIRE BY AGE 30 AND RETIRE BY AGE 50.** (See Figure 13 below.) That's all it said, nothing fancy, no comments or suggestions about how to do it, just a simple statement about what I would do and when I would do it. It became the goal that would direct my life for the next 30 years. I folded the note, laid it on the nightstand, which was a cardboard box with a cloth draped over it, and then I climbed back into bed and went to sleep.

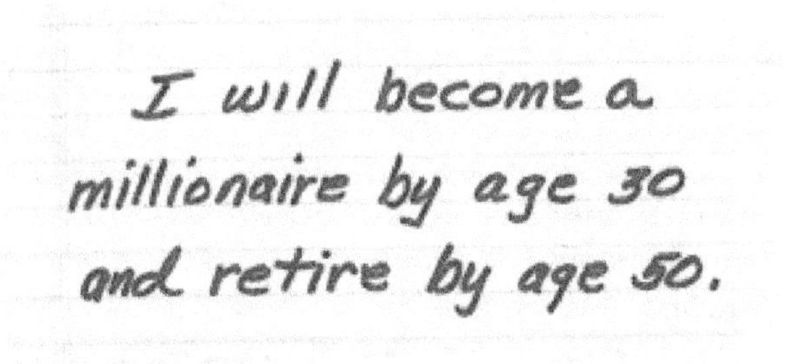

I will become a millionaire by age 30 and retire by age 50.

Fig. 13

The next morning, I picked up the note, unfolded it, and looked at what I had written. **I WILL BECOME A MILLIONAIRE BY AGE 30 AND RETIRE BY AGE 50.** As I stared at the words and contemplated the possibilities, a chilling thought passed through my mind, "Is this really possible, or am I just kidding myself?" Then I thought of the $80 weekly salary I'd been making. I took out a pencil and multiplied it by 52 weeks. It came to $4,160! That was my salary for a whole year. When I divided it into $1,000,000, I couldn't help but laugh at the result. Based on what I was making at the factory, it would take a little over 240 years just to earn a million dollars, let alone be worth that much, and for the first time I understood the power of goals. The written goal to become a millionaire by age 30 let me see that finding another $80-a-week factory job was not the way to go. It didn't tell me what I should do, but it definitely showed me what not to do.

Recalling the advice my mother had given me as a child, "If you want it badly enough, you'll find a way to get it," I knew that if I wanted to be successful, I would have to **learn from winners, not losers.** If my goal was to build wealth and become financially independent, I would need to seek advice from people who knew something about the subject. The only suggestion I had received from the laid-off plant workers was to go apply for unemployment. I needed to seek advice from successful people, ones who had achieved success, or at least ones who understood what success was. I most assuredly wouldn't find these people in the unemployment lines.

During my final week of employment at the plant, I discussed my goal with Dr. Godfrey. When I showed him the paper where I had written down the goal, it brought a bit of a chuckle, and the comment, "Well, I wish you luck."

I laughed with him, but as I started out the door, I turned and said, "I didn't mean to bother you, but I'm going to have to do something other than what I'm doing now. Last night I figured out that it would take me over 240 years just to earn a million dollars at what I'm making here. I thought you might have a suggestion or two."

"Mike, having goals is great, but they need to be realistic. Do you really believe you can become a millionaire by age 30?"

"I don't know," I replied. "The idea came to me a few nights ago. I wrote it down, and now I'm looking for ways that can help me make it happen. I know it seems impossible right now, but unless I give it my best effort, I'll never know for sure whether it's possible or not. Right now, I'm exploring all my options and looking for the best way to get started."

"Have you thought of going into business for yourself?" Dr. Godfrey asked.

"No," I answered. "What kind of business could I go into?"

"Have you thought of starting a sign business?" he replied. "You've been making signs for the plant, and they're quite good. Maybe you could do that for other businesses and create a good business for yourself. I don't know if it will make you a millionaire, but if you work hard and are successful, you can probably make more than you're making here."

That comment started me thinking. I had thought about continuing to make signs as a sideline to supplement my other income, but I hadn't thought of making it my full-time business. I decided to research the idea. The rest of that week, as soon as I got off work, I started visiting businesses throughout the area. I talked with the owners of restaurants, car dealerships, motels, real estate companies, and any other business owners who would spend a few minutes with me. All of them encouraged me to start a sign business and promised to give me work if I did. Finally, I called my mother who lived in Virginia.

"Mom, I've got a bit of news for you," I said. "I've been laid off from my job. Friday was my last day, but don't worry; I think I'm going to go into business for myself."

"Doing what?" she asked.

"I've been making signs for the plant for the last several months, so what I've decided to do is start a sign company," I said. "They gave me $300 in severance pay, and I've decided to use it to buy a van to work out of and a few supplies to get me started. I've talked with several business people, and they all encouraged me and said they would give me work to do, but that's not the main reason for my call. What I'm more excited about is the goal I've set for myself."

"And what's that?" she asked.

"Mom, I'm going to become a millionaire by age 30 and retire by age 50," I replied. "What do you think of that?"

Then just as I anticipated, she said, "That's a pretty big goal, but if you think you can do it, I'll bet you will find a way."

When I hung up with my mother, I placed one more call, this one to my father, to whom I had hardly spoken since I moved out to take the job with the encyclopedia company. I didn't call looking for approval of my decision; I merely wanted to inform my dad about what had happened with my secure factory job. The conversation was short and to the point. I told my dad about being laid off from the plant, and the response I received was not unexpected.

"So what are you going to do now?" my dad asked.

"I've decided to go into business for myself," I replied.

That brought the same question my mother had asked, "Doing what?"

"I've been painting signs at the plant for the past few months, so I've decided to go in business making signs for businesses."

"That's the biggest crock of &%#$ I've ever heard of," my dad yelled into the phone. "You'd better get a job and go to work. That's even worse than that stupid idea you had about selling encyclopedias."

And with that discouraging comment, I began a trek that would take me on a wild and sometimes frightening journey to becoming a millionaire. The contrasting opinions I had gotten from these back-to-back calls allowed me to see just how encouraging or discouraging other people's opinions could be. From that day forward, I vowed to never let negative people influence my decisions again. As a result, I would not talk with my father again for more than three years.

Key points from this chapter:

- Avoid people who spend their time complaining and griping; surround yourself with ones who are inspirational.
- If you don't have goals, you don't have direction.
- Wishes are not goals; goals are what make wishes come true.

- Set specific goals and let them guide you on your journey through life.

- Determine if what you are doing will get you to where you want to go in life. If not, make adjustments.

20

Financial Success Requires Investment of Time and Money

When life deals unexpected disappointments, difficulties, hardships, adversities, and other sufferings, it can be very discouraging. When dreams are shattered, it can be a devastating blow, if you let it. Everyone has bad things happen that they didn't expect. It may be the loss of a job, an accident, an illness, divorce, the loss of a loved one, or any of a thousand other unfortunate occurrences that disrupt their lives. It's up to each person, based upon each person's character, to decide whether that disruption will be temporary or permanent.

Some people have a run of bad luck and use it as an excuse to give up on life. They're easy to spot by their hangdog looks and lack of enthusiasm. The problem is that these people become so focused on looking backward that they run head-on into new problems and disappointments that could easily have been avoided had they been looking forward. What has happened in the past cannot be changed. No matter how much you focus on past events, they will still be the same. The past is of no value unless you learn from it. Then its value only arises if you apply what you learn to make better decisions today, because it is today's successes that bury past disappointments and bring brighter futures.

As I have mentioned several times already, I hope you are reading this with a notepad at your side. As I take you through some of the experiences that taught me valuable life lessons, if these stories trigger thoughts about experiences from your past, I want you to make notes. I keep reminding you because this is an important exercise. You are going to learn how to use the events from your life to change your thinking and develop your own path to financial independence.

My first year in business was difficult. I expended far more time, energy, and effort than I had the previous year, yet after 12 exhausting months, I had earned only $3,400, considerably less than my annual salary at the plant. I was struggling just to keep food on the table. At this point, it would have been very easy to give up and quit, especially after having failed in the management position at the encyclopedia company, been laid off from my last job, and now hit with declining income when I was trying to start my own business. But I didn't think that way; although I wasn't aware of it at the time, I was gradually developing the toughness and tenacity I would need to achieve success later.

Sure, my income was down, but my knowledge was up and my spirits were high. I think this was because I had decided to **believe in myself and cancel the pity party.** Unlike my last two jobs, I was in control of this one. I didn't have to worry about being fired or downsized, what I had to guard against was succumbing to the negative influence of other people. Had I been focused on the past, I may have been tempted to quit, but instead of being discouraged, I viewed this first year as an investment, one that would pay dividends in the future.

The biggest lesson I learned from this first year was also one of the simplest: **INVESTING REQUIRES SACRIFICE.** Whether it is time or money, investing means setting aside for future benefit. If you invest time in learning a skill, that same time can't be used to go fishing, watch a movie, or do some other fun activity. If you invest money in equipment to start a business, that money can't be used to buy a boat or a motorcycle or purchase some other fun toy. As I explained in Chapter 7, getting from birth to death has a cost. What you spend today pays for today, but what you invest today is what pays for tomorrow.

I looked at my first year as an investment, because during that year, much of my time had been spent learning the business. I learned that there was a special type of paint that was used for signs, that there were special brushes made just for lettering, that there was a special type of plywood with a smooth coating made especially for signs, and using these resulted in much higher quality signs. I spent hours practicing lettering techniques, learning different lettering styles, learning how to lay out designs with balance and easy readability. I learned that quality was crucial when it came to signs. They were to a business like clothes are to people; they provided the look from which customers formed first impressions and often made decisions on whether or not to patronize the establishment. Imagine how you would feel about eating in a restaurant if its sign looked amateurishly made, was dirty, and the paint was peeling. It wouldn't present a very appetizing appearance, would it?

Fig. 14

Soon after starting my business, I got this message loud and clear. My first attempt to advertise my new business, Figure 14, was a disaster. I made this hand-drawn flyer and got several copies made. I made several calls on businesses throughout the area that used a lot of signs and gave them copies of my flyer. I was proud of it, so I couldn't understand why I wasn't getting any calls. When I was trying to learn how to price my work, I had made anonymous calls to several established sign companies to get price quotes, so I knew that the prices I was quoting were less than what the companies were currently paying. Finally, I just pointedly asked the owner of a real estate company why they kept getting their signs elsewhere when they could get them from me cheaper. The answer I got changed my entire outlook on business.

"Mike, I like you, but your work is a little rough for me," the broker said. "These signs are my image to the public, and I'm willing to pay a higher price for a more professional look."

That comment convinced me that I needed to invest time in learning the sign business and improving the quality of my work. As I mentioned in Chapter 6, with youthful naiveté I paid a visit to one of the established sign shops in the area where I met the owner, Dave Cheadle. When I explained that I was trying to get started in business, Dave welcomed me into his shop and spent hours helping and encouraging me. He showed me the right materials to use, explained how to lay the signs out for good balance, taught me the best color combinations to use for good readability, and even offered to let me make some signs in his shop so he could provide hands-on guidance. There was never a hint that he viewed me as a competitive threat to his business.

All of the time I spent learning and practicing the techniques Dave taught me was time I wasn't earning any income. It was time invested. The new brushes, paint, and other supplies I bought cost money, but it was money invested. The time that Dave spent helping a youngster get started was also time invested, but not an investment for which he ever expected to receive monetary compensation. As I would learn years later, Dave Cheadle was one of those rare individuals who placed helping others above helping himself. He must subscribe to the idea that success stops when you do, because, in his 80s, Dave still was going to work each day at the sign shop where he taught me so much, more than 45 years ago. Unfortunately, Dave passed on, but his sons still run the sign business and they occasionally do work for me today.

I was different; my idea of success was spelled out in my written goal: **I WILL BECOME A MILLIONAIRE BY AGE 30 AND RETIRE BY AGE 50.** I was quickly learning that accomplishing that goal would be impossible without investing a tremendous amount of time, energy, and money. That's why I wasn't discouraged by the meager $3,400 I earned my first year in business. I had made a substantial investment and was looking forward to the coming year, a year that would prove to pay big dividends and from which I would both earn more and learn more on my journey to becoming a millionaire.

Key points from this chapter:

- Bad things happen to everyone. It's your character that determines whether this will be a brief setback or a permanent disruption to your life.

- Don't use bad luck as an excuse to drop out of life. Take a brief look back to learn from what you did wrong and then focus on the future.

- Believe in yourself and don't join the pity parties you find all around you.

- Investing in your future means using some of your time and your assets to make your future better even if it reduces what you can do today.

- Remember that investing requires sacrifice.
- Have the courage to ask other people to help you.
- Don't be discouraged if progress toward your goal is slow at first. The fact that you are making progress is more important in the beginning than the amount of progress you are making.

21

Accept Responsibility and Do the Right Thing

My second year in business was a testament to the investment of time and energy made during my first year. By the end of year two, my profits were slightly over $12,600, which was nearly four times the prior year and the most for any year since I began working. My profits would have been substantially more had I not made a big blunder.

Early in the year, I landed my first "big job." Up until this time, all of my work had been small incidental signs that only brought in a few dollars each, but the learning and practice I had done during my first year had finally begun to pay off. A local restaurant owner contracted with me to paint the word RESTAURANT in large letters down the entire side of their building. The building was made of masonry block that had been painted a light gray. The side of the building that faced the highway was a solid wall with no windows, and the owner wanted RESTAURANT painted in red letters down the entire side. The job would bring in several hundred dollars.

I was excited that I would finally have the opportunity to prove to the business community that I could do a large job as well as the small token jobs I had been doing. The letters on the building would be five feet tall and extend nearly 50 feet down the side of the building. Since I had only two ladders with a walk board between them from which to work, I decided I would start in the middle of the wall and letter in both directions to get the word centered on the wall. I was about to learn the meaning of the old saying, "Measure twice; cut once."

Maybe because I was caught up in the enthusiasm of getting to do such a big job, or maybe I was already counting my money, but for some reason when I located the center point of the wall, I laid out the letter "T" on the left side of centerline and the letter "R" on the right side. I then continued to work to the right adding the letters "ANT" and then moved back to the "T" and continued to the left adding the letters "SER" in that sequence. When I finished the final letter "R," I stepped back to admire my work and nearly had a heart attack. The job looked great, except for the fact that neatly lettered down the side of the building was the word "RESTRANT." My heart was pounding. I didn't know what to do.

Before I could get up the courage to go inside and tell the restaurant owner what I had done, a customer pulled up in the parking lot and yelled, "Hey, you spelled RESTAURANT wrong!" That was the last thing I needed to hear.

With my head down and butterflies in my stomach, I walked into the restaurant with the customer. When the restaurant owner greeted us, he must have sensed something was amiss because he looked at me and said, "What's wrong?"

"I've really screwed up," I said.

"What happened?" the restaurant owner asked.

"I wish I had an excuse," I began, "but the bottom line is, I just screwed up. I spelled RESTAURANT wrong."

"You did what?"

"I spelled RESTAURANT wrong," I repeated. "I left the AU out of the middle."

We walked out to look and I learned once again that **PEOPLE HELP THOSE WILLING TO HELP THEMSELVES.** Business people are not all greedy, self-centered, abusive individuals the way many people try to portray them. The generosity Dave Cheadle had shown me when I was trying to learn the business is a good example of this. If they've been in business any length of time and had any success, they've made some mistakes too.

The restaurant owner could have blown up and started screaming at me, but he just looked at the wall and laughed, "It looks like you're a better sign painter than you are speller," he said.

"I'm really sorry," I said. "Whatever it takes, I'll fix it."

At this point, I experienced another example of people helping people who are willing to help themselves.

"Don't worry about it," the restaurant owner said. "I've got a couple of gallons of paint that were left over from when we painted the outside. You can use it to cover up the mistake and then letter it again."

I was so relieved that I immediately took the leftover building paint and quickly covered up my error where the lettering was dry enough to paint over. By the end of the day, I had it all covered. I waited until the next day to give the paint time to dry, but when I returned to re-letter the wall, I noticed that the old lettering was still showing through. There wasn't enough leftover paint to put on a second coat, so I took the partial bucket that was left to the paint store and purchased two additional gallons. I returned to the restaurant and applied a second coat over the lettering.

The following day, it was very obvious where I had covered the old lettering; not because the lettering was still showing through, but because the fresh paint was nice and clean and the rest of the wall was weathered. I remembered the real estate broker's comment about signs representing his image to the public and his willingness to pay more for a professional job. I returned to the paint store, purchased additional paint, and repainted the entire side of the building.

When I finished re-lettering the word RESTAURANT on the building, I gave the restaurant owner an invoice for my work and two fresh gallons of the building paint to replace what I had used correcting my mistake. The restaurant owner was so impressed with the way I had handled the mistake that he gave me a letter of recommendation and told me to feel free to have anyone call him if I needed a personal reference.

By the time I finished the job, what was to have been a several-hundred-dollar profit turned into a sizable loss, but the experience was invaluable. Sure, it was a disappointment to lose money on my first big job, and although I received a great deal of personal satisfaction from correcting my mistake, the real benefits were yet to come.

I didn't know it at the time, but there was a local business group that met once a month for breakfast at the restaurant. At their next meeting, the restaurant owner stood up and told the story about what had happened to the side of his building. One of the people attending that meeting later told me that the owner had given me the highest of praise for my handling of the mistake and urged everyone in attendance to give me all of their sign work. This same businessman invited me to attend their next meeting as his guest.

When I showed up for the meeting, I was greeted with open arms. It seemed that everyone wanted to rib me about spelling RESTAURANT wrong, but it was all in fun. Once the meeting began, I was introduced and asked to say a few words about my new business. Although I was nervous when I got up in front of this group of businesspeople, I began by giving them a brief accounting of how I got started making signs for the plant. I followed by telling them about being laid off from my job and my decision to go into business for myself. I also discussed my first year in business and explained how I had nearly starved to death trying to learn the business. I also explained how I had learned the importance of doing quality work.

I once again learned that **PEOPLE HELP THOSE WILLING TO HELP THEMSELVES.** Before I left the meeting that morning, eight business owners had given me their cards and asked me to call on them about doing their sign work. This was the beginning of a dramatic increase in business that resulted in increasing my profits nearly fourfold my second year.

When I stopped to reflect on my success, I was excited and extremely enthusiastic until I compared it with my written goals. My $12,600 profits were great, but it had taken nearly all of my time to produce the work. Just as I did when I was contemplating the future after being laid off from the plant, I took out my goal sheet, which I still have in my wallet, looked at it, and divided $12,600 into $1,000,000. Wow, I had really made an improvement; at this rate it would only take me a little over 79 years instead of 240 years just to earn a million dollars. But, becoming a millionaire meant having a net worth of a million dollars . . . quite a difference.

Once again, when I focused on my goal sheet, I saw that I had earned nearly four times as much my second year as I did my first. I took out a calculator and did some multiplication. Four times $12,600 is $50,400. Four times $50,400 is $201,600. Four times $201,600 is $806,400. Four times $806,400 is $3,225,600. That's just four years of quadrupling profits. I still had six years before I would turn 30. Could I do it?

When I looked at the numbers, I knew that my goal was very optimistic, but I had faith in myself. I saw that I would have to spend my time doing more profitable jobs and at the same time find a way to invest part of my time in the creation of assets that would pay me into the future.

Although this is the last chapter in the section about The Transition/Learning Years, it doesn't mean that you stop learning. As I transition to the next section, The Earning Years, you will see that there are still lessons to be learned, but these lessons merely enhance earnings; they are not a search for earnings like what I experienced when I was trying to "find myself." I had set a huge goal, established the course I would take to achieve this goal, and was now ready to tackle the challenge.

Key points from this chapter:

- You're responsible for cleaning up your own messes. If you make a mistake, admit it and fix it quickly, whatever it costs you.

- Treat people right, and they will become your biggest supporters.

- People help people willing to help themselves.
- If you are given a chance to stand up in front of a group and tell them what you do for a living, jump at it, even it scares you half to death.
- Check your progress against your goals regularly to measure your progress, and make adjustments so you can keep moving toward them.

PART IV

The Earning Years

The earning years, as I define them, begin when individuals commit to career decisions and settle into consistent courses of action that determine the kind of future they will experience. Most of us attempt a number of jobs in our youth before we settle into a career. While I worked in construction, textiles, selling encyclopedias, and in a defense-related research lab before making my commitment to the sign business, some people try 5, 10, 15, or more jobs before settling into a career. Some enter the earning years early, some late, and, unfortunately, some never make it.

This book is designed to help you develop the thought process through which ordinary working people can build wealth without sacrificing happiness and can ultimately become millionaires if they so desire. The career you choose is not as important as the choices you make throughout your life. Developing this thought process entails accepting personal responsibility, establishing a pattern of investing, tracking where your money goes, developing a plan for success, keeping on track, repelling negative influences, and continuing to learn. In this section I will take you through a number of situations that will teach you how to make the kinds of decisions that will propel you to financial success.

The journey to financial independence is a slow and often difficult one, but one everyone can enjoy if he or she has the right mindset. As I've learned, goal setting is critical to this journey. I'm mentioning it again to help you better understand the importance of this section.

One of the great tragedies I've observed throughout the years is the number of people who remain in their Learning Years most if not all of their lives because they lack goals. I watch them start down one career path, hit an obstacle, change careers, hit another obstacle, and change careers again and again and again. They never stick with anything long enough to realize success. Have you ever noticed that there are people who have become very wealthy in virtually every enterprise you can name? Have you also noticed that whatever the venture, there are usually many more people just surviving than becoming wealthy? Why? Could it be that the successful ones have goals and the unsuccessful ones only have wishes and dreams?

My life changed when I set the goal to become a millionaire by age 30 and retire by age 50. As I take you through this section, you will learn that I never lost focus on my goal. When I encountered obstacles, I found ways to go through them, over them, or around them. When faced with problems, I looked for solutions, not excuses. One of the more important things I did was continue to learn, but equally important was to continually measure my performance. Even more important was the fact that I didn't measure my progress against what others were doing, but against my own prior performance, which I then compared with my personal goals.

As I addressed in the last section, if I had compared my first year's performance with that of other people in the area who were in the sign business, I would have seen myself as a dismal failure. Although much improved, if I had compared my second year's performance with others, I still would have looked like a failure. But because I compared MY second year with MY first year, I was enthused and excited with the progress instead of being depressed. Without the goal to guide me, I may have quit before the end of my first year. Having my goal forced me to measure where I was against where I wanted to be so I could determine if I was on track or what adjustments I needed to make. It was during the examination of my first year's performance that I determined much of my time had been invested in improving myself so that I could perform better in future years. Likewise, the examination of my second year's performance, compared with the first, revealed just how much that investment had paid off. The improvement showed me I was on track, but the distance I remained from my goal showed me that I still had much more to do.

Financial success is achieved one step at a time; it doesn't come overnight. One of the big fallacies people have is that wealthy people are just lucky. Sure, some were lucky enough to be born into wealth, but they're not the people for whom this book is written. Wealth doesn't just happen! Ask those who have created wealth through their own initiative, first generation earners, and they will tell you it didn't happen overnight. They laid one small success on top of another until they became a big success. That's what working for financial security is all about; it's developing the right frame of mind to "build" success rather than "attain" success. You can't arrive without taking the journey, and that's what I will teach you in this section.

The basic fundamentals of my financial success were established during my Formative Years and Learning Years. In my Earning Years, I simply perfected and polished these fundamentals as I laid one small success on top of another. As you will see, most of my success came from the consistent application of these fundamentals, not because I hit some lucky jackpot or had divine revelations come to me later in life. From this section, you will learn that building wealth and becoming a millionaire is something every working person can accomplish if he or she has patience, persistence, and a plan of action. Yes, setbacks can and will happen, but whether they are just setbacks or turn into catastrophes depends entirely on how you respond when they occur.

22

Accepting Personal Responsibility Is More Than Apologizing

Accepting personal responsibility means different things to different people. For some, it merely means admitting mistakes when they make them. This is such a depressing connotation, because with it usually comes an apology and an acceptance of whatever punishment is meted out. In the end, the perpetrators feel absolved of further responsibility and cleansed because they admitted their mistakes and paid the price for them.

Accepting personal responsibility for mistakes is one thing, but for wealth builders, it is quite different. When they set goals and commit to them, they accept responsibility for overcoming obstacles in order to complete the journey to achieving the goals. Mistakes are considered a part of that journey, not a reason to abandon it. A big part of achieving financial independence involves understanding this concept. When people make mistakes, offer their apology, accept their punishment but lack the courage to try again, they will never become wealth builders. That's one of the reasons why so many people change careers over and over and over. They just can't seem to face their peers after making a mistake or being reprimanded for shortcomings.

Many people allow those around them to determine their destiny. They refuse to accept personal responsibility, are afraid to attempt new ventures without the approval of their friends or relatives, and, as my dearly departed friend Zig Ziglar said, they become "SNIOPed": Stymied by the Negative Influence of Other People.

Until you learn to accept personal responsibility for your actions, knowing that you will sporadically make mistakes, you will never understand that occasionally, even when everyone you know disagrees with you, it just means that all the fools are on the same side. If Christopher Columbus had failed to understand this concept, we may still be afraid to venture out to sea for fear of sailing off the edge of the world. Having goals and the commitment to achieve them gives you confidence to make decisions and accept responsibility, without fearing that some of your decisions may be wrong. It opens your mind and allows you to learn from your errors, correct them, and avoid making similar mistakes in the future.

As I began my third year in business, an incident occurred that illustrates how accepting personal responsibility had a profound effect on the rest of my life. Bowling was a hobby that allowed me a bit of recreation in my otherwise busy life. It was a sport at which I became very proficient, bowling only the second perfect game in western North Carolina history and eventually becoming a member of the Professional Bowlers Association (PBA). But this story isn't about my bowling abilities; it's about an incident while I was bowling that demonstrated how far I had drifted away from the advice the psychiatrist had given me in high school. It's about how I accepted responsibility and in doing so changed my life for the better.

At the center where I bowled, there was a men's group called the Executive League that was made up entirely of businessmen. It consisted of 10 four-man teams, and since I was in business for myself, I had been invited to join one of the teams. Right from the start, I carried the highest average in the league and was recognized as a fiery competitor. My competitiveness and quick temper also made me the target of occasional unkind words from the other businessmen. One evening, I was on a long string of strikes thinking of another possible perfect game. I rolled a ball perfectly into the pocket between the number one and three pins, which should have produced another strike. Instead, it blasted all of the pins into the pit, except for the eight pin, which didn't move.

"Dammit," I yelled as I turned around and kicked the ball return.

The bowler on the lane next to me was a small, mild-mannered man named Don Collins, who was in the mobile-home business. When I kicked the ball return, it disrupted Don's approach, and he rolled his ball into the gutter. When I came back to the ball return, I was still fuming over the eight pin as I waited for my ball to return so I could attempt the spare.

Don, who seemed to never get upset or raise his voice, turned to me and said, "Why don't you stop acting like an ignorant fool and just enjoy the game."

"Sorry," I replied sarcastically. "I didn't mean to make you mad."

"You didn't make me mad," Don said very calmly. "It takes someone smarter than me to make me mad."

Stung by Don's comment, for which I didn't have a comeback, I rolled my ball, made the spare, and sat down. Finally, what Don had said sunk in. It takes someone smarter than me to make me mad, was a sentence that would stick with me for the rest of my life. Sure, I had been mad when I kicked the ball return; I was known throughout the league for my hot temper and short fuse. When Don told me that it took someone smarter than him to make him mad, he made the right choice. Unlike him, I had been making poor choices and allowing little things to upset me. That was my fault, not anyone else's, yet I was subjecting people around me to bad behavior because of my poor choices.

Don had made a better choice. Rather than engage in a heated altercation, he let me know, in a not-so-subtle way, that he wasn't going to allow my mocking behavior to intimidate him or cause him to react negatively. It was a staggering experience that I would not forget. It brought back memories of the advice the psychiatrist had given me in high school many years earlier: say "positive, positive, positive" before responding, and if you can't come up with something positive, just don't say anything.

I sat quietly between frames as we concluded the evening's match before going up to Don and apologizing for my behavior. Don graciously accepted the apology but never knew the profound impact the incident had on me. From that moment forward, I vowed to take personal responsibility for my actions and never again let others think they were smart enough to get under my skin and cause me to lose control of my emotions. Since that day, I have used that same line many times with hotheads who tried to engage me in heated discussions.

This incident is just one of many that taught me the power of accepting personal responsibility in my life. The more I assumed responsibility for control of my actions, the more my business career flourished. I was also learning that accepting responsibility encompassed much more than just controlling my temper and making a few decisions. It also included accepting personal responsibility for developing the right mindset if I expected to reach my goals. Part of this responsibility was expunging any negative mental baggage I might still be carrying.

As my third year in business was drawing to a close, I found myself struggling with some of this mental baggage. Although it was years in the past, the bad memories I harbored of my stepfather Paul Kiser and the estrangement from my natural father both weighed heavily on my mind. The animosity and hard feelings of the past were still lingering, and they were burdens I needed to unload. I had proven I could make it on my own, so it no longer mattered what my father thought of my career choice. The hatred I once held for Paul didn't seem to matter anymore either. What mattered was the strained relationship with my family. I decided to take personal responsibility for everything that had happened, and I set out to mend fences.

As soon as I completed the accounting for year three of my business, I took my financial statements and went to visit my dad, who was still working as a bookkeeper. When I laid out my statements showing $3,400 profits my first year, Dad wasn't impressed. When I then laid down the statement for my second year showing that I had made $12,600, Dad's eyes looked up. That was more than he had made at his bookkeeping job. But when I laid down the statement for my third year showing profits of more than $55,000, he was shocked.

"That's not bad, boy," he said.

"Well, I just wanted you to know that I wasn't starving to death," I replied. I paused long enough for my dad to look at the statement again, and then I continued, "As you can see, the business is growing, and I'm doing quite well, but that's not the real reason for my visit. I just wanted to come by and let you know that I have no hard feelings about the problems we had earlier. We just had different opinions, and I don't think either of us knew how to deal with them. I'd like to put those feelings behind us and discuss a business proposition with you.

"My business is doing so well that I'm going to need a bookkeeper before too long. I'd like for you to consider coming to work for me. I don't want an answer now, but I'd just like for you to be thinking about it. I'd also like to invite you to come by and visit the business so you can see what I'm doing."

"Well, Son, I don't know what to say," Dad responded.

"You don't have to say anything," I replied. "I just wanted to clear the air between us and ask you to think about it. You don't need to tell me anything until you feel comfortable about it."

That brief discussion reopened the relationship between us and took one of the burdens off my mind. One thing I noticed was that my dad had referred to me as "son" for the first time. (Note: Dad came to work for me two years later and worked for me until his death 10 years later in 1986.)

After exceeding my goal of quadrupling my earnings from year two, I decided I could afford to purchase a small sign crane for use in the business. I used this purchase as an excuse to attempt to heal the wounds with my stepfather. I had purchased a used truck in Asheville and made a deal to buy a used crane from a company in Kansas. That meant I would have to drive the truck to Kansas, a two-day trip, wait for the crane to be mounted on the truck, then drive it back. I telephoned my stepfather Paul and asked if he would make the trip with me to keep me company. I knew we would be together at least six days, which I hoped would give us adequate time to hash out our differences. Paul accepted my offer and agreed to drive down from Bluefield, Virginia, to go with me.

We left Asheville on Saturday heading west on Interstate 40 toward Tennessee. The plan was to make it across the state of Tennessee and on to Sikeston, Missouri, the first day, and then complete the drive to Ottawa, Kansas, on Sunday. I wanted to have the truck at the factory so they could start work first thing Monday morning.

From the time Paul accepted my invitation, I knew the first day of the trip would be difficult, and it was. Our conversations were strained from the beginning, and neither of us could keep a conversation going for any length of time. One of us would ask a question, the other would give a terse response, and then there would be silence until one of us could think of another question to ask. The normal type of ongoing dialog most people would enjoy when traveling was nonexistent. We were both uncomfortable, and it showed.

As the day wore on, and I do mean "wore" on, the situation became increasingly uncomfortable. We stopped to stretch our legs and get lunch at a McDonald's in central Tennessee. We went inside, ordered, and ate in the restaurant. Neither of us said a word to the other over lunch. When we climbed back into the truck and headed west again, I knew I wanted to try to clear the air between us, but I didn't know how to begin. Paul was probably just as uncomfortable, but he didn't make any effort to change things either. We rode along for nearly an hour with hardly a word spoken between us. I used this period of silence to contemplate the best way to open a dialogue about the subject I had invited Paul along to discuss. Finally, I realized that it was me that had invited him, not the other way around. I would have to take personal responsibility for not only opening the dialogue, but also for bringing it to a satisfactory conclusion if I expected to relieve myself of the burden I had been carrying.

"This is crazy," I finally said as I broke the silence.

"What?" Paul replied.

"The way we are acting; here we are, two grown men riding together on a long trip and not even speaking to each other."

"I thought that was the way you wanted it," he said.

At this point, I decided there wasn't a good or tactful way to broach the subject, so I decided to just jump in, speak my mind, and see what happened.

"The reason I invited you to come with me is because I want to talk about the feelings I've had toward you and why I left the way I did," I began. "I hated your guts growing up. I felt like you were totally unfair and even abusive at times. When I ran off at Grandma Sallie's, I vowed that I would never live with you again, nor would I ever have anything to do with you. I was so bitter my insides were boiling with anger.

"But, that was a long time ago, and I've since learned that a lot of my problems were self-initiated. I never let you know about it, but I went to a psychiatrist while I was in school in Abingdon. My anger was so intense that it caused problems for me there just as it had in Bluefield. I've never forgotten that visit to the psychiatrist or the advice he gave me. He helped me understand that my negative reactions usually made my problems worse. Once I started thinking positively and reacting accordingly, things actually did start getting better.

"I don't want to go back and rehash the past; I don't see that it would serve any purpose. I invited you to come on this trip so we could try to put the past behind us and let bygones be bygones. Now that I look back, I'm sure some of the things you did were caused by my behavior. I just want you to know that I accept full responsibility for all the problems we had, and I apologize. Even if some of them were your fault, I forgive you. I just want to unburden myself with the guilt I've been carrying because of our strained relationship and the difficult position in which it has put my mother. I love her very much, and I want to be able to visit her and not feel uncomfortable when I do."

"I don't know what to say," Paul replied.

"No reply is needed," I said. "I've gotten what I wanted to say off my chest; I've put the past behind me and sincerely apologized; that's all I can do. Now it's up to you whether or not you choose to accept my apology and put the past behind you."

Paul just sat there looking sort of stunned for a few moments. Then he shifted around in his seat so he could face me and said, "You don't need to apologize. I was probably as much at fault as you were. I don't know when it started, but the older you got, the harder it was for me to deal with you. I know I did some things I probably shouldn't have done also, so I'll apologize as well."

"Apology accepted," I said.

"I'm glad we are having this discussion," Paul continued. "I've been troubled by the way we parted also. In fact, I accepted the offer to go with you hoping we could resolve our differences. I never meant to be unreasonable or abusive; I just didn't know how to handle you, and the fact that you were my stepson made it even more difficult. It seemed like every time I had to get on you about your behavior, it caused me to question whether or not I was being fair."

"Well, that was all in the past, and like I said earlier, I've put the past behind me," I said.

"That's a good idea," he replied. "I'll try to do the same."

"Truce?" I said as I turned and stuck out my hand.

"Truce!" Paul said as he shook it.

For the next five days, the two of us had an ongoing conversation about the future. I talked about my business, my goals, what I had learned since leaving home, my newfound hobbies, and an endless variety of other topics. Paul spent a lot of time sharing the concerns he had for the rest of his family. He had suffered two massive heart attacks and was thankful that he had lived long enough to take early retirement at age 62. He laughed about the trip being the first thing he had done since retiring. He talked about how he had learned to better control his temper, and he looked forward to retirement without the pressure he had been under while working. The experience was a cleansing one for both of us. (Note: Paul and my mother eventually moved to Asheville, North Carolina, to be closer to me as they grew older. Paul and I maintained a good relationship throughout the years until his death in 1999 at age 90.)

These three experiences proved to me that taking personal responsibility was much more than just admitting mistakes and accepting the consequences. When I decided to take full responsibility for my own happiness and stopped blaming others when things didn't go my way, I grew immeasurably. My confidence grew, my attitude improved and my business relationships were enhanced once I finally understood that it was me who controlled my destiny, not others. By learning to control my temper, repairing my relationship with my father and stepfather, and taking control of my actions, it released a surge of energy that had been suppressed for years. This energy propelled me into a period of strong Earning Years.

Key points from this chapter:

- Accepting responsibility doesn't mean just apologizing for your mistakes and taking the punishment.

- It's not how many mistakes you make, but how quickly you learn to avoid making the same ones again that leads to success.

- Just because everyone disagrees with you doesn't automatically mean that you are wrong.

- Don't let the negative influence of others ruin your life.
- When you lose your temper, it's because you weren't smart enough to maintain control of your emotions.
- Have the courage to reach out to the people who have hurt you in the past and do whatever it takes to get rid of your animosities.
- Don't harbor bad feelings; they do nothing but sap your strength and minimize your ability to perform at your optimum level.

23

An Easy Way to Start Saving

During my first few years in business, I saw an increasing stream of revenue flowing through my bank account, yet I always seemed to come to the end of the money before I got to the end of the month. I was not alone. Many people have this experience whether they are in business or not. Many days, I would spend hours riding around trying to collect money for work I had already completed just so I could pay my bills. This was not only an unpleasant, time-consuming experience for me, but also often an inconvenience and an interruption for my good customers, the ones who paid within a few days when they could. What could I do? Shorter months were not an option. More income would solve the problem, but I was already working as hard as I could. It soon became clear that the problem was that I had very little cash reserves from which to operate.

I resolved to find out what was happening with my money. I had never viewed myself as a spendthrift, but for some reason no matter how much I made, it always seemed to slip away from me. I knew I needed to start building some cash reserves, but I couldn't figure out how I could do that when I was always out of money. Eventually I took a small spiral-bound notebook that I could carry in my shirt pocket and began writing down every penny I spent. If I bought a soft drink, I wrote it down. If I bought a candy bar, I wrote it down. Everything! Groceries, gas, cigarettes (yes, unfortunately I smoked at the time), clothes, bowling, even a piece of bubble gum; no matter how small the purchase, I wrote it all down. I continued this exercise for an entire month before I sat down to analyze my spending.

My analysis was simple; I categorized each outlay into one of two categories, necessary or unnecessary. Loan payments, utilities, food, and similar such expenditures fell into the necessary category. Unnecessary meant it was something I wanted enough to purchase, but something I could have done without. Cigarettes, candy, soft drinks, records, a new pocketknife, and a new bowling ball were among the items that showed up on the unnecessary list that month. I was shocked when I totaled up the items on the list. I discovered that in just one month, I had spent more than $600 on unnecessary items.

This exercise accomplished three things. First, it identified a pool of money from which I could start building cash reserves or use to start investing. Secondly, it caused me to pay much greater attention to my spending habits. But the third and the most important thing that it showed me was you have to **KNOW WHERE YOUR MONEY GOES** if you expect to achieve financial success.

When I teach this concept in a live program, a few people will acknowledge they waste a little money, but most take a defensive posture and deny that they spend frivolously. The tighter their finances, the more adamant they are that they don't waste money. Invariably they blame their problems on others; prices are too high; they don't make enough to cover expenses; or they've just had a run of bad luck. They remind me of functioning alcoholics who continue to deny they have a problem.

Everyone wastes money; some people just waste more than others, and until you're willing to face this fact, it will be very difficult for you to put yourself on the road to financial independence. Don't get me wrong. I'm not advocating that you live an austere life with no frivolous spending and no fun in order to achieve financial success. That's the image most people have of misers, and that's the last thing I want you to become. Once you begin getting control of your finances, you will find that it is possible to build wealth and be happy. One is not mutually exclusive of the other.

Once you **KNOW WHERE YOUR MONEY GOES,** you have options. After identifying exactly the amount of your unnecessary spending, you can begin making life-changing decisions. You get to decide what portion of this money you want to redirect into building cash reserves or making other investments. I'm not suggesting that anyone attempt to redirect all of his or her discretionary money. For most, redirecting a third to half of it is enough to produce life-changing results if done consistently over time and invested wisely.

In my case, once I saw how much I was spending on unnecessary items, I came up with a novel idea to redirect part of it. I decided that I would pay for all purchases with bills and any change I received I would bring home and put in a jar. You may think, "That's a silly idea." But after the first month, my loose change totaled more than $50. The second month it was once again over $50, and my experiment of paying with bills and saving the change was becoming a habit, one that has stuck with me until this day.

After several months of saving change and watching it accumulate from a few nickels, dimes, and quarters to several hundred dollars, it dawned on me that I hadn't missed the money. I couldn't think of anything I had sacrificed, yet I had accumulated more than I had ever been able to save before. It wasn't the amount I saved; it was the way I did it that made the difference.

In the beginning, I would roll the change and take it to the bank and deposit it into a savings account, but as the years passed, I began to enjoy watching the growing pile of change, and I decided I'd just keep it. Granted, this was not a good investment strategy, but I used it as a reminder of what could happen by putting aside a only few coins each day. It gave me encouragement and let me see the results of what I was doing. I still continue this habit today and have accumulated many thousands of dollars in change dating back over 40 years.

By only paying with bills, I noticed another phenomenon that helped me manage my money. I found myself becoming less and less willing to break a large bill to make a frivolous purchase like buying a candy bar or a soft drink. By religiously refusing to spend my change for these small items and adhering to my vow not to break a large bill to get them, I saved even more money. Without knowing it, I was training myself to be more responsible with my discretionary spending, and the results started to show. Each month I seemed to have a little extra money in addition to the change I was saving.

This small exercise in thriftiness quickly turned into a habit that was the first of many similar experiments during my Earning Years that would become part of the thought process that led to my financial success. It helped me discover the true power of the three Ds of success. I had the Desire to curb my unnecessary spending. I had the Discipline to pay for each purchase, no matter how small, with a bill. And, I had the Dedication to continue saving my change until it became a habit. The results have been outstanding; I have saved more than $100,000 throughout my career using just this one small, insignificant habit. Many people never accumulate this much cash in a lifetime of conscious saving, let alone by doing something so insignificant as saving change.

I have dedicated this entire chapter to discussing the importance of **KNOWING WHERE YOUR MONEY GOES** because I believe that it is essential to building wealth. Many people think wealth comes from what you earn. Wealth is not accumulated by what you earn; it is accumulated by what you save and invest. If you make a million dollars a year and spend a million dollars a year, are you any better off at the end of the year than someone who makes fifty thousand a year and spends fifty thousand? At the end of the year, both people must earn additional money to live the following year. By **KNOWING WHERE YOUR MONEY GOES,** you are able to redirect portions of your earnings into investments that can pay you for the rest of your life. That's one of the benefits that come from developing habits that lead to saving and investing.

Now, hold that thought as we move to the next chapter, where I will discuss developing a pattern of investing.

Key points from this chapter:

- You cannot operate efficiently without cash reserves.
- Start by analyzing every penny you spend.
- Categorize all of your expenditures into necessary and unnecessary.
- Turn unnecessary expenses into cash reserves or working capital.
- Paying only with bills and saving the coins is a painless way to start saving.
- If you have to break a big bill to buy a small item, let it be a red flag. Do you really need it?
- Knowing where your money goes is essential to building wealth.
- Keep working the three "Ds": Discipline, Dedication, and Desire in everything you do.

24

Big Success from Small Savings and Investments

As I mentioned in the previous chapter, the habit I developed of paying for purchases with bills and saving the loose change caused me to be more responsible with my discretionary spending. This gave me my first investment capital. I was early into my Earning Years, and the temptations of youth were strong. I had the same desires that most young people have to spend these funds rather than invest them, but I found myself pouring every penny I could back into my business.

As I mentioned in Chapter 6, I began building highway signs to rent rather than sell. Each new billboard was another investment that would provide me with a growing income stream, but each one also cost hundreds of dollars to construct. Unlike the ease with which I saved loose change and watched it grow, it was difficult to find large sums of money with which to build signs. For years, I endured a continuing struggle with my banks. When I tried to borrow money to invest in new signs, none of my bankers understood my business. They didn't know how to collateralize a loan with signs built on leased property and rented to clients for which they didn't have financial information.

I tried everything to get more financing. I wrote proposals; I prepared projections; I called on every bank in town; I even went to the local university and took a course titled "The Economics of Money and Banking." I was obsessed with finding the money to continue to invest in building more signs to rent. One day I was talking with one of my good customers, a fine gentleman named George Duke who had moved to North Carolina from Florida and purchased a local campground. I had done extensive sign work for the campground for more than a year and had developed a close friendship with George. During our discussion, I expressed my frustration over not being able to obtain bank financing when I had plenty of clients ready and willing to rent signs if I could only get the money to build them.

"How much are you trying to borrow," George asked.

"About $30,000," I replied.

"And how long do you need it for."

"I could easily pay it back in three years," I said.

"Well, banks can be difficult to do business with at times," George responded. "I know, I was in the building business in Florida, and I had to deal with them all the time. Tell you what; I've seen how hard you work, you do a good job, and you've always been fair with me, so I'd like to help you if I can. Why don't you check with your bank and see if they will let you have the money if I co-sign the note with you."

"You'd actually do that?" I exclaimed.

"I'd be happy to; just check with the bank and see if that will work."

This was the break I needed. It didn't happen because I was lucky; it happened because I had demonstrated to someone who was in a position to help me that I was responsible and could do quality work. With George's guarantee, the bank made the loan, and I was quickly able to construct several new signs. The signs produced substantially more income than the payments on the loan. I was on my way to financial success.

I should mention here that George was extraordinarily generous and trusting in co-signing for the loan. Very few people would have done that, because there's a real danger that they would not only lose the money but also ruin their credit rating, which is far more serious. Had he not known me well enough to be comfortable that I would repay the loan, he might have been better off just loaning me the $30,000 himself. By co-signing the bank loan, he not only allowed me to get the money I needed, but also to demonstrate my responsibility to the bank and build my credit rating.

By building and owning signs to rent, I was learning the power of investing. My business kept growing, and soon I had to hire my first employee, a talented sign painter named Joe Letterman (yes, that is his real name). Joe did most of the work to produce the signs that I rented.

Now in my fourth year of business and still on track to achieve my goal of becoming a millionaire by age 30, I found myself in a situation where business growth was easily consuming all my profits plus any additional money I could borrow. Unfortunately, another event occurred that caused me to think that maybe I should consider investing at least a little money into something other than my company. The passage of the

Highway Beautification Act, also known as the Lady Bird Johnson Act, caused a bit of concern because it regulated billboards and limited where new ones could be built.

In the summer of 1973, shortly after the new regulations went into effect, I visited my mother and Paul in Bluefield. Since I had repaired my relationship with Paul, I felt comfortable talking with him about my business concerns. Paul, who had been in the life insurance business, suggested that I take out an insurance policy insuring my life. He explained that a whole life policy would not only provide insurance that might make my banks more comfortable, but it would act as a forced savings plan as well. He showed me how he had been able to borrow against his own life insurance to purchase his cars and how he was able to do it at a much lower rate than he could get from the banks. He described how these policies began building cash value after a couple of years and could even provide for retirement income in the future.

Although he was retired at the time, Paul was still able to write insurance, so I decided to purchase a $100,000 policy through him and have the $106.87 premium deducted directly from my bank account. I recalled how I had been able to save over $50 per month, without even noticing it, just by saving my loose change. Now that my business was doing better, I was sure I wouldn't miss the insurance premium and it would give me another way of saving a little money outside of the business, but the main reason I bought the insurance was because I felt it might also give my bankers the added security of knowing that if something happened to me, they would get paid. When I finished completing the application, I left for the return trip to Asheville.

As I drove along, I began thinking about the insurance. I was proud of myself for making the commitment to invest more than $100 per month into the insurance, but the longer I thought about it, the more I wished I had doubled the amount. This thought kept running through my mind for a month, especially after I saw how thrilled my bankers were to learn that I now had life insurance. I knew I would be borrowing much more money, so I decided to buy another $100,000 policy. This time, I talked with the agent who carried my business insurance and found that I could get a policy comparable to the one I had already purchased for just $101.90 per month. These policies were issued in September and October 1973.

By the following spring, business was booming, I had been able to secure two more bank loans to invest in new sign construction, and I had hardly missed the insurance premiums that had been deducted monthly from my account. In May, I was once again visiting my mother and Paul. I told Paul about buying the second $100,000 policy and how I had hardly noticed the premiums being deducted from my account. We also talked about the two new loans I had gotten from my banks. Eventually, I got around to telling Paul that I would like to purchase another $250,000 policy.

"I know it's not the best investment as far as getting a high return, but having the premium deducted directly from my account becomes a habit. I don't miss it. It reminds me of the loose change I still save every day. If I don't have it, I don't spend it." I told him.

"Well, I think you're making a smart move," Paul replied. "If you keep the insurance, you'll be surprised at what it will be worth as you get older, plus it will give you security and peace of mind."

The $250,000 policy was issued in June 1974, and little did either of us realize the impact this insurance would have in just two short years. I won't bore you with the details here, but two years later, I was able to negotiate the purchase of another billboard company with no money down and full owner financing. The seller accepted a pledge of my insurance policies instead of a cash-down payment as collateral for the purchase. This was a huge step for me, but the deal was so favorable, it enabled me to reach my goal of becoming a millionaire, not by age 30, but by age 28.

Most people would think that the big loans I took out to finance the growth of my billboard investments were the reason I reached my goal two years ahead of schedule. But if you want the truth, I learned more from saving loose change than from all the difficult meetings I had with bankers. Sure the bank loans enabled me to grow the business, but the effects of patiently accomplishing a little each day, every day, was far more responsible for my development of the mindset for success than any of my bigger accomplishments. In fact, it was the little things I learned from this process that made the bigger successes possible. Just learning that I didn't have to do everything at once, that doing a little each and every day could add up to a lot over time was knowledge that was priceless.

Throughout my career, I have never forgotten the lesson I learned from saving loose change: that if I could only invest a little each day and, keep doing it consistently, day after day, it could add up to quite a sum over a long period of time. This is the message that investment counselors try to drum into clients when they talk about investing in IRA and 401k accounts or other retirement plans. Most people have a difficult time grasping this concept when they can't touch or feel their investments. For me, watching the ever-increasing volume of coins grow provided visible reinforcement and encouraged me to continue doing the other things that weren't so visible.

I have applied this concept throughout life. When it was announced that effective January 1, 1990, US Savings bonds would earn interest tax-free if used for education, I began purchasing a $100 bond each week for my two sons, who would not enter college until more than a decade later. Just as with the loose change and the insurance premiums, the money I put into the bonds went practically unnoticed. I adjusted my lifestyle to life with what was left after I made the purchases. This, too, soon became a habit, and I didn't miss a week buying the bonds. As with the loose change, I watched the stack of bonds continue to grow higher and higher year after year. When my son Jason entered Florida State University in the fall of 2000, the cost of his entire four-year college education was in hand. Furthermore, I continued purchasing the bonds even after my youngest son, Matt, entered college in 2002, and I didn't stop until 2004, when I determined that I had more than enough savings to cover their education.

Once again I learned a very valuable lesson from making this sacrifice. When my sons graduated from high school and left for college, many of their friends did the same, but when I talked with their parents, there was a big difference. Almost all of them who were trying to help their children with their education had to go into debt to do so. They had not made the sacrifice required to save for this expense, even though they had known since their child's birth that it was coming. While they had to reduce their standard of living to make payments on the loans, I was able to increase my standard of living because I no longer needed to purchase the bonds each week. College for my children became a financial relief for me, while it was a burden for many of their friends' parents.

Go back to Chapter 4 and review the chart in Figure 6 where I showed how you can drive a Chevrolet or a Cadillac for the same amount of earned income. The Cadillac owner and the Chevrolet owner paid the same amount for their cars. The only difference was that the Cadillac owner saved for his car, "earned" interest on the money, and paid cash. The Chevrolet owner borrowed the money to buy his car and "paid" interest for the use of the bank's money. The notable difference is that the Cadillac was five years newer than the Chevrolet! The way I saved to pay for my son's college education is a perfect example of this concept of saving to spend rather than borrowing to spend. Most people wait until the money is needed, and then they go into debt to help their children, or the children have to take out student loans to pay for their education. This negatively impacts their standard of living long after graduation while they pay off the debt. On the other hand, I was able to improve my standard of living because I was able to stop buying the bonds two years before my youngest son graduated, plus I had the comfort of knowing that his education was already paid for. This is another example of the positive effects of living the Lifestyle of Success described in Chapter 2.

If you have read this far, you already know that achieving financial success is rooted in patience and persistence. Throughout my Earning Years, I lived on a salary from my billboard business, but it was what I did with my salary and my spare time that ultimately brought me true success. Saving loose change, paying premiums on cash-building life insurance and buying US Savings bonds are examples of the many ways working people save money, but they rarely bring financial success because most people lack the stick-to-itiveness to turn these actions into habits. Even if they do, it's still difficult to save your way to financial success.

In the late 1970s, the billboard business was becoming more and more volatile, and the uncertainty of its future was causing me some major concerns. My bankers were becoming increasingly nervous each time a new ordinance was passed, and my accountant and lawyer expressed doubts about the future of the industry and recommended that I begin diversifying my investments. At the time, the loose change I had saved and the cash value of my life insurance accounted for less than 1 percent of my assets. Everything else I owned was invested in my company, which was still consuming all of my profits plus what I could borrow to keep it growing.

I had a discussion with my CPA, John Kledis, about investment options that might be available to me. I told John that I didn't have any extra money to invest and I certainly couldn't take any out of my billboard business. It's hard to diversify when you don't have any money. John told me that I might want to look into investing in rental real estate. He said it was very similar to investing in signs, except that every city and county around wasn't trying to pass regulations to do away with houses. He went on to explain that many times real estate could be purchased with very little or no money down by simply assuming someone else's loan or getting the seller to finance the purchase. (Back then you could assume real estate loans without having to qualify.) This conversation sparked my interest and enticed me to want to learn more about it. Little did I realize at the time that this conversation would eventually lead to real estate investing's becoming a far larger part of my success than the billboard business.

I didn't have any extra money, but I did have a little time. I began using some of my spare time on the weekends to look at houses that were for sale and started making offers that I could handle if one was accepted. It took me nearly a year to buy my first rental house, but when I bought it, I only had to come up with a few dollars to close the deal. The spare time I invested in looking at houses and making offers soon became like the loose change and the insurance premiums; it developed into a habit. Although the results were anything but spectacular, I came to enjoy the time I spent inspecting properties and making offers. Over time, I was able to purchase a second rental house and then a third.

I set up a separate bank account in which to deposit my rental income and from which to pay the expenses. I obtained amortization schedules on each mortgage loan. These schedules showed how much of each payment was interest and how much went to pay down the loan balance. Every month, when I made the payment, I would circle the principal and interest amounts and the loan balance and write down the date and check number with which I paid the payment. Each month I noticed that a little more went to principal and a little less to interest. Monitoring the declining loan balances and increasing rents soon became a game, much like playing the board game Monopoly . . . for keeps.

When I said earlier that what I learned from saving loose change taught me more than what I learned from high-powered meetings with my bankers, I was talking about the value of patience and persistence. Watching the loan balances decline each month was similar to watching the loose change fill up in the jar, only this time other people were making the deposits, namely my tenants when they paid their rent. It was like having employees that got up each day and went to work, but someone else supervised them, paid the taxes on them, and dealt with any problems that arose; and when they paid their rent each month, they were making deposits into my future. I liked that!

I soon acquired a fourth and a fifth house, and then a sixth and seventh. Each month as I recorded the income and expenses, I watched my debt go down and the value of my assets go up as rents increased. (You can learn how to build wealth investing in real estate by reading my book co-authored with Roger Dawson titled *The Weekend Millionaire's Secrets of Investing in Real Estate: How to Become Wealthy in Your Spare Time* (McGraw-Hill 2003). This truly was like the Monopoly games I remembered playing as a child. I recalled the times I would be flat broke during a game when everyone else had loads of cash and all I had were properties. But, this also brought to mind the number of those games I ultimately won as the people who hoarded their cash and didn't invest began landing on my properties and having to pay rent. I saw no reason why I couldn't do the same thing in real life, and that's what I eventually did. By 1997, my real estate had become so profitable that I sold the sign business and retired at age 50, just as I had planned. Since that time, I have been playing Monopoly for keeps.

This chapter is designed to teach you the value of **DEVELOPING A**

PATTERN OF INVESTING. It's not nearly as important how much you invest as it is how consistently and over what duration you invest. As I said earlier, "A mouse can eat an elephant if you give it long enough." It's the habits you acquire when you **DEVELOP A PATTERN OF INVESTING** that ultimately bring financial success. It's amazing what ordinary people can accomplish when these principles are applied.

Key points from this chapter:

- Saving a little bit regularly is the key to building investment funds. Even if it's only the change from your pockets or purse.

- Persistence is the key to success; don't quit just because you encounter an obstacle. Keep at it until you find a way to overcome the obstacle.

- Develop the habit of regularly saving, whether it's by purchasing life insurance, savings bonds, or other investments; the importance is to do it consistently.

- Plan for large expenditures such as college tuition or replacing automobiles, and start saving the money now so you won't have to go in debt later. You're going to have to make the payments one way or another, so why not make them before the purchase rather than after?

- The effect of saving can be greatly multiplied by investing in rental properties because the rent from your tenants will pay down the mortgages instead of your having to earn the money to do so.

- There are many ways to invest other than real estate; I only mention real estate because that's what I know best. If you choose another way of investing, just be sure to learn all you can about it before putting your money into it.

- Saving and investing are essential to building wealth; the sooner you develop these habits, the quicker you will begin moving toward financial independence.

25

Personal Budgeting Is Key to Financial Independence

I've covered many different topics and events that contribute to developing the thought process required to achieve financial independence, but until you start tracking where your money goes, you will find it difficult to stay on course. You've probably heard the saying, "The road to hell is paved with good intentions." What you may not have heard is, "The road to financial ruin is paved with 'I'm gonna's' and 'wish I hadda's.' " If you are serious about building wealth and becoming financially independent, you have to make a lifelong commitment to understanding where your money goes.

The key to building wealth is being aware of what you can buy and when you can buy it, not the amount of money you make. I've seen people making huge salaries file bankruptcy because they spent more than they made. Why? I think the reason is simple. They don't have a plan, but they do have an "I want it now" mentality, and this causes them to buy things before they can afford them. As a result, they finance the purchases and pay exorbitant amounts of their hard-earned income in fees and finance charges. I firmly believe that **MOST ORDINARY WORKING PEOPLE PAY ENOUGH IN INTEREST AND FINANCING-RELATED FEES OVER THEIR LIFETIMES TO BECOME MILLIONAIRES.**

The sad part is that these purchases are not all big, expensive items. More often than not, they are small things like going to a movie, eating out in a restaurant, buying a new dress, or any of the thousands of other things they charge on their credit cards. Instead of asking, "Can I afford this," they ask, "Can I make the payments?" At this point, I urge you to go back and reread Chapter 6, **How Debt Impacts Your Journey**. In this chapter, I'm going to teach you how to avoid destructive debt, which is debt to purchase things that don't produce income and that go down in value the longer you own them.

In Chapter 23, I discussed an exercise in which I wrote down every expenditure I made for a full month in order to determine where I was spending my money. This is a valuable exercise, and you should try it. Before you can establish a plan to achieve financial independence, you must be honest about what you are currently doing with your money. You can't just "wing it" and expect positive results. This exercise is important because it may let you see that you are already living above your means, and if that is the case, no matter how well-intentioned you are, you can't build wealth as long as you spend more than you make.

First, let me dispel a myth many people have about budgeting: a budget is not a device to keep you from doing the things you'd like to do. You need to understand that budgeting is flexible. Preparing a budget is merely establishing what you plan to do with your money. It becomes the benchmark against which you compare what you actually did with what you planned to do. If worked properly and consistently, a budget can become a tool that helps you make the kind of financial decisions that will lift you from the Lifestyle of Ordinary to the Lifestyle of Success.

I believe that the biggest reason ordinary people have a problem with financial planning is because they try to make it too complicated. Have you ever met with a financial planner and walked away from the meeting wondering what he or she said? Could it be that if they simplified things you wouldn't need them? First, I want you to understand that financial planning is different from debt counseling and investment counseling. Debt counseling helps you get out of debt if you are already in the hole. Financial planning is what you use to put your financial house in order. Investment counseling helps you decide where and how to invest your money once your financial house is in order.

The system I'm going to teach you in this chapter is simple. It's a way to evaluate your personal finances to determine the course of action you will need to take to achieve financial independence. Some of you will see that you have adequate income; you just need to manage it better. Some of you may find that you have to reduce your standard of living temporarily or that you have to earn more if that's easier than giving up things to which you've grown accustomed. No matter what your situation, I'm going to teach you how to improve it and how to establish a course of action that will lead you toward financial independence. I call this flexible budgeting because it is adjusted each month.

The first thing you are going to need for this exercise is a columnar pad or an electronic spreadsheet program on your computer. The best type of pad for this use is an accountant's three-column pad that can be purchased at any office-supply store. You will need several sheets, on which the columns should be labeled as shown in Figure 15.

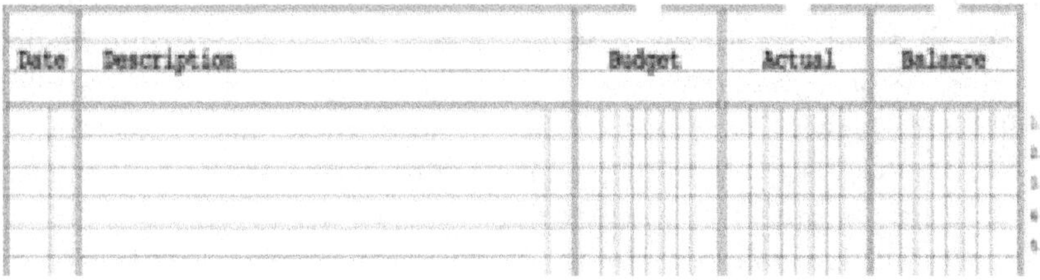

Date	Description	Budget	Actual	Balance

Fig. 15

The picture in Figure 15 shows you how your sheets should be laid out. Most of the columnar pads come pre-punched to fit in a three-ring notebook style binder, which I recommend you use. It will take a little time to set up this system initially, but you will find it is well worth the effort.

I'm going to show you how to set this up by hand, the old-fashioned way, because not everyone is familiar with using electronic spreadsheets on a computer. If you are computer savvy and would be more comfortable using an electronic spreadsheet program like Microsoft Excel, by all means do so. The principle and results are the same whether you do it by hand or on a computer.

Start by making out a sheet for each payment you pay on a regular basis, including those items you pay quarterly, semiannually, or annually. Put the name of the account on the top of the sheet, and label the columns as shown in Figure 15. You will eventually need to set up some additional sheets, but for now let's just make ones for the things you "have to pay." Here's a partial list to help you get started: Electric, Water, Gas/Heating Oil, Phone, Cell Phone, Cable TV, Trash Collection, Groceries, Clothing, Newspaper, Credit Card (one sheet for each credit card), Other Credit Accounts (one for each account), House Payment/ Rent, Car Payment (one sheet for each car loan), Gasoline, Homeowners/ Renters Insurance, Car Insurance, Hospitalization Insurance, Life Insurance, Property Taxes, etc. You will also want to set up a "contingency" account for unforeseen expenses, such as car or home repairs, accidents, etc. Whatever you put into this Contingency Account is money you won't have to come up with when those unexpected expenses arise.

Each person's situation is different. You may need accounts not on the above list or there may be ones on the list that don't apply to you. This list is just a suggestion to help you take the first step toward putting your financial house in order, so at this time make sheets only for recurring payments. I'll discuss other sheets you might want to add a little later.

For these illustrations, I'm going to assume we are starting at the beginning of a calendar year, so the first entry on all my examples will be for January; however, it doesn't matter which month you begin. Once you've completed a sheet for each of your recurring payments, let's select one with which to get started. Since nearly everyone has an electric bill, I'm going to choose the first one on the list, Electric, to use as an example. Now, I want you to do a little research. Check your back records and try to determine what your average electric bill has been over the past several months. If you don't have records, make your best educated guess or call your power company and ask them to give you your average monthly amount for the last year. Then enter this amount on the first line as the "budget" for the month from which you will be starting. Of course, if you've been paying bills on your computer already, you'll quickly be able to pull up a list of your paid bills. Your sheet will look like this:

Electric Company Name

Date	Description	Budget	Actual	Balance
Jan. 1	January	$235.00		$235.00

As you can see from the example above, I selected $235.00 as the budgeted amount for electricity for the month of January. Your entry will be the amount you determined to be your average monthly electric cost. Now, stop and complete a sheet like this for each one of your accounts. For items that you pay quarterly, semiannually, or annually, enter the amount you would need to set aside each month between now and the next due date in order to have the money on hand to pay the bill when it comes due.

When you have completed all of your sheets, add up the total budgeted amounts from all of your sheets. This total will be the minimum amount you will need to earn for the month to be solvent. I say the minimum amount, because you have not yet allowed for any discretionary spending. If you cannot earn this amount during the month, you need to stop right here and re-evaluate your spending. Unless you adjust your standard of living to fit your income, you are heading for financial disaster, and it's better to find out now than to wait until you're so deep in the hole you can't get out.

I recommend that you set up a special bank account from which to pay your bills. Once you have established the amount you will need to cover your minimum expenses, you will need to deposit that amount into the account. This is known as funding your budget. With this amount in the account, when the actual bills come in, you pay them from this account and note the date and amount you pay on the next line below your first entry. Your sheets should then look like this:

Electric Company

Date	Description	Budget	Actual	Balance
Jan. 1	January	$235.00		$235.00
Jan. 14	January payment		$231.25	$3.75

Again using the Electric Company sheet as an example, you can see that the actual amount was less than what was budgeted. When you subtracted the actual from the budgeted amount, it left $3.75 remaining in the account. You will leave this amount in the account and budget an additional $235.00 for the month of February. After doing that, your sheet now looks like this:

Electric Company

Date	Description	Budget	Actual	Balance
Jan. 1	January	$235.00		$235.00
Jan. 14	January payment		$231.25	$3.75
Feb. 1	February	$235.00		$238.75

As you can see, your electric account now has $238.75 budgeted for February. "But," you say, "What if my electric bill is more than what I budgeted?" Good question! Let's continue with the assumption that that's exactly what happens in February. After paying the bill, your sheet should look like this:

Electric Company

Date	Description	Budget	Actual	Balance
Jan. 1	January	$235.00		$235.00
Jan. 14	January payment		$231.25	$3.75
Feb. 1	February	$235.00		$238.75
Feb. 14	February payment		$247.65	$ -8.90

As you can see, your account is now in the negative by $8.90. When this happens, what you need to do is budget another $235.00 for the upcoming month plus the shortage from the prior month. When you do this, your sheet should look as follows:

Electric Company

Date	Description	Budget	Actual	Balance
Jan. 1	January	$235.00		$235.00
Jan. 14	January payment		$231.25	$3.75
Feb. 1	February	$235.00		$238.75
Feb. 14	February payment		$247.65	$ -8.90
Mar. 1	March	$243.90		$235.00

For March, you needed to put more into the electric account than you did in the previous months just to get the balance back to your regular monthly budgeted amount. That's why I refer to this as flexible budgeting. It allows you to correct shortages immediately rather than having them unknowingly accumulate until they cause problems. You should leave any overages in the accounts to help compensate for future shortages that may arise. If you consistently run short each month, you will need to adjust your budgeted amount upward. Likewise, if you budget more than you need for several months, you can adjust what you put in the account to a lower amount. You will do this for each of your accounts each month. When you total the amount you will need to meet you regular expenses, you will find that it fluctuates up and down a little each month.

For those accounts that you pay quarterly, semiannually, or annually, your sheets will look a little different. The following is an example of what your sheet for auto insurance may look like if you pay the premium semiannually in June and December.

Auto Insurance – Premium due $435.00 in June and December

Date	Description	Budget	Actual	Balance
Jan. 1	January budget	$72.50		$72.50
Feb. 1	February budget	$72.50		$145.00
Mar. 1	March budget	$72.50		$217.50
Apr. 1	April budget	$72.50		$290.00
May 1	May budget	$72.50		$362.50
June 1	June budget	$72.50		$435.50
June 10	Semiannual payment		$435.00	$ 0
July 1	July budget	$72.50		$72.50

In this example, one-sixth of the semiannual premium was budgeted each month. This amount was placed into the bank account to cover the premium when it came due. When you plan this way, you avoid being caught in a bind when these larger, less frequent expenses come due. With this system, you always know how much of the money in your bank account is needed to cover these larger expenses. By adding up the amounts in the balance column of all your sheets. you can know at any given time how much money should be in your bank account to meet your upcoming obligations. This is important, because even if your intentions are good, without a system like this in place, it is very easy to spend the money and then come up short when the large bills come due.

So far I've discussed planning for regularly occurring expenses, but you can use the same method to plan for items like clothing or other irregularly occurring expenses. These are the expenditures that blow most people's budgets because they don't plan for them, and then the expenses get charged to the credit cards. The way to avoid this is to set up a sheet and budget an amount for irregularly occurring expenses each month just as you do for your other expenses that aren't paid monthly. You may not purchase anything for several months, but you will be accumulating funds to pay for your purchases when you do make them. If you want to buy a new outfit, all you need to do is refer to your budget sheet and see if you have accumulated enough to do so without going into debt. If the money isn't there, simply delay the purchase until it is.

This system can really help you when it comes to automobiles. We all have transportation expenses, whether we have a car payment or not. Here's a tip! If you are making a car payment and you have it in your budget, continue to budget the payment amount even after you pay off the loan. By doing so, you will begin accumulating funds for your next purchase. Try, if at all possible, to wait until you accumulate enough to trade cars and pay cash for the difference, but if you can't, the funds you are able to save will enable you to finance less when you do trade. By financing less, you can keep the same payment you've become accustomed to making and pay off the new vehicle quicker. In any event, this car account will enable you to make better decisions about when to trade rather than letting your emotions decide for you.

Let's now take things a step further. Up to this point, we have only dealt with mandatory expenses, and you are probably thinking, "What about discretionary spending, things like dining out, recreation, vacations, etc.? What about savings?" The reason I left these items until last is because I wanted you to determine if you had any extra money before discussing them. If, when budgeting for mandatory expenses, you found that you had no extra money; you are left with just three alternatives. You can earn more, spend less, or go into debt. Of these options, going into debt is the one that is sure to cause future difficulties and result in one of the other two options being forced upon you.

If you're like most people, you will find that you have some discretionary funds. The amount will vary depending on your income and the standard of living you have chosen, but most responsible people, especially the vast majority who are living the Lifestyle of Ordinary, have some extra money after paying their bills. What you do with these funds is what determines if or when you will achieve financial independence.

Many people view life as a drudgery and complain that they are simply working day after day just to survive. The pressure this places on them mentally often results in binge spending, which invariably puts them deeper in the hole and subjects them to an even more depressing life of hard work and toil. It's a vicious cycle that becomes as difficult to break as a drug or alcohol habit.

If you're already caught in this cycle, I'm going to show you how to break out of it. If you aren't, I'm going to help you avoid it. Everyone needs to have some pleasure in life. Things like dining out, vacations, recreational activities, and hobbies are as important to a healthy and happy life as anything else. You've heard it said that there's more to life than just making money. I totally agree. There's also nothing more stabilizing in life than having solid control over your finances and seeing the security that comes with watching your financial nest egg grow. With my simple flexible budgeting system you will be able to achieve all of these things and more.

Once you have established your budget for mandatory expenses and adjusted your standard of living, if necessary, to ensure that you have some discretionary funds, here's what you do next. Set up a sheet for long-term savings. (This really should be the first item you fund!) This can be an amount budgeted for your IRA, 401k, or other retirement account. Later on, you may want to set up an account you can use to purchase other investments that can give you higher returns, as I did with real estate. It is money that you don't plan to touch until you're ready to retire. Then you set up additional sheets for other savings that you will use for shorter-term expenditures like Dining Out, Vacations, Recreation, or any other activity that brings you pleasure. Set up a savings sheet for Christmas expenditures and another for Miscellaneous Gifts like birthdays and anniversaries. Probably the most important item you can plan for is the unplanned. To handle these unexpected expenses, set up a sheet for Contingency Fund and use it to accumulate money to cover these unforeseen expenses so you aren't forced to dip into your retirement funds when they arise. The key is to avoid being caught short when unplanned expenses arise.

Using these sheets will allow you to secure your future while planning for activities, without going into debt. I recommend that you establish a budget for your retirement account first. Be as generous as possible when you set your budgeted amount because the more you budget, the quicker you will achieve financial independence, but don't try to budget so much that you can't have a little fun in life too. If you do, you'll constantly be tempted to dip into your retirement account to fill your emotional needs for merriment.

Once you've established your budget for retirement and contingencies, look at the money you have remaining, and allocate it to discretionary spending. You may want to spread it over several discretionary accounts. For this example, I'll use the Dining Out account to demonstrate how this works. You will set up a sheet titled Dining Out just as you did for the other expense accounts. Select an amount based on your remaining funds that you would like to spend on dining each month. Your sheet may look similar to the example below:

Dining Out

Date	Description	Budget	Actual	Balance
Jan. 1	January budget	$100.00		$100.00
Jan. 8	Dinner at ??		$42.50	$57.50
Jan. 22	Dinner at ??		$32.65	$24.85
Jan. 26	Lunch at ??		$12.50	$12.35
Feb. 1	February budget	$100.00		$112.35
Feb. 14	Dinner at ??		$58.85	$53.50
Feb. 22	Dinner at ??		$28.25	$25.25
Mar. 1	March budget	$100.00		$125.25
Mar. 6	Lunch at ??		$13.50	$11.75
Mar. 12	Lunch at ??		$16.35	$95.40
Mar. 20	Dinner at ??		$56.45	$38.95

In this example, you budgeted $100.00 per month to dine out. Each time you ate out, you recorded the expenditure on the Dining Out sheet and deducted the amount you spent from what was in the account. Since you planned on spending a budgeted amount of $100.00 per month, by keeping your sheet current, whenever you get the urge to go out for dinner, you can refer to the sheet and make an informed decision as to whether you can afford it and, if so, how much you can spend without having to charge it.

By using this method to budget discretionary spending, not only will you be able to see if you have the money for an expenditure, but in the event you don't, you will be able to determine how soon you will have it based on the amount you are budgeting. You should use the same method to budget for buying a new piece of furniture, a boat, or other large-ticket item. If you want to get it sooner than the projected budget will allow, you can re-evaluate your other discretionary spending accounts and make adjustments so you can either put more into the account or transfer funds from one of the other accounts. You may decide to eat out less or skip a vacation or other recreational activity and transfer the money you would spend on these items to the account for some other big item so you can get it sooner.

The bottom line is that this simple budgeting system allows you to take total control of your finances, it enables you to know when and how much you can spend, and it prevents you from making hasty and often expensive mistakes. Sure, it requires a little time and effort to maintain, but you will soon learn that the value you receive will far and away offset any inconvenience.

Now for one last tip before moving on to the next chapter: I recommend that you set up a cover sheet to bring forward the totals from your individual account sheets. On the first of each month, sit down with your calculator and total the budgeted amounts from each sheet and bring this total forward to the cover sheet. On the last day of each month, do the same with the actual expenditures you paid out during the month. This will allow you to see at a glance where you stand. You can use multiple sheets of the three-column paper you use for the individual sheets, or you can get a pad of sheets with 13 columns and use it to show an entire year on a single page. Your cover sheet should look like this:

Budget Reconciliation Sheet

Description	January	February	March	April
Beginning bank balance	$500.00	$1,150.00	$1,380.00	$850.00
Budgeted amount (memo)	$3,500.00	$3,650.00	$3,600.00	$3,550.00
Amount deposited	$3,500.00	$3,650.00	$3,600.00	$3,550.00
Actual expenditures	$2,850.00	$3,420.00	$4,130.00	$2,975.00
Ending bank balance	$1,150.00	$1,380.00	$850.00	$1,425.00

This cover sheet gives you a quick snapshot of how you did each month and shows you how much money you should have in your bank account from which to pay your bills. Let's take a minute and analyze the information in the above example. You can see that you started with a Beginning Bank Balance in January of $500. Your budget for the month was $3,500. You funded your budget by depositing that amount into the bank account. Although you budgeted and funded $3,500 for the month, you spent only $2,850. The difference was money representing a month's share of your quarterly, semiannual, and annual payments plus any other budgeted funds you didn't spend. Since you didn't pay out these amounts in January, your bank balance grew from $500 to $1,150. At this point, without your budget, you might be tempted to spend this extra money.

In February, you carried forward the Ending Bank Balance from January and posted it as the Beginning Bank Balance for February. When you totaled your sheets for February, you found that your flexible budgeting system increased your budget by $150 to $3,650.

Once again, in February you didn't spend the full amount, so your bank balance grew to $1,380. Again, without the budget, you might think you have extra money and be tempted to spend it on an emotional purchase that was not planned.

Just as you did the previous month, you carry the Ending Bank Balance from February forward to the Beginning Bank Balance for March. Once again, your budgeted amount changed. This time it dropped $50 to $3,600. You again funded the budget by depositing this amount into your bank account, but this month Actual Expenditures were $4,130, which is $530 more than you budgeted. This could have been due to one or more of your larger infrequent payments coming due, but it did not create a problem. The only effect it had was reducing your bank balance from $1,380 at the beginning of the month to $850 at the end of the month. You had already planned for the extra $530, and your budget caused you to reserve the funds to pay it, so it didn't present a cash-flow problem.

I'd like to share a couple more thoughts before leaving this subject. First, some people prefer to keep out a bit of cash each month to use as "mad money." And others prefer to track this as well. If you want to track it, set up a Cash Account sheet just as you did for other expenditures. Budget yourself an amount of miscellaneous cash to spend as you please. Post this budgeted amount to the sheet, and include it in what you deposit into your bank account. When you withdraw part or all of it, write yourself a check or visit the ATM, and then deduct the amount from the sheet. You don't have to keep up with what you spend the cash on, just the fact that you took it out of the account. As with your other expenditures, you can look at the sheet and know how much, if any, "mad money" you still have left at any given time. Keep in mind that any money left over after you fund your budget can be considered mad money.

Secondly, the amounts I have used in these examples are for illustration purposes only. Your numbers will be different, but whether your monthly budget is $2,000 or $20,000, the system works the same. It allows you to maintain complete control of your finances.

Finally, I want to remind you again that keeping up with this system may take a little time and effort, but the security and confidence you will gain by getting control of your finances will make it well worth the effort. You can't achieve financial independence by just "winging it" any more than you can jump in your car and reach a destination when you haven't decided where you want to go.

Key points from this chapter:

- Make a lifelong commitment to understanding where your money goes.

- Prepare a flexible budget that will accommodate every item on which you spend money.

- Most people spend enough money on finance charges and fees to become millionaires over their lifetimes.

- What you buy is not nearly as important as when you buy it.

- Planning for savings enables you to accumulate the seed money you will need to acquire investments that bring financial independence.

- Planning for purchases in advance helps you to avoid accumulating destructive consumer debt.

- It is most important to set up an account for long-term savings.

- Don't overlook setting up a Contingency Account for those unexpected expenses.

- Be sure to plan for a little "mad money."

- Setting up and working a flexible budget is an investment of time that will pay dividends, just as investing money does.

26

A Caution about Corporations' Positive or Negative Influence

Throughout this book, I have driven home the importance of being positive, of surrounding yourself with positive people and staying focused on your goals. I've discussed the way people respond when you're trying to climb the ladder of success, how some will give you a boost up while others will try to drag you down. So far I've dealt primarily with how individuals can positively or negatively influence your success. In this chapter, I want to take it a step further and show you how corporations, as impersonal as they can seem, often do the same thing.

In the late 1990s, I undertook a large multimillion-dollar construction project in which numerous vendors and subcontractors were involved. The project spanned a 4½ -year period. As with any large project, occasionally problems arise, and this project was no different. Two vendors, Lutron Electronics Incorporated and Philips Products, provided materials that were not satisfactory. The contrasting way these companies handled the problems provides a wonderful example of what makes some corporations a joy with which to do business and others to be avoided whenever possible. Poor customer service can make your blood boil and negatively impact your performance if you allow it to do so.

The first example I'll discuss involves Lutron Electronics' Maestro® line of incandescent/halogen dimmer switches. These switches offer consumers a wide array of features in a flat-faced decorative switch. They allow you to set wide ranges of lighting levels that you can return to with the touch of a button. They also allow you to adjust levels up or down with the simple touch of another button. They are very attractive and offer additional options beyond simply being a dimmer switch. I installed dozens of these switches throughout my construction project.

The problem arose before the project was even completed. I began noticing that some of the switches were malfunctioning. It appeared that a spring inside the switch was breaking or coming loose, preventing the on/off button from working properly. I called the electric supply house where I had purchased the switches and described the problem. They advised me that they would have the Lutron sales representative call within the next few days when he came by on his next scheduled visit to their store.

True to their word, the following week I received a call from the Lutron sales representative. The first thing he did was to ask if he could come by and inspect the bad switches. When he arrived, he only had to look at two of the switches before telling me that I should not be having the problem with them. He inspected the other broken switches and quickly apologized for the problem. He told me that Lutron would cover the cost of replacing them.

What happened next is what makes this such a wonderful story to tell. Before the bad switches could be replaced, two additional ones failed. I called the Lutron rep, who had left me his business card with his office and cell-phone numbers when he had visited. When I told him that two more of the switches had failed, he said he would like to make a call to his company and would call me back after he talked with them. The following day, he phoned to say that his company didn't know why the switches were failing, but they wanted to make it right. He said that in case there may have been a defective production run, the company wanted to replace all of the switches in the project with new ones. He further advised that it would not only provide new switches, but would cover the cost of the labor to replace them as well.

Within days, the new switches arrived at the electric supply house where the original ones had been purchased and Lutron contacted the electrical company that had originally installed them and contracted with them to replace all of the switches. What impressed me most was the fact that they replaced switches that were functioning perfectly, rather than risk more of them failing. The positive effect of their customer service was immeasurable, and you can bet that I will continue to use Lutron Electronics' products on future projects and will recommend them to everyone when I have the opportunity.

By contrast, Philips Products supplied dozens of windows for the project through their Malta Windows division. All of the windows they supplied were satisfactory with the exception of just five. These five windows arrived in a separate shipment and were eventually installed in five upstairs dormers. Shortly after their installation, a driving rainstorm blew water against their face, and I noticed leakage coming into the building. I didn't think much of it at the time because the roof shingles and exterior siding had not been completed. Although the leakage was unusual, I wasn't that concerned.

Over the next several weeks, additional leakage was noticed each time windblown rain pelted the face of the windows. Eventually, the exterior siding and roofing was completed, and I assumed it would solve the problem. Wrong! The first driving rain that occurred, water continued to pour into the building and run down the walls below the windows.

Just as I had done with the dimmer switches, I called the vendor from whom I had purchased the windows. They sent a service person to inspect the installation, and he advised that the roofer had not properly installed the flashing around the base of the dormers and that was why the water was coming into the building. Relying upon this information, I called the roofer and told him what the window company's service technician had told me.

The roofer immediately came to the project and tore off the shingles around one of the dormers to reveal properly installed copper flashing. This involved considerable work and the reinstallation of several shingles, but the roofer did not charge for the trip. He wanted to be sure his work was not the problem.

I once again called the window vendor and reported what the roofer had found. They once again sent people to look at the problem. On this trip, their service people connected a water hose and pulled it up on the roof so they could spray water on the face of the windows. When they did, it poured into the inside of the building. This time they told me that the windows were not properly installed and that the water must be coming in around the nailing flange of the windows.

The windows had been installed in exactly the same manner as dozens more had been, but I called the building contractor and told him what the window company's service people had said. Just as the roofer had done, the building contractor, a man with more than 40 years' experience, immediately came to the project to inspect his work. He took off all of the trim around one of the windows and revealed a properly installed window. I could readily see that it would be virtually impossible for water to come in around the nailing flange.

The next time a blowing rain occurred, water again poured into the now finished interior of the building. I called the vendor once again to report the problem. They informed me that they no longer sold the windows. They provided me with the phone number and a name to contact at the window manufacturer, Philip Products. When I called and explained the problem to the Philips representative, I was told I would have to complete their warranty claim forms and provide proper documentation before anything could be done.

The forms, which consisted of several pages, were sent to me. I completed them and returned them with all of the requested documentation, including copies of the invoices showing where I had purchased the windows and what I had paid. Finally, Philips agreed to send its Division service manager from the home office in Elkhart, Indiana, to look at the problem. All the while, water was continuing to pour into the finished room and run down the face of expensive woodwork.

Once an appointment was set for the Division service manager to visit the project, I also arranged for the roofer and building contractor to be present at the same time to avoid any more buck passing. With everyone present, numerous tests were conducted on the windows, most of which involved spraying them with high-pressure water from a hose. Eventually the trim from one of the windows was completely removed along with the shingles and copper flashing so the Philips representative could see what the contractor and roofer had previously inspected.

He then began pointing out ways the windows could be reinstalled to prevent leakage. I stopped him and suggested another test. This time plastic sheeting was duct-taped all the way around the outer frame of a window in such a way that only its face was exposed and no water could be sprayed so that it could get over, under, or around the plastic. When this test was conducted, water still leaked through into the inside of the building.

At this point, I advised the Philips Division manager that I was tired of excuses and delays. I said the potential damage to the interior was so great that I wanted the windows replaced. In the presence of the other subcontractors, the Philips representative told me to get the windows replaced and send him copies of the bills.

It took some extensive searching, but I eventually found a window manufactured by a different company that matched the profile of the Philips windows. It took six weeks from the time I placed the order for the new windows to arrive and another two weeks for them to be installed. This resulted in eight additional weeks of mopping up water each time a blowing rain occurred. When the Philips windows were removed, the flaw was obvious. The bottom of the windows had moisture trails showing where water had entered around the sashes and flowed out from the bottom of the windows into the building.

The new windows were installed exactly as the Philips windows had been. Even though I had already paid the bills, I waited several months to confirm that the windows had been the problem, not the installation or the roofing. Had the problem persisted with the new windows, I would gladly have apologized to Philips, but after numerous hard blowing rains there was no further leaking. I sent the bills to Philips Division service manager as I had been instructed. I waited patiently for my reimbursement, but after several weeks with no reply, I called the Division manager to see when I could expect a check. To my surprise, the Division manager told me he had not received the bills. This time, I sent the documents Certified Mail, Return Receipt Requested.

Two additional weeks passed after the letter was received before I got a letter from the Division manager denying that he had agreed there was a problem, denying that he had agreed to pay for replacing the windows, and advising that he was forwarding my correspondence to the company's legal department.

My initial reaction was to just turn the matter over to my attorney and sue the company. I even went so far as to send my files to the attorney with instructions to begin the legal process. Then I realized that I was allowing the company to negatively impact my life by occupying so much of my time with an issue that was insignificantly small in relation to the overall size of the project. Eventually I visited the Philips website at www.philipsproducts.com and gained a better understanding of their methods. On the website was a page titled "Our Company." On this page I found an interesting explanation for their behavior. The text on the page described the weakening economy and rising interest rates of the 1980s, but the following sentence told the story. "Our organization reacted to this change by pursuing every approach to increase profitability and throughout the '80s, Philips found ways to cut costs and save creatively . . ."

I then realized that one of these creative cost-cutting measures must have been to blame others and avoid taking responsibility with unsatisfied customers. As any large company would know, the cost of litigation deters most people, thereby allowing it to escape financial responsibility. This tactic may be good for the bottom line in the short run, but can you imagine what it must be like to work for a company who backs up its products this way. Imagine being a salesperson and trying to earn a living representing a company this shortsighted.

Philips is one of the country's leading manufacturers of replacement vinyl windows, something I use in large quantities in the maintenance of my investment properties, but do you think I will ever purchase another one of its products? In my case, the company may have won the battle, but it definitely lost the war. Although it cost me several thousand dollars to replace the windows, I did just what the company wanted and decided that it wasn't worth my time to keep arguing with them. What I would spend in time and legal fees I could easily replace by focusing on more productive endeavors.

Can you see how these contrasting examples demonstrate the positive and negative influence corporations can have on your time and energy? Can you see why I would want to sing the praises of Lutron Electronics but want to purge myself from any future dealings with Philips Products? Corporations are no different from individuals. Some give you a boost up and hope you will remember them on your climb to the top, while others will attempt to hold you back or drag you down to their level. Just as I discussed in Chapter 14, it's how you respond to these negative people or corporations that determine how well you will perform on your journey to financial independence.

In neither of these illustrations was the amount of money involved enough to make a noticeable difference in either my lifestyle or the corporations' bottom lines. But the long-term effects of these differing behavior patterns can be significant. The lesson to be learned from these experiences is that to achieve financial independence and be happy, you must **REPEL NEGATIVE INFLUENCES AND FOCUS ON THE POSITIVES.** Don't get bogged down in minor skirmishes over insignificant matters. Sure, it sometimes means walking away from a situation and cutting your losses, but maintaining control over your emotions when adversity strikes will always serve you better.

Key points from this chapter:

- Corporations, like individuals, have good and bad character and varying ethical standards.

- Give individuals and companies the opportunity to remedy problems before choosing not to do business with them.

- Praise and support those who do the right thing.

- Avoid getting dragged down emotionally by individuals or companies whose merchandise or services are inferior and who won't stand behind their products.

- Learn to repel negative influences and focus on the positives.

27

Use Spare Time to Gain Knowledge and Improve Skills

The vast majority of people who win large lottery prizes end up broke or nearly so within a few years of receiving their millions. Why? Could it be that the same reason most ordinary working people fail to achieve financial independence is the same reason so many lottery winners end up broke after becoming instant millionaires? I think so, and I think I know what that reason is and how to deal with it.

What do you think would happen if you took a professional truck driver used to making numerous trips across the country in a semi truck, but one who had never flown in an airplane, and suddenly put him or her in the cockpit of the simplest single-engine airplane and said, "I need you to fly this from New York to Los Angeles?" Not only would the truck driver be unable to fly across country, but he or she may not even know how to start the engine. The truck driver, who may be well into his or her Earning Years and eminently qualified to drive a truck, would probably be baffled by the simplest of airplanes.

Although piloting a large commercial airplane pays several times as much as driving a truck, without the corresponding increase in knowledge required to fly a plane, even a truck driver who could get one started would stand a better-than-average chance of crashing and being killed before completing the first flight. Winning the lottery is much like putting a truck driver in the cockpit of an airplane. Without knowing how to handle money, a lottery winner stands a better-than-average chance of crashing and burning financially. Just as the lottery winner may lose the newfound wealth, the ordinary working person will never attain wealth without first acquiring a corresponding increase in knowledge. That's where the application of audio learning can make such a difference as you aspire to becoming financially independent.

In Chapter 18, I discussed the advice Dr. Godfrey gave me when I was working at the defense plant:

"If you will read an hour a day about something you know nothing about, within five years you will be amazed at the impact it will have on your life."

This advice was given to me in the late 1960s, and I've followed it religiously. I readily attribute my ability to start and build a business to this valuable guidance, which I still follow to this day. But, another event occurred years later in the early 1980s that expanded upon this advice and carried me to even greater success.

By this time, I had purchased a few single-family homes as investment properties. One day I received a call from my property manager asking if I would like to go with him to Charlotte, North Carolina, to hear Zig Ziglar speak to a Realtor's group of which he was a member. I had never heard of Zig Ziglar, so I initially declined the offer, but when my property manager told me that Zig was the country's leading motivational speaker and someone I would surely learn from, I decided to go. That was my first such experience, and one I will never forget.

Zig absolutely awed the audience, including me, with his total command of the stage and his inspiring motivational message. His enthusiasm was contagious, and when he closed the program with an invitation to purchase his audiocassette programs, I was at the head of the line to buy. This was my first experience with audio learning, but far from my last.

On the return trip from Charlotte, my property manager and I listened to several of the tapes, and on one of them Zig stressed that you needed to listen to each tape at least 16 times to grasp its full content. The message was so positive and so uplifting that I vowed to do just that. Each day my commute to and from my office was about 30 minutes each way. I began listening to the tapes every day. When I came to the last tape in the series, I put a mark on the album cover and started over. Each time I completed all the tapes I added another mark to the cover and once again went back to tape one. I was determined to listen 16 times as Zig had recommended. It wasn't long before I realized why listening repeatedly over and over was so important. Each time I went through the program, I heard something I had missed in my previous listening. Sometimes I heard things but didn't fully understand them until after I had an experience in which they applied.

It wasn't until a few years later that I began to fully grasp the power of audio learning. One of the tapes I had gotten from Zig was a music tape titled *Born to Win*, which was the title of its lead song. I thought the collection of positive motivational songs would be good listening for my young children, so I gave the tape to my wife, who began playing it in the car as she transported them to and from play school.

A few months later, we decided to go to dinner with a young couple and their three daughters who had recently moved to town. The new friends and their children met at our house prior to dinner for a visit and to allow the children to play. When we loaded up to go to dinner, the other father and I went in one car with his two oldest daughters and my older son, Jason. My wife and the other mother took the two younger children with them in a second car.

As we were driving to the restaurant, I was talking with the other father, and the children were in the back seat talking. Jason, who was about four at the time, was younger than the girls, who were seven and nine. Being new to town, the girls began telling Jason where they were born.

The oldest said, "I was born in Gainesville, Florida."

Then the younger girl chimed in, "Me too. I was born in Gainesville too."

The older girl turned to Jason and asked, "Where were you born?"

Jason proudly swelled out his little chest and proclaimed, "I was born to win."

When my friend and I finally were able to stop laughing, I told the story about how my boys had been listening to Zig Ziglar's *Born to Win* tape. That's when I realized the subliminal effects that repeat listening to audiotapes could have on even young children. It's also when I realized how different I was from most ordinary people who waste hours riding around in their cars listening to radio programs that teach them absolutely nothing. What a waste of time. As Zig would say, "It's like chewing gum for the ears."

Following my experience with Zig Ziglar's audio program, I began to seek out other audio programs from which I could expand my knowledge. I discovered Nightingale-Conant Corporation, the country's largest producer of self-help programs, and it was through them that I eventually met and became close friends with Roger Dawson. One of the first tape programs I purchased was his *Secrets of Power Negotiating*. It only took one time listening to this program for me to realize that the people in my industry could greatly benefit from hearing Roger speak.

At the time, I was president of the North Carolina Outdoor Advertising Association, so I contacted Nightingale-Conant and arranged to book Roger to speak at our next state conference. This led to another speaking engagement with the Outdoor Advertising Association of America and a budding friendship that would grow and endure to this day. It eventually led to Roger and me combining our talents to produce the Weekend Millionaire series of books (McGraw-Hill) and an eight-hour audio programs produced by Nightingale-Conant.

In my quest to learn more, I also purchased Carleton Sheets' *No Money Down* real estate investing program, a purchase that would lead to another long-term friendship and greatly enhance my growing real estate portfolio. In fact, I have continued to read and listen and learn throughout my entire Earning Years. If you visit my home and office, you will find extensive libraries of books and audio and video programs that reflect my continuing desire to learn and improve my performance.

Now, here's a little secret I want to share with everyone who reads this book. There are books and audio and video learning programs on virtually every subject imaginable. Unlike formal education, which can often be boring and dull, especially when you can't see its purpose, these tools allow you to acquire skills as you need them, when you need them, so you can apply them immediately.

When I failed at my first management job, I read numerous books on management and later purchased several audio programs on the subject to avoid repeating my mistakes. When I struggled with obtaining bank financing for my business, I studied books and tape programs on economics, money, and banking and finance to gain a better understanding of things from a banker's perspective. I studied programs on psychology, motivation, creative thinking, ambition, peak performance, and self-esteem. As my real estate investing career took off, I not only studied Carleton Sheets' *No Money Down* program, but every other real estate investing program I could find, plus programs on negotiating, sales, and any other subject that could enhance my abilities as an investor. When I reached a point at which I felt overwhelmed with work, I studied time-management programs to learn how to get things done more efficiently. I found that if I could learn just one thing I could use from an eight-hour audio program or a several-hundred-page book, it was worth the time it took to listen or read.

Believe it or not, no matter how well-versed I was on a given subject, I've never read an educational book, listened to an educational audio program, or watched an educational video on the subject without learning something new I could put to use. I've found that even the most bizarre authors occasionally slip up and say or write something profound. No matter how much you know, don't ever think you know it all. In many endeavors, it takes only one tidbit of new information to make the difference between success and failure.

This is the reason why while I was in the outdoor advertising business, I encouraged my employees to continue expanding their knowledge and skills just as I was doing. I offered them an opportunity to use payroll deductions to build their own self-improvement libraries. I allowed my employees to sign up for as large or as small a payroll deduction as they wanted, and I agreed to match it, provided the money was spent on self-improvement materials. I also ordered the books or tapes my employees wanted and passed on any discounts the company received. By matching money with the employees, I gave them an opportunity, not a handout. I learned very quickly that the employees would use materials when they had a financial investment in them but wouldn't if the materials were given to them free.

I was constantly bewildered by the number of employees who complained about their finances but refused to do anything to improve them, until one day I overheard a conversation in which several of my least productive employees were chiding another one about wasting money on the audio program he had in his car. I believe that the negative influence of other people keeps more people from achieving success than any other single thing. Sure, books and audio programs cost money to buy and time to study, but as I said earlier, if you get just one idea from each one that you can put to use, it's well worth the time and money. Think of it as going to a gem mine; until you learn to look for the gems, all you see are mounds of dirt and rocks.

I'll leave you with this thought; imagine what could happen if everyone suddenly decided to use the time he or she spends riding in a car or the few minutes just before going to sleep or just after waking in the morning to improve his or her knowledge and skills. Would we have more financially secure people? Absolutely! Would we have more emotionally secure people? You bet we would! Would we see a growing number of people achieving financial independence rather than being buried in debt? Would they be happier? I think so, because I know that your mind is like a muscle: when you use it, it expands and gets stronger, when you don't, it withers and fades away.

Key points from this chapter:

- Whether you inherit wealth, hit the lottery, or simply want to build financial independence, you have to learn money-management skills if you expect to be successful.

- Use otherwise unproductive time like driving to and from work to learn by listening to audio programs.

- Spaced repetition is a powerful tool, and listening to audiotapes over and over implants messages in your subconscious mind that become part of you.

- Approach every book and audio or video program with the goal of finding at least one new idea you can put to work to improve your performance.

- Feed your mind regularly just as you do your body, because it's like a muscle that needs to be nourished and exercised every day.

28

Conquering Frustration and Rejection

I have been describing the way experiences from my Formative Years, my Learning Years, and my Earning Years helped me reach the goals I set at age 20 and achieve financial independence. I have described events that have shaped my outlook on life, my approach to problem solving, and my quest for knowledge. In the final two chapters of this section, I will conclude by discussing two problems that prevent many ordinary people from achieving the financial success they would like.

Being unwilling to practice and succumbing to frustrations can sink even the best of us. Many people know what to do but refuse to practice long enough to master it. They become frustrated when things don't go perfectly the first time they try, and they lack the determination to keep practicing long enough to get it right. They let small failures and insignificant shortcomings keep them from doing great things. Let me give you some examples.

I have had many opportunities to let frustration get in the way of success, but throughout my life I have resisted that temptation. Possibly it began as early as my experience with buying that first bicycle in War, West Virginia. It could have been any of the other frustrations I worked through during my early years. I'm not sure when it started, but I attribute much of the success I have enjoyed to my ability to cope with frustrations without allowing them to deter me from my goals. I wasn't born with this talent; I didn't learn it in the classroom; I think I must have developed it over the many years I studied at the University of Hard Knocks.

People from all walks of life experience frustrations, and they aren't just limited to major events. Learning to deal with aggravations, even small ones, can make life more fun as well as make you more enjoyable to be around. A few years ago I was involved in an incident that demonstrates what I'm talking about.

The day after New Year's Day 2005, I took my sons Jason and Matt, together with their girlfriends and two of my young nieces, bowling. Although I had bowled professionally when I was in my 20s, I had not bowled in years and had never taken up the game with my sons. We got two lanes at the bowling center and put the girls on one lane and the guys on the other. We arranged for the girls' lane to have bumpers put up to keep their balls from going into the gutters, but the guys, being the macho men that we were, didn't use the bumpers.

The first game, Jason had trouble keeping his ball on the lane and ended up having the lowest score of everyone. With each ball he rolled, he was becoming more and more frustrated. By the latter part of the second game, he was stomping and huffing to the point that it was becoming annoying to everyone around him. Finally, I called him over, and told him to sit down and cool off, that it was only a game.

"Yeah, I know," Jason said. "But it is so frustrating, I can't enjoy it."

"Would you like some coaching?" I asked.

"It won't do any good," he huffed. "I'm just no good at bowling."

"Well, will you at least try something to see if it works?"

He huffed and puffed some more and finally said, "What?"

"Come on," I said when Jason's next turn came. "I'm going up on the lane with you, and I want you to try something just once or twice and see what happens."

I then took him up on the approach and lined him up near the center of the lane and pointed to the arrows that were painted several feet down the lane. "I want you to start here," I said and pointed out a spot on the approach. "Then I want you to take your time, walk straight toward the second arrow from the right gutter, and roll the ball directly over it. Forget about the pins way down at the end of the lane, just try to roll the ball to the arrow, and let's see what happens."

Jason stood on the spot I had pointed out and slowly approached the foul line. He rolled the ball, and it went right over the second arrow. The ball went down the lane and hit the head pin dead center. All of the pins went down except the six pin. When he turned around and started back from the foul line, he had a big grin on his face. "How'd I do that?" he said.

I then went back up on the approach with him, pointed out a spot about four boards to the left of where he had started when he rolled the first ball and said, "I want you to stand right here and once again roll the ball over the second arrow from the right gutter."

"But won't that make the ball go more to the left," he asked.

"Just try it and see what happens."

Once again, he approached the foul line slowly and rolled the ball directly over the second arrow. This time the ball went toward the right side of the lane and hit the six pin solidly. It was the first spare he had made in nearly two games. This time when he came off the lane, he had a really big grin on his face.

After he experienced this success, I sat him down and explained that the dots and arrows on the approach and out on the lane were like the sights on a rifle, that if he could find the right spot on the approach to start and roll the ball consistently over the same spot on the lane, the ball would go to the same spot down at the pins every time. Then by adjusting where he started on the lane (the back sight) and continuing to hit the same spot on the lane (the front sight), he could make just about any spare he might leave. It truly was like the sights on a gun: you adjust the back sight to line up where the bullet hits. That's why it's called "sighting in" the gun. In life, knowledge is the back sight and your goal is the front sight. Increasing your knowledge is what moves the back sight so you can home in on and eventually hit your goals.

Before his next turn, I told Jason, "If you will just trust me and try to do what I tell you each time you roll a ball, I think you will begin to figure out that the game is not that difficult."

Throughout the rest of the second game and all through the third game Jason did exactly what I told him. Sure, like the rest of us, he didn't always hit his target, but by the end of the third game, he had gone from being the worst bowler of the group to having the second-highest score, and he had totally different attitude. His frustrations were calmed by learning more about the game. Understanding how to use the markings dramatically improved his score. By the end of the third game, he was no longer stomping and huffing around the way he had been earlier. When he focused on learning about the things that would improve his score and started concentrating on them, not on the score itself, he began to conquer his frustrations.

The way Jason liberated himself from his bowling frustrations is the same way you can deal with bigger frustrations. When you learn more and practice what you learn, you get better and it makes you happier and causes you to feel better about yourself. I had a bigger frustration during my early years as a pilot. In July 1978, after having earned my private pilot certificate years before, I wanted to add an instrument rating to the license. I had finally completed the required classroom and flight training, passed the FAA written exam, and was within a couple of hours of the minimum 200 hours of flight time I needed to take the flight test.

I was planning an extended vacation later in the month and wanted to be instrument rated before I left home.

On July 12, 1978, my flight instructor signed my log book stating that I was ready to take the flight test I would need to pass to obtain the rating and arranged for me to fly to Morristown, Tennessee, to take my check ride. My examiner was the legendary pilot and FAA examiner Evelyn Bryan Johnson, nicknamed "Mamma Bird." The flight to Morristown gave me the additional time I needed to log the required 200 hours.

From the minute I first saw her, I could tell that Ms. Johnson, who looked to be in her late 60s, was an all-business, tough-as-nails examiner. After giving me a route to fly and the procedures to expect, she had me file an instrument flight plan with the Federal Aviation Administration Flight Service Station. It took another hour or so of questioning on the ground before she announced that we were ready to fly.

We got in my single-engine Piper Cherokee Arrow, cranked the engine, taxied out to the end of the runway, and took off. For the next two hours, she put me through a series of maneuvers and approaches, which I flew perfectly while wearing a hood that restricted my vision to just the instrument panel. It prevented me from looking outside the cockpit for reference. She even took the controls and put the airplane in several unusual attitudes and then had me make the corrections necessary to bring the plane back to normal flight configuration. Finally, she had me make an unexpected flight to Knoxville, 27 miles away, covered up part of the instruments to simulate their failure and instructed me to fly back to Morristown using only partial instruments and then make an approach to the airport. (I had never heard of an FAA check pilot requiring such a procedure and haven't since.) When I thought I had arrived at the missed approach point at Morristown, she told me to lift the hood from my head and look outside. I was several hundred feet to the left of the runway.

She told me to go ahead and land the airplane but didn't say anything else. We landed, taxied in to the ramp, and shut down the plane's engine. Finally she said, "You didn't pass."

I was devastated. I was counting on having the instrument rating before I left on my trip. "What did I do wrong?" I asked.

"You need to go back and do some more primary (no gyro) work," she said and so noted in my logbook.

I knew this was nonsense. I had flown the route and approaches for the flight plan she had asked me to file perfectly. It was not until after that test flight was over that she suddenly told me go to Knoxville to make a 27-mile partial panel approach and even at that, I had arrived within a few hundred feet of the runway and at a safe altitude to make any needed corrections before landing. I was furious and frustrated.

When I returned to Asheville and talked with my instructor, he couldn't believe that she had failed me. "We can go fly some partial panel approaches, but I don't know how much good it will do," my instructor said.

"The problem is, I'm leaving on a trip to go out West and then to the Bahamas, and I don't have time to go back for another check ride," I said.

"Well, if I were you, I'd go ahead with your trip and just be careful. Without your instrument rating, you won't be legal to fly in bad weather, but it's usually good this time of year. If you should get caught in poor conditions, I feel comfortable that you know enough to get out of it," my instructor replied.

And that's just what I did. I flew from Asheville to Kansas City, Missouri; Medicine Bow, Wyoming; Salt Lake City, Las Vegas; Alamosa, Colorado; Ashland, Kansas; Fort Smith, Arkansas; Mobile, Alabama; Bartow and West Palm Beach, Florida; then on to Bimini, Freeport and Nassau in the Bahamas before returning to Savannah, Georgia, and then back to Asheville. It was an extended sightseeing and pleasure trip that added nearly 100 hours to my flight time. I won't say whether or not I fudged a bit when it came to getting through some weather fronts I encountered, but the trip went well, and when I returned, I was ready to retake the instrument flight test.

This time I flew to Morristown ready to take on Ms. Evelyn Bryan Johnson once again. I expected another brutal check ride, but all she did was to have me take off, fly one time around the airport, make a single approach and land. As we taxied in, I looked over at her and asked, "What did I do wrong this time?"

"Nothing," she replied with a smile. "You passed."

"Well why didn't I have to do all that stuff you had me do before?" I asked.

"Didn't need to," she said. "You did fine before, I just don't give instrument ratings to people with minimum time. I know that doesn't seem fair, but that's the way I do it. From the looks of your logbook, it didn't keep you from flying all over the country. Did you enjoy your trip?"

I had to admit that I was a much better pilot than I had been when I took my first check ride. Although I had been frustrated with my failure on the first attempt, it had made me hone my skills to the point where I felt comfortable I could fly that same 27-mile partial panel approach again and nail it.

Understanding a simple concept is a big part of becoming financially independent. Losers get frustrated and quit when they think they've been treated unfairly. Winners swallow their pride and get back in the game with an even stronger resolve. I'm sure the accumulations of experiences I've described in this book have helped me develop this resolve. I'm also sure that had I succumbed to some of the early frustrations I experienced, I'd probably be unhappy and broke instead of writing this book.

I could write another entire book on dealing with frustrations, but I think you get the point from these few stories. If you let frustrations deter you, you will never be able to achieve financial success and probably very little success with anything else you attempt. When frustrations arise, deal with them by learning more and practicing what you learn. You will find the frustrations, no matter how great, will slowly subside and eventually go away if you approach them in this manner. Now let's move on the last chapter of this section and talk about practicing what you learn.

Key points from this chapter:

- Just because things are tough, don't give up. Giving up never gets you anywhere. Successful people are the ones who battle on and find a way to overcome problems.

- You're never too old or too smart that a little coaching won't help.

- Just as learning how the marks on a bowling lane help guide you to a strike, the more you learn about a difficult task, the easier it becomes.

- Don't let stinging and unfair rejections stop you from continuing to try; choosing to quit before you master a task leaves you feeling dejected and apprehensive and discourages you from trying other new things.

29

Wealth and Happiness Require Practice, Practice, Practice

I'm flabbergasted at the number of people who want to play the game but don't want to practice. Athletes in every sport love to play the game but hate to go to practice. Football players hate to hit tackling dummies but will gladly give it their best shot in a game. Basketball players hate to run sprints in the gym but will gladly give it their best shot in a game. Baseball players hate to chase fly balls for hours during practice but will gladly give it their best shot during a game. Tennis players hate to spend time hitting balls thrown to them by a machine but will gladly give it their best shot during a match. The problem is that their best shot is seldom good enough to win against those who regularly practice.

This same phenomenon holds true not just for athletics but also for almost any endeavor. People who seek perfection and practice the hardest are the ones who usually rise to the top whether it's in sports, business, entertainment, or any other enterprise. So why are people so reluctant to practice? Could it be because practice tends to highlight weaknesses rather than strengths? When you practice, you are looking for ways to improve, which means you, or your coach, or your adviser is looking for weaknesses that you can improve. When you perfect one weakness, it usually means you immediately move on to another and another. In the beginning, little emphasis is placed on what you do well. It's not until you are already accomplished that the emphasis begins to shift from strengthening weaknesses to enhancing strengths.

The reluctance to practice derails many good intentions. Hardly anyone likes to do things they aren't very good at doing, so they avoid their weaknesses and focus on their strengths. Unfortunately, a balanced and successful life is much like a chain; it's no stronger than its weakest link. Until you replace its weakest link, the chain can never be used to its full potential. Likewise, unless you are willing to practice and improve upon your areas of weaknesses, you will always be vulnerable to disappointments and failures. If you're trying to achieve financial independence and your weakness is earning money, you won't make it by becoming the biggest tightwad in town. Likewise, if you're great at earning money, but your weakness is that you're a spendthrift, you won't get there by focusing on additional earnings. It takes strengthening your weaknesses to build a stronger future, and that requires practice.

Practice is important in every area of life. If you want to be a better athlete, you have to practice; if you want to be a better teacher, you have to practice; if you want to be a better speaker, you have to practice. Whenever you want to get better at doing anything, you have to practice. Practice will not only improve whatever you are doing, it may even save your life, as I learned several years ago.

As I mentioned in the previous chapter, I am a licensed pilot. When I travel, I pilot my own airplane to the destination. In January 1989, I had flown my twin-engine Beechcraft King Air to a maintenance facility in Greer, South Carolina, for some minor repairs. I had other business in the area, so I didn't return to the airport until the next day after eight o'clock in the evening. I had spoken with the maintenance facility's foreman earlier in the day and had been informed that my plane was ready and would be waiting for me on the ramp at the private terminal.

When I arrived at the airport, it was dark and weather conditions were deteriorating. Conditions at Asheville and Greer were similar. Both airports were reporting ceilings at 400 feet, overcast, with one-mile visibility, light rain, and fog. There was no severe weather in the forecast, only low ceilings with light rain and fog. I had flown many flights in this kind of weather, so I felt comfortable filing an instrument flight plan for the short 36-mile trip back to Asheville.

I boarded the plane and started the engines. While they were warming up, I called ground control to obtain my clearance. I was cleared as filed, to fly the runway heading until reaching 2,000 feet, then make a climbing right turn to the north, continue climbing to 5,000 feet, and proceed direct to Asheville. The field elevation at Greer is just less than 1,000 feet, but at Asheville, which is in the mountains of western North Carolina, it is almost 2,200 feet. Five thousand feet was the minimum altitude for an aircraft approaching Asheville from the south when flying in instrument flight conditions.

I taxied out to the end of the runway and was cleared for takeoff. Everything was normal throughout the takeoff roll, climb, and turn toward Asheville. Almost immediately after takeoff, I entered the clouds and was still in them upon reaching 5,000 feet. Light rain was pelting the windshield, but the ride was smooth and nothing was showing on the weather radar. I expected a normal flight that would take less than 15 minutes.

Shortly after reaching 5,000 feet, and just as I was approaching the edge of the mountains, Greer Departure radioed, giving me a new radio frequency and advising me to contact Asheville Approach Control. I acknowledged the change and put the handheld microphone back on its hook while I switched radio frequencies. Before I could pick the microphone back up, the plane suddenly pitched up violently and started a rapid roll to the right. It was as though a big gorilla had grabbed it and was throwing it around.

I forgot about the radio and grabbed the yoke with both hands, trying to regain control of the plane. Within seconds, the plane had rolled until the wings were perpendicular to the artificial horizon on the instrument panel; altitude was passing 6,000 feet and climbing at a rate of more than 8,000 feet per minute. I had the controls all the way to the stops in the opposite direction, but the plane was continuing to roll, when just as suddenly as it began, the plane shuddered, and then the roll stopped as if it had hit something hard. The stop was so sudden that it slammed my head against the metal post framing the side window of the cockpit, opening a gash beside and above my left eye.

Almost instantly, the plane shook violently and began to rapidly roll in the opposite direction and started a rapid descent. I didn't even notice the blood pouring down the side of my face. My only thoughts were to get the wings level and regain control of the airplane. Although the instruments were blurred, I could see that the plane was descending more than 5,000 feet per minute, even with its nose in a climb attitude. I pushed the throttles forward and started to lift the nose a little more trying to arrest the descent, but the plane was continuing to roll left in spite of the fact that I now had the controls locked as far as they would go to the right.

Within seconds, my altitude had fallen below 5,000 feet and the wings had rolled to the left until once again they were beyond perpendicular with the artificial horizon. I was just on the verge of moving the controls to roll the plane a full 360 degrees in an attempt to get it back upright, when just as it had done before, it abruptly stopped rolling. This time the change was so sudden that it tore loose the nylon netting holding my overnight bag in place in the luggage area at the rear of the cabin. A small handheld recorder I had laid in one of the seats in the cabin was thrown into the cockpit.

Fortunately, the roll to the left stopped, and as I was leveling the wings, the plane began another rapid ascent. The roll had stopped, but now with the engines running at full power from when I had pushed the throttles forward, airspeed was rapidly increasing even though the plane's nose was above the horizon and it was climbing at a rate of more than 10,000 feet per minute.

I reached over and pulled the throttles back to idle, but the airspeed kept increasing. Since the plane was climbing, I kept the wings level and pulled back on the controls to lift the nose and try to slow down the airspeed. Throughout the ordeal, I kept recalling what my instructor had made me practice over and over in training when he would put the plane in an unusual attitude and then tell me to correct the condition. He drummed into me that the most important thing was to keep the wings level and control the airspeed. When I saw the needle on the airspeed indicator go well past red line with the power pulled all the way back and the nose up, I yelled out, "My God, this is easier said than done."

No sooner had the words escaped my mouth than the plane suddenly stopped climbing and started back down again. The overnight bag that had torn loose in the baggage area now came floating through the cabin door and hit the instrument panel. I shoved it toward the empty co-pilot's seat and looked back at the airspeed indicator. Now the needle was rapidly falling and the airspeed was approaching stall speed. When a plane's momentum doesn't support the angle of climb, it won't fly anymore. It flutters like a dead bird and falls to the ground. I pushed the nose forward and reapplied full power. This descent was not as intense as the previous one, and I became aware that I was getting out of the turbulence. After getting quite a scare, I heard the voice of a controller from the Asheville airport coming from the speaker above my head.

Apparently information transmitted by reporting instruments on the plane had allowed the controller to see on his radar screen that the aircraft was experiencing sudden and rapid altitude changes. That could only mean problems. Evidently he had been trying to contact me but received no response, because when he came on the air he calmly said, "November 28 Mike Sierra, Asheville Approach. If you copy, you are cleared for the ILS approach to runway 34 and cleared to land. You need not acknowledge."

That was good to know, because by that time I was beginning to regain control of the plane, but I had no idea where my microphone was. It had jumped off its hook, and apparently its weight flying around in the cockpit had pulled the plug loose that connected it to the transmitter. Gradually I flew out of the turbulent air and quickly set the instruments to make the approach to the airport. My route was taking me across the initial approach fix, and when I passed it, I began a descent down the glide path to the airport. I was beginning to recover my composure from the violent experience, when I noticed my face stinging just above the eye. I reached up to touch it and felt the blood running down my cheek and dripping off my chin onto my pants. That was the least of my worries at the moment; I still had to get the airplane safely on the ground in less than desirable weather conditions.

As I continued down the approach, I was totally focused on keeping the glide path and runway centerline in the crosshairs of my instruments. Finally, just a little over 300 feet from the ground, I exited the base of the clouds and saw the runway stretching out directly in front of me. The wheels touched, and the plane rolled down the runway until speed slowed enough for me to turn it off the runway. As soon as I hit the taxiway, I stopped the plane, located the microphone, plugged it back in, and called Asheville Ground Control. The first thing they said was, "What happened out there?"

"You don't even want to know," I said. Then to break the tension I was feeling, I added, "I think Ms. Evelyn Bryan Johnson just gave me another instrument competency check ride."

Although it was said in jest at a very stressful time, my comment reflected my newfound respect for the lady who didn't want me flying under instrument conditions until I had more experience. I would hate to think what the outcome would have been that night had this experience happened earlier in my flying career. Now, thousands of flying hours later, the experience reinforced my belief in practice. Had I not continued to receive recurrent training every year and practiced emergency procedures, I would probably not be around to talk about the experience today. I have no doubt that practice had truly saved my life.

I felt lucky to have survived the ordeal. Then I remembered what I had often told others, "Luck is really just preparation meeting opportunity."

There are many additional sidebars to this story that would make for interesting reading, but the lesson from the experience is that **PRACTICE IS THE KEY TO POWER PERFORMANCE.** Whether it's practicing flying skills, buying skills, speaking skills, writing skills, or any of the other skills I have been fortunate to develop, I wouldn't be where I am today if I hadn't been willing to practice. No matter what you do, practice will make you better. No matter what your goals, practice will enable you to reach them faster and enjoy them more when you get there. Just never doubt that **PRACTICE, PRACTICE, PRACTICE IS THE KEY TO POWER PERFORMANCE.**

Since this book is about how to build wealth and be happy, this is the perfect place to remind you that it takes practicing to accomplish either one. Wealth building and happiness are journeys, not destinations. Setbacks, disappointments, and failures are the obstacles life presents that give you the opportunity to learn and improve your performance in order to have successes along the journey. The level of achievement you attain will be directly related to your willingness to devote time and effort into learning and practicing the skills you will need to overcome life's challenges. Don't be misled by all the stories you hear about people who became rich and happy overnight . . . it just doesn't happen that way. Joy and happiness are the emotional rewards that come with accomplishments, and wealth is the monetary reward you receive when you succeed. If done correctly, the two go hand in hand and you can build wealth and be happy.

Key points from this chapter:

- Don't wait until you're in a crisis situation to start practicing.

- Practice implants the practiced performance into your subconscious mind, thereby making it second nature when reaction time dictates immediate action.

- If you can't make a speech, write a letter, negotiate a deal, or fly an airplane when you're not under pressure, you sure won't be able to do it when the pressure is on.

- Luck is the word many use to describe the coming together of preparation and opportunity.

- You build a more balanced life by strengthening your weaknesses than by focusing only on your strengths.

- Practice is what makes it possible to become wealthy and be happy.

PART V

Applying What You've Learned

Your journey to financial security and independence follows a path that depends on your motivation and your skills. As the old song goes, "You can't have one without the other." While having motivation and skills is crucial to success, practical application of certain traits is even more important. Let's explore this a bit more.

I've talked much about how motivation is strengthened by the three Ds of success: DESIRE, DISCIPLINE, and DEDICATION. You have to have enough creative discontent in your life to set goals that clearly define where you want to be and have a realistic time frame to get there. Without meaningful goals, it is difficult, if not impossible, to develop the DESIRE to actually make major changes in your life. It's hard to get excited about a journey if you aren't sure where you are going. Goals provide the destination. Discontent is the crucible in which DESIRE is created. Your DESIRE must be strong enough to persuade you to find the DISCIPLINE needed to keep moving forward even when the going gets tough. And, finally, once you have the DESIRE and the DISCIPLINE, it takes DEDICATION to stick with it until you arrive at a successful conclusion. Sounds simple, but is it?

Some motivational speakers can lead you to believe that enthusiasm is *all* you need. I respectfully disagree. Sure, enthusiasm is important, but developing skills is equally important, if not more so, if you want to become financially independent. If you have enthusiasm but lack the skills you need, you're like the roadrunner in the old cartoons; you're a bundle of energy and you stir up a lot of dust, but once it settles, you're still right where you started. If you have the skills, but lack the motivation, you tend to analyze situations to death and take no action. I call this suffering from the paralysis of analysis.

Motivation, enthusiasm, and skills are vital to success, but these have to be properly channeled and appropriately applied. In this section I'm going to discuss a number of additional ways to apply the lessons we've covered up to this point and give you several tips we haven't covered. Throughout this section you will find many small things you can do to change your financial situation and move you closer to financial independence. Just as a brick wall is built one brick at a time, your journey to financial freedom must be taken one small step after another.

As you read the chapters in this section and learn additional ways to apply the lessons you've learned up to this point, it will encourage you and help you to become motivated. Remember, you can change your world by changing the way you think, but financial independence involves much more than just a lot of rah-rah-rah and hand clapping. You have to do your part by actually applying what you learn.

In this section I'm going to lay out a smorgasbord of ideas and tips that you can either use as I describe or you can take bits and pieces from several of them to come up with ideas of your own. I've had many experiences and learned a lot, but I certainly don't have all the answers. As I've said several times throughout the book, if any of the events I describe trigger similar events from your life, make a note of them. I want you to eventually learn to extract the life lessons from your own experiences and put them to work to enhance your life. I want to help you overcome the fears and anxieties that hold many people back from enjoying the success they could experience.

The only thing in life that is the same for everyone is that we are all born and we will all die. It's the decisions we make and the actions we take in between these events that determine our quality of life. So, read on as I share some more ideas and actions for you to consider.

30

Managing Cash Flow

In previous chapters I've already discussed budgeting and cash reserves, but a few years ago I discovered something on my property that gave a more graphic representation of this concept than anything I could write. When you are always able pay your bills on time, it not only improves your credit rating, it gives you peace of mind and reduces stress. The discovery I made taught me how cash reserves can do for financial stability what storage reservoirs do for the dependability of water systems. Let me explain.

I live on the top of a hill and have a spring on one side of my property. Many years ago it supplied drinking water to several houses in the valley below. When I bought the property, I had no idea the spring even existed. I certainly didn't know that it supplied a water system I would unearth several years later. The spring is located in a wooded depression north of my house. It had been buried by decades of decaying leaves and the silt that heavy rains had washed into it.

One day I was operating a small bulldozer on the 25 wooded acres that surround my home. I was building trails for my young sons to have a place to ride their dirt bikes. When I made a cut below the depression, I hit an old pipe buried in the ground. Water was seeping from it, but it obviously was not coming from an active water line. I had no idea why this water pipe was buried in my woods, so I decided to find out. I climbed up the hill to see if I could find its source, and what I discovered was amazing.

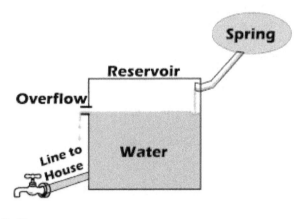

Fig. 16

Less than a hundred feet up the hill I found a water system that functioned like the one depicted in Figure 16 above. I unearthed the corner of a large concrete structure buried in the ground and began clearing the dirt from it. In the process, I uncovered a concrete lid that was covering a large access hole in its top. I slid the lid back to reveal a large tank partially filled with water. The pipe I had broken was coming from a spot about a foot above the bottom of the tank. There was a second pipe, with water trickling from it, coming into the tank near its top on the uphill side. A third pipe was sticking out of the tank on the downhill side near the top. I dug around the upper pipe and found that it ran a few feet up the hill to a smaller concrete bowl that was completely filled with mud and silt and covered with a large flat rock. When I cleaned out the bowl, it revealed a spring with water flowing from under a large rock into the concrete bowl.

When I cleaned out the spring, a larger stream of water began to flow into the bowl. It took several minutes for the bowl to fill, but when it did, the water started running freely through the pipe down the hill into the storage tank. I plugged off the flow going into the pipe from the bowl and went back down to dip the water from the big tank and clean out the mud and silt from its bottom. When I let the water flow back into the tank, it took the rest of the day for the trickle to fill it back to the point where water again flowed into the pipe running down the hill. The next morning when I checked the pipe where I had broken it, the flow coming from it was about the same as the flow coming from the spring into the big tank.

I went back to the house and got some tools to cut and thread the end of the broken pipe and then attached a faucet to shut off the flow of water. It took a couple more days for the tank to fill, and when it did, the flow from the overflow pipe near the top of the tank was running at about the same volume as the flow from the spring. Once the tank was full, when I opened the faucet, a strong stream of water gushed forth. The volume of water in the tank pressurized the flow from the faucet down below and provided a strong continuous flow as long as the tank had water a few inches above the line to the faucet. When the tank was partially drained, I could close the faucet and the trickle coming from the spring would refill it. If, however, I left the faucet open continuously, the tank would gradually empty down to the lower line and the flow from the faucet would be reduced to the trickle coming from the spring. I now understood how the system had been designed to work.

The more I thought about it, the more I realized that this primitive water system that regulated the supply of water to the houses operated very much the same way cash reserves regulate your day-to-day financial needs. Here's the same figure, but with the labels on it changed.

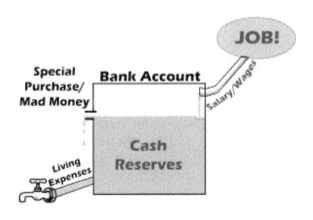

Fig. 17

Do you see the similarity? In Figure 17, the spring is depicted as your job or source of income, and the pipe into the tank is your salary or wages. The reservoir is your bank account in which you build up cash reserves. Money flows from your job into the bank account. The line coming from near the bottom of the reservoir is the flow of funds that pays for your living expenses. When the faucet is opened, demand for water from the houses below is greater than the flow from the spring. When it is closed the rest of the time, the trickle from the spring is keeping the tank refilled. Living expenses are the same way; they are paid intermittently and often require more money in a week or month than you make. That's why your cash reserves must be maintained at a level that can meet the higher demand when it is arises.

When the reservoir in the water system is full, the trickle from the spring dumps the excess water out the overflow pipe until it is needed to refill the reservoir. You could do whatever you want with this excess water without impacting the supply to the houses below. You could save it by channeling it into another reservoir, or you could just let it run down the hill and soak into the ground. Either way, it doesn't affect the flow of water to the houses as long as the main reservoir is kept full.

Your cash reserve reservoir works the same way. When it is full, the overflow can be your "mad money." You can save it until you have enough for those larger purchases, the things you want but don't really need, or you can use it to just have some fun. The important point to keep in mind is that whenever the funds in your cash reserve get pulled down, you have to stop the frivolous spending until they are replenished. It works just like the water system; it allows you to handle your financial obligations promptly when they come due without having to worry. Think of cash reserves as your financial stress reliever.

Imagine what would happen if the houses turned on their faucets and let them run continuously. Eventually the water in the reservoir would drop down to the level of the supply line to the houses and the flow of water would be reduced to the same trickle coming in from the spring. Figure 18 below depicts how the flow of money to cover living expenses coming from the faucet would be the same as the flow of salary or wages from your job unless you allow some to build up cash reserves. In financial terms, this is called living from paycheck to paycheck. When you live this way, any little unexpected expense becomes a problem. When you consistently spend more than you make, it can become a major problem. Everyone needs to have some "mad money," but when spending frivolously comes at the expense of building cash reserves, it will ultimately become quite depressing!

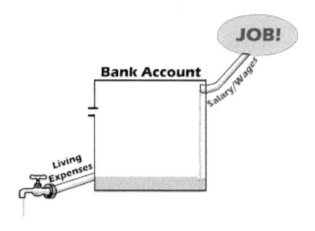

Fig. 18

Unless you like living paycheck to paycheck and having no financial security, the flow of living expenses as shown in Figure 18 has to be reduced to less than your flow of income. There are two ways to do this: earn more or spend less. Either one requires an adjustment in the way you live. You simply must put more in the bank account than you take out, or you will never have the security that comes with having cash reserves.

Without cash reserves the flow of money from the faucet can never be greater than the flow of income from your job. If you spend everything you make as fast as you make it, it's impossible to make large purchases or handle unexpected expenses without incurring debt. Once in debt, payments on the debt then become a drain on your finances and reduce your standard of living. Credit cards are especially destructive because the debt grows little by little month after month. An evening out for dinner and a movie, when charged to your credit card and not paid off when the statement comes, adds to the drain. Little purchases, made month after month, soon become a big debt.

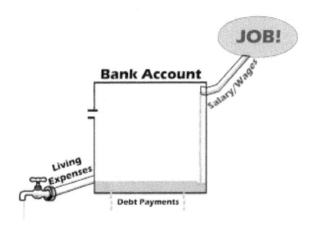

Fig. 19

As shown in Figure 19 above, debt payments have the same effect that having cracks in a water reservoir would have. If you left the faucet open, eventually the flow of water from it would be reduced to less than the trickle coming in from the spring because of what escaped through the leaks. Even after the faucet is closed, the leaks would still cause it to take substantially longer for the reservoir to refill.

The way to avoid becoming caught in this trap is to put part of your earnings into a savings account as soon as you get paid and then adjust your lifestyle to live on what's left. By making regular deposits, you will slowly build up cash reserves that can act as a cushion to help you cover intermittent or unexpected expenses without having to go into debt. Once your cash reserve account is adequately filled, you can start saving the extra funds and use them to treat yourself to some of the nicer things in life without having to resort to debt. I understand that adjusting your lifestyle to accomplish what we've just discussed may be difficult, especially if you've become accustomed to living paycheck to paycheck, but when you spend everything you make, you're like the people below the spring would be if they tried to live without the storage tank. They would go through life struggling to survive on the small trickle from the spring, and when drought reduced the flow, they could be forced to seek help from others.

If you're finding it difficult to save, it's because you're already living above your means. Unless you are willing to temporarily lower of your standard of living in order to save, it will be hard to avoid the burden of consumer debt and the forced lowering of your standard of living that comes with it. The problem is, once you start overspending, it's easy to slip into habits that can lead to financial distress or bankruptcy, and this can totally ruin your standard of living.

The old saying, "An ounce of prevention is worth a pound of cure," is never truer than when it comes to building cash reserves. Putting aside a little from each paycheck, even $5 to $10, will gradually help you build the reserves that will enable you to pay your bills timely, strengthen your credit rating, and give you peace of mind. Try it and see if it doesn't work for you too.

Key points from this chapter:

- Cash reserves give you peace of mind and reduce stress by enabling you to always pay your bills on time and be prepared for unexpected expenses.
- Use the "overflow" money left over after your reserves are established to purchase fun things.
- Unless you stop frivolous spending and live on less than what you earn, you'll never fill up your cash reservoir.
- Living paycheck to paycheck leaves you vulnerable to unexpected expenses and the temptation of bad (unproductive) debt.
- Without cash reserves, the flow of money from your living expenses faucet can never be greater than the flow of income from your job.
- Debt payments are like cracks in your reservoir; they reduce the flow of money from your living expenses and cause it to take substantially longer to fill up the reservoir, even if you reduce spending and increase your income.
- Each time you get paid, put part of your money in a savings account FIRST, and then live on the rest.

[31]

Wealth Building Requires Full-Throttle

I've been flying airplanes for more than 40 years, and I never cease to be amazed at the similarities between flying and wealth building. After taxiing an airplane into position for takeoff, you point the nose down the runway and give it full power until the speed builds up enough for it to lift off. Once off the ground, you keep giving it maximum power while it climbs to cruising altitude. Throughout the climb, the airplane flies at reduced speed and often encounters turbulence. Only after leveling off at the desired cruising altitude does the plane begin to accelerate and you are able to establish your cruise speed and then ease back on the power.

Now, imagine what would happen if you pointed the nose down the runway and only brought the power up to half throttle. The plane would start down the runway and gain some speed, but not enough to ever create the lift required to get off the ground. Eventually it would run out of runway and crash into whatever terrain lay ahead.

Wealth building works this way. In the beginning, it requires maximum effort, often with little or no visible rewards while you are getting started. Once things begin to move, it still requires maximum effort, often for years, as you climb the ladder of success. Just as airplanes encounter turbulence, wealth building encounters its setbacks and disappointments too.

Even after you get off the ground, what would happen if the pilot encountered turbulence on the climb out and he or she said, "This is harder than I thought," and pulled the power levers back to idle, or even worse shut off the engines? You know the answer. The nose would pitch forward, the plane would start down, and unless power was reintroduced, the plane would do the same thing it would do if adequate power was never applied in the beginning: it would eventually have a very unpleasant encounter with Mother Earth.

Everyone knows what would happen to an airplane in this situation, so why are so few people able to understand that the same phenomenon occurs with wealth building or achieving excellence in virtually any other endeavor one might undertake in life? Great artists, musicians, athletes, business executives, and others who excel in any area of life had to devote thousands of hours, endure many disappointments, do things they didn't want to do, and still keep moving forward before they were able to fully enjoy success. The ladder of success has to be climbed one rung at a time, but the higher one climbs, the less competition there is. Granted, the competition at the highest levels may be stiffer, but there aren't as many of them because the weaklings have already given up.

I know you have watched the space shuttle lift off. When the engines first light off, it sits on the pad and tremendous flames and smoke pour from its base as power builds up. Then slowly it begins to creep upward. The power required to lift this giant vehicle off its launch pad is enormous, but as it blasts into the thinning air of the upper atmosphere, resistance decreases and speed increases until it eventually breaks the pull of gravity and goes into orbit. At this point, the engines shut down and the great ship coasts through space.

Wealth is not built by trading labor for money. Translate that to mean working a J-O-B. Wealth comes from investing time and money into assets that produce passive income, income for which you don't have to trade time or money. In the beginning, the more time and earned income you can invest into these types of assets, the quicker the stream of passive income grows. As I described in Chapter 2, once passive or investment income equals or exceeds what you earn, you have reached functional retirement. Your life becomes like the space shuttle in orbit. You get to sit back and coast, unless you want to continue working.

Reaching this point gives you options. If you want to increase your standard of living dramatically, you can continue working, live off your earnings, and keep reinvesting the passive income until it grows large enough to support whatever lifestyle you desire. Once you are able to live the way you want without having to work, you have achieved financial independence.

One of the most difficult things for working people to comprehend is that you get ahead financially from the money you invest, not the money you make or from what you spend. Granted, when you spend everything you make, it lets you enjoy a bit more at the moment, but it limits you to never being able to enjoy more than what your current earnings can support. For those who think that earning more enables you to enjoy more, I would simply ask, What happens when you are no longer able to work and earn?

Many high-wage earners live in exclusive homes, drive fancy cars, wear the finest clothes, belong to country clubs, and take expensive vacations with very little thought put into what they will do when they can no longer work. Maybe they think they will be able to work forever, but far too often they are forced to give up the things they enjoy when faced with forced retirement and limited income. This doesn't have to happen to you.

Even average wage earners can live luxurious lives in retirement if they will start early, work hard, live on less than what they make, and invest the difference. It isn't magic; its common sense. Wealth building takes time. Your earning years equate to the takeoff and climb phase of an airplane flight, which is why the sooner you start and the more effort you put into it, the sooner you can reach altitude (financial independence) and start to cruise.

For those of you who have steady jobs and are reading this thinking you can't invest anything now because you're barely able to pay the bills, go back and reread the previous chapter. You're already living above your means. Unless you adjust your lifestyle and live on less than what you make, you'll never be able to invest and reach a point in life where you are able to cruise. All you need to do is visit a few fast-food restaurants or big-box stores to see the elderly people still working meager jobs to support their retirement.

The sooner you start, the higher percentage of your earnings you invest, the quicker you will be able to reach your financial cruising altitude and be able to start coasting. One of my greatest thrills has been watching my investments grow and counting down the days until I was able to face my golden years with security, knowing I didn't have to worry about where my next meal would be coming from. It's unfortunate that in this great country, too few people are ever able to enjoy this feeling.

Key points from this chapter:

- Reaching financial independence requires maximum effort in the beginning.

- During the climb, an airplane trades speed for altitude. Climbing the financial ladder of success requires trading some of today's fun for tomorrow's well-being.

- If you slack off on effort before reaching your desired financial plateau, it would be like pulling back on the power in an airplane during its climb.

- The sacrifices made today that enable you to invest for the future are what make it possible to reach financial independence.

- Living above your means impacts your life the same way trying to take off without enough power impacts an airplane.

- One of life's biggest joys is being able to watch and measure the increasing stream of passive income from your investments.

32

The Magic Money Game—Financial Literacy for Children

Many parents spend a great deal of time teaching children in their early formative years to feed and dress themselves, they potty train them, and they get excited as they learn to walk and talk. Then around age five, children enter kindergarten, and parents often miss a golden opportunity by abdicating much of their teaching responsibilities to schoolteachers. Sure, they may help with homework, encourage them to read, and offer enticements for good grades, but many fail to use this time, when children can be molded like a piece of clay, to teach them valuable lessons about financial responsibility, lessons I had to learn the hard way, through trial and error. In this chapter, I will share a few thoughts and ideas you might want to use to help your children grow into more financially literate adults.

You may question how elementary-age school children can learn about financial responsibility when many haven't even learned to count. How can they learn to handle money when they still can't make change? Well, believe it or not, young children can learn, and learn a lot. Granted their math skills may be lacking, but you can bet that long before they enter kindergarten they know it takes money to buy things and without money they can't.

I often take our public education system to task for turning out financially illiterate graduates, ones who don't understand the effects of credit, who can't balance a bank account or prepare a budget, but I can't lay all the blame on schoolteachers. Parents must accept a role in this shortcoming as well.

I believe the time to start teaching the importance of saving and investing is when children are in elementary school, when their minds are porous and hungry to soak up knowledge. This is an age when they can be taught to live within their means and to be patient and wait for things they can't afford rather than going into debt to get them. This is also an age when financial mistakes aren't devastating the way they can be later in life. By following the advice in this chapter, parents can teach basic money management principles with as little as five dollars a week or even less, plus they may learn a thing or two themselves in the process.

In most households, preschool children notice one or both parents going off to work each day, and they may occasionally ask why Mommy or Daddy has to leave. Here's a great opportunity to start teaching them about life. Parents can explain that they have to go to work to make money so they can buy food, clothes, a home, etc. Then they can tell their children that they will soon get to go to work too. Their first job will be at school where they will learn how to get a real job like Mommy and Daddy. This can be made to sound exciting rather than something to fear.

Children love to play games. If you've prepped them properly, instead of the first day of school being a traumatic experience, children will look forward to it with great anticipation. This is the time when you can introduce them to what I call The Magic Money Game. This is a game you can use to teach them a great deal about the real game of life. Here's how it works. In the weeks leading up to the first day of school, make school sound thrilling. Encourage them to look forward to it as the start of their first job, one which will let them go to work each day just like Mommy and Daddy. Instead of giving them an allowance, let them "earn" money by going to school. Pay them a dollar for each day they attend school. Fridays can be payday, as it is for many workers. *(I use a dollar in this example for illustrative purposes only. Use whatever amount you are comfortable with; it could be a quarter, a dollar, or five dollars per day. The amount is not important; it's the principle you will be teaching that will have the lasting value.)*

A good idea is to go to a bank and purchase a quantity of the new gold Sacagawea or presidential dollar coins. These are slightly larger coins that are easy for children to handle, and they really like the golden color. On Friday pay children for their week's "work" with a coin for each day they attended school that week. This is where the learning really begins.

Get two clear containers, ones where you can see what's inside. Mark one "Savings" and the other "Toys." Explain to your children that each week they must put one coin in the "Savings" container and two in the "Toys" container. As much as possible, let the children decide what to do with the other two dollars. This is also a good opportunity to introduce them to the relationship of one denomination coin to another. I suggest that you take the child to the bank and let them see how they can trade one of their dollar coins for 100 pennies, 20 nickels, 10 dimes, or four quarters. You can take some of these smaller coins home and use them to teach the relationship of one denomination coin to another; one nickel equals five pennies, one dime equals 10 pennies or two nickels, etc.

Now, back to the containers. Explain that the money in the "Savings" container will always be saved, but the money in the "Toys" container is different. The children can watch it accumulate, and when it contains enough, that money can be used to buy a favorite toy or game that may cost several dollars. Over time, children will learn the value of long-term savings as they watch the coins in the "Savings" container continue to grow. They get to experience the excitement that comes with saving for larger purchases when the money in the "Toys" container enables them to buy an expensive toy. And finally, they develop the confidence that comes with having "earned" money not just for the new toy, but to spend on other little things they may want right now.

The possibilities to teach life lessons with this game are endless. The Magic Money Game can be used to teach children financial responsibility all the way through high school. Read on, and we'll discuss how the coins can become bills and the bills can lead to bank accounts, and how to introduce children to the effects of credit. Just remember, however, that all of these possibilities require parental involvement and helpful oversight. The question is, are you up to the task, or are you going to let your children enter the workplace as financial illiterates.

Imagine the learning opportunities this game can provide. As with a real job, it can be used to teach children that they get paid for work (that's the days they attend school), for holidays and vacation days, including summer vacation, but not for the days they don't work (miss school). You can give them small pay raises as the years pass . . . children need more money as they get older. The game needn't be a financial burden, because children can be taught to use their "own" money to pay for some of the things parents would otherwise buy anyway. It can be used to teach the value of money and to appreciate having to work for what they get.

The life lessons that can be taught with this game are endless. As children grow, the coins you paid them in elementary school can be switched to bills as they reach middle school. Eventually the money in the "Savings" container could be used to open a savings account at a bank or credit union where they could continue depositing a portion of their money into savings. As the children watch their savings grow, they can be taught how banks work as they receive their monthly statements. They can learn that their savings earn interest, which is money for which they don't have to work.

The effects of credit can be introduced by occasionally loaning them a week or two-week's pay when they want to buy something today without having enough to pay for it. You can then withhold part of their future pay until they pay back the loan. In real life, isn't that what happens? When you borrow money to buy something today, you then have to repay the loan with payments from tomorrow's income. This lesson teaches children that buying on credit means having to do without things they could otherwise enjoy until the loan is repaid. Many people still haven't learned this lesson by adulthood.

Here's another idea! Being promoted from elementary to middle school is a big deal, and it provides a golden opportunity to celebrate by giving your children a raise to go along with the promotion. This teaches them another life lesson. If they've been "earning" a dollar a day going to elementary school, you could reward them with two dollars a day when they start middle school. Explain that with their promotion comes more income. Just as on that first day they entered school, when children move from the nurturing environment of elementary school to the raging hormones that are rampant in middle school, it can cause a great deal of apprehension. It's much like the apprehension that comes with a new job or big promotion, so it should be rewarded accordingly.

Throughout the summer break, parents can encourage children by discussing their promotion to middle school and the big raise that will come with it. They can discuss how with more money, they will have additional responsibilities. Remember, it's not the amount of money, but the principle that's important. Whatever students have been receiving in elementary school, doubling this when they enter middle school equates to a big raise. What's important is that parents continue to provide guidance and insist on the money being allocated based on the same percentages used before the increase. When the money doubles, so should the savings. Hopefully it will become a habit, because this is a principle that should be applied throughout life.

Instead of paying with the gold dollar coins I recommended using during the elementary years, students can now be paid with dollar bills. If they will be receiving 10 dollars per week instead of five, students should put two in their savings account, four in the clear container (whose name you will change from "toys" to "special purchases"), leaving the remaining four dollars for discretionary spending. By middle school, children are old enough to understand the concept of charitable giving.

Parents may want to encourage them to give to their church, or civic or other charitable organization, but they need to understand that it's also important to let young people make some financial mistakes and pay for them. There's no better teacher than a bad experience.

As savings deposits continue to grow, young people will slowly see the effects of investing for the future . . . you don't want to mention retirement at this age, because in their minds, they're never going to get old. The four dollars per week they put into the "special purchases" container helps teach them the concept of saving for more expensive items and allows them to experience the excitement and anticipation that comes as they get closer and closer to being able to make that "special purchase." The contrast between the euphoric feelings that come with finally having saved enough to make a purchase and the dismal feelings of having to do without to repay a loan if they borrowed to get it a little earlier is dramatic. This experience can be invaluable in later years when they get their first credit card.

Using The Magic Money Game is a simple way to teach children the basic money-management skills they will need to become financially successful later in life. Again, the suggestions offered here for middle school students are just to give you some ideas. I'm sure you will come up with many more ways to apply the game, but now let's move on and discuss ways you might use the game to prepare high school students for college and the workplace. Once again, I want to remind you that this game teaches children skills they will not learn in school, but it requires parental involvement. Are you up to the task? If so, it will help your children grow into productive and financially secure adults.

Now, we come to the hard part . . . high school. This is a time when children often think they know everything but are able to do very little. Friends are more important than parents or teachers, and with this attitude come problems resulting from peer pressure. Financially speaking, the transition to young adulthood is much easier for those students whose parents have worked with them throughout the elementary and middle school years. Unfortunately, they are few and far between.

Talking with children about money is taboo in many households. Some parents are reluctant to discuss finances because they feel children don't need to be concerned with money while they're still in school. Others avoid the subject entirely because of embarrassment over the financial messes they've made of their own lives. And still others know so little about money management they don't know where to begin.

Rather than avoiding financial discussions, these are all good reasons to work with children throughout their youth, but having an ongoing dialogue with teenagers about money is critically important. If they are allowed to leave the protective custody of parents and enter adulthood lacking monetary knowledge, they are gullible prey for savvy financial predators.

Unfortunately, during high school, students reach the age when they can drop out and not continue their education. Those who do graduate soon leave home to attend college or enter the workplace. Regardless of a child's career choice after high school, knowing how to manage money, how to set financial goals, how to pay bills, and how to create and execute financial plans is a vital part of building a successful life. Parents who have consistently and successfully played The Magic Money Game with their children in the early grades will find it will be much easier to continue working with them when they become teenagers.

Children who have been introduced to the concept of earning money for their efforts, saving, investing, planning for larger purchases, experienced the effects of borrowing, and accepted limitations on frivolous spending have a much better understanding of the importance of learning additional money-management techniques. Playing The Magic Money Game with small amounts of money while children are young is a great way to teach them long before they reach high school.

The key element of The Magic Money Game is treating school as children's job, one that will prepare them to get better jobs later in life. Paying them a daily rate to attend school rather than just doling out allowances lets them feel rewarded for their effort. Paying them for vacation days and holidays is consistent with a job, as is not paying them if they don't attend school. The numbers of subtle lessons that are embedded in this game are enormous.

The promotion from middle school to high school is another huge step in a child's growth. Just as with middle school, this promotion should be rewarded; however, parents should base the amount they increase their teenagers' pay on the responsibilities that will be transferred along with the money. Students' needs are greater in high school than they were in elementary and middle school, so what might have been one or two dollars per day in the lower grades may become five or ten dollars a day or more in high school. The increase in pay should be accompanied by an increase in responsibility. They should be expected to use a substantial portion of the money to pay for items parents would otherwise be paying for. School lunches, clothes, movies, dating, fuel for the car, etc. are a few examples of expenses that could be transferred to students. To have maximum effect, it's extremely important that once a financial responsibility has been transferred, it not be subsidized if the students waste the money on other things and comes up short. That's hard for many parents to do, but it's an important part of the learning process.

Whatever amount parents decide to pay, they should work with their children to encourage long-term savings and short-term savings for large purchases (*a car for example*) and still give them the freedom to be frivolous with a little of the money (That's youth!). The recommended mix is still 20% to long-term savings, 40% to short-term savings, and 40% mad money. Encourage charitable giving, but teach them to take the funds from the short-term savings or the mad money, not the long-term savings. If the students take on part-time jobs, encourage them to pool those earnings with their school earnings and allocate them in the same manner.

I encourage you to go back and read this chapter several times and think of other ways you can use the game to teach financial responsibility. Parents who work with their teenagers and teach them to handle money before they enter the workplace will not only find it rewarding, but may learn from it themselves. Not only will they find it rewarding to see their children learn, but parents often improve their own financial management skills while teaching their children tasks like balancing bank statements, keeping up with credit and debit card receipts, preparing budgets for how to spend their money, starting to invest their long-term savings, and learning to handle other financial transactions they will need to know as adults.

An entire book would be required to go into all the details about how parents could use The Magic Money Game to teach their children personal financial literacy, but one thing is certain, parents who spend time teaching their children about money produce young adults who are more likely to become productive members of society than those who let their children enter the world as financial illiterates. Again I ask, "Are you up to the task?"

33

Tracking Your Financial Progress

I think it only fair to let you know that when I first entered the workforce, I was like most young people; I got a job, went to work, received a paycheck, paid my bills, and didn't have a clue whether I was getting ahead or not. If I had money left over, I usually found something on which to spend it and then looked forward with anticipation to my next paycheck. I was renting another small house (not the one I lived in when I set my life's goals), when an unusual opportunity presented itself that enabled me to buy my first home.

My next-door neighbor had lost his job and was in dire financial difficulties. His misfortune was my good fortune because it placed him in a situation in which he had to sell his home quickly. He saw me in my yard one evening and came over to explain his situation. He said he was behind on his payments and asked if I would be interested in buying his home before the bank foreclosed on his loan. He said if I would give him $500 and assume his mortgage, he would let me buy the house. (That was back in the late 1960s before the advent of the "due on sale" clause in mortgages.) He explained that this would get him out from under the debt and help him salvage his credit.

Although I was a total greenhorn when it came to buying real estate, I was able to come up with the $500 plus closing costs, and I bought the property. I didn't realize it at the time, but this transaction inadvertently taught me some very valuable financial lessons. At the closing, the attorney was going over the note and deed of trust documents and having me sign everything, when he handed me an amortization schedule for the loan.

Keep in mind, my financial knowledge was very limited at the time. I looked at the document, turned to the attorney, and said, "What's this?"

I'd never seen an amortization schedule and didn't know what it was. The attorney explained that it listed each scheduled payment on the mortgage loan and showed the amount of each payment that would be applied to interest and the amount that would go toward reducing the outstanding balance of the loan.

I studied the document for a minute and then said, "So, if I follow this schedule and mark off each payment as I make it, I will be able to watch the loan balance go down, right?"

"That's correct," he replied. "Think of it this way, when you pay rent, all of the money goes to someone else. When you make a payment on your mortgage, part of it goes to the bank as interest, but the rest reduces your loan balance. Paying down the loan is similar to taking money out of one pocket and putting it in the other; you don't have the cash, but your equity in the property increases by the amount of the principal payment, but," he continued, "even the interest that goes to the bank will help you because it is deductible on your tax return. You can use it to offset part of your income, and you won't have to pay tax on that money."

That brief discussion started me down a road that eventually led to carefully tracking my financial progress. When I made the first payment, I circled the principal and interest amounts as well as the new balance. I continued doing this after each payment was made. Beside each monthly entry, I wrote the date I paid and the check number I used to make the payments. I soon noticed that as the loan balance got smaller, less of each payment went to pay interest and more to paying off the loan.

This was my first introduction to tracking financial progress. While it was exciting to watch the loan balance go down each month, it was even more inspiring when I saw the nice refund I got when I filed my taxes the first year.

This led me to start thinking about the other payments I was making. I had a car loan and two credit cards, so I decided it might be fun to track those payments as well. I didn't have an amortization schedule on those debts, so I started a ledger sheet on each outstanding debt. Just as on the amortization schedule, I had a column for interest, principal, and balance. As I made each payment, I put the interest in one column and the rest of the payment in the principal column. I reduced the outstanding balance by the amount in the principal column. The first month, I learned that I needed to add a column to my credit card sheets to add the amount of any new purchases I made during the month and would have to add this amount to the outstanding balance. When I charged more than I paid in principal, the balance went up instead of down. This revelation led me to think before I charged things to the credit cards and soon resulted in my paying off the credit card debt.

That was more than 40 years ago, and as soon as I paid off the debt, I haven't carried an outstanding credit card balance since. The process of tracking the repayment of my debts showed me the value of keeping up with my financial progress, but keeping up with debt reduction is just a part of tracking your financial progress.

After suffering the embarrassment of bouncing a few checks to close friends and stores with whom I did business, I learned the importance of keeping track of my spending as well. The stiff overdraft fees and returned check charges from the merchants didn't help make the situation any better. Until this happened, I had never thought about balancing my bank statements. In my head I kept a loose running total of where I stood, and if I wasn't sure, I just called the bank and asked how much money I had. That's what many people do. I even heard that some actually think that as long as they still have checks, they must have money.

When I bounced the checks, I went to the bank to see what had caused the problem. The bank officer explained it very simply when she said, "You wrote checks for more money than you have in your account."

She then explained the importance of balancing my bank account each month when the statement arrived. This is a simple task that I had not been doing. I've since learned that, unfortunately, not enough people, especially young people, take time to perform this task.

I've had numerous discussions with people who have asked me, "Why balance my checking account? All I need to do is call the bank or go online to see how much money I have."

Well, it's not that simple. When you open a bank account, whether it's a checking, savings, money market, or CD account, don't rely on the bank to keep up with your money. Machines make mistakes, people make mistakes, and the banks have plenty of both. I know you may find this hard to believe, but we occasionally make mistakes too. Balancing your accounts is how you discover and correct these mistakes, no matter who makes them.

If you want to improve your finances, the first thing I recommend you do is to get a handle on your money. Balancing your bank accounts is an integral part of this process, and here's why.

Whenever you write checks, make deposits, use an ATM card, have automatic drafts taken from your accounts, or perform any other activity that puts money in or takes money out of your account, you should keep a record of it. This gives you a running record of the amount you should have in the account. When your statement arrives, balancing your account is simply comparing your records with the bank's. If they don't balance, you have to find out where the mistake has been made and correct it. If you have trouble doing this, you can take your records to the bank, and they will be happy to help you. Finding and correcting mistakes is known as reconciling the account.

Here's why it is important to do this. Suppose the bank's equipment makes a mistake in reading the magnetic bar coding on one of your checks or a teller transposes a number when recording a deposit. Or, suppose you make an addition error that causes you to show that you have more money in an account than you actually have. All of these mistakes happen and happen much more frequently than you may think.

In addition to mistakes, other irregularities can occur that make balancing important. If you have automatic drafts taken from your account, the fixed amount may change. There may be unauthorized charges debited from your account, bank fees, chargebacks for checks that do not clear, and overdraft protection that automatically deposits funds to your account if you inadvertently overdraw the account. Any of these are transactions that can cause your records to be out of balance with the bank's records. When you rely solely on the bank's records, you'll never know when it makes a mistake. Without keeping your own records and balancing them with the bank's, you have to accept its accounting errors even when they aren't not in your favor . . . and they usually aren't. I deal with a number of banks, and it's rare that a month goes by that I don't find a mistake in one or more of my accounts.

Catching mistakes is only part of the reason for balancing your accounts each month. What if a mistake, either yours or the bank's, causes you to bounce checks? Not only do you have the mistake to correct, but it often results in big fees being charged by both the bank and the companies to which you wrote the checks. If it's due to a bank's error, you can usually get the fees credited back to your account, but you still have to pay the fees charged by the merchants.

Another problem with relying on the bank's records occurs if you have overdraft protection that automatically makes deposits to your account. Unless you reconcile each month, you may call the bank and get a balance that is much larger than you expect and assume that you've made a mistake. Then you spend the extra money and eventually find out that you owe several hundred dollars on your overdraft line of credit.

As you can see, there are many reasons to keep track of your personal financial records and make sure they agree with the ones being kept by the banks. If you're doing this, chances are good that you're better off financially than your friends who don't. Problems that come with sloppy record keeping always hurt you more than they do the bank.

If you've never balanced a bank statement, there's no better time to start than now. Get out your last statement, flip it over, and follow the instructions on the back. Do the best you can to reconcile your records with the bank's, but if you can't, don't worry. Just getting started is what's important. If your records don't agree with the bank's, and the difference is small, make an adjusting entry to reconcile your records with theirs. Now you have established a starting point!

From today forward, be sure to list every check, deposit, debit card transaction, or other activity in your register and keep a running balance of the amount in your account. When the next statement arrives, do the same thing you did before. Flip it over and follow the instruction on the back. If the adjusting entry you made the previous month when you were getting started was incorrect, you should be able to find any errors and correct them this month. Folks, it's not that hard, but if you're still having trouble, take your statement and records to the bank and ask them to help. Banks are usually very good about helping customers learn to reconcile their accounts.

In today's age of computers, there are programs like Quicken and Microsoft Money that make keeping up with finances a snap. You simply keep your records on the computer, and when your bank statements arrive, you can reconcile them in minutes. Plus the computer programs also allow you to track your spending and income by category, compare these to a budget if you so desire, and have the information needed to file your taxes at the click of a mouse.

For those of you who say, "I don't have time to do all that," try taking some of the time you use whining and complaining about money and put it to work doing something to improve your finances. Tracking your finances is one of the most important tasks you can do if you expect to eventually achieve financial independence. Let me give you an example of why this is so important.

A few years ago, I conducted an interesting experiment. I visited three very busy convenience stores, where I just hung out watching people come and go and observing what they bought. Each time, it was late in the day, around the time people were getting off work. Most of them appeared to be working people on their way home. Many were still in their work clothes. Some wore company uniforms with their names emblazoned above the shirt pockets. There were fast-food employees in their colorful work outfits; construction workers in jeans and boots, who were driving their company trucks; and numerous others who were obviously wage earners. A few had the brisk walk and snappy dress that would lead one to believe they were executives or professionals. But it wasn't the starched shirts or scuffed work boots that caught my attention. It was their pattern of spending.

For the most part, the ones who were neatly dressed and had an air of professionalism drove the nicer vehicles and purchased little more than gasoline, which they usually paid for at the pump. When they did go into the store, their purchases tended to be milk, bread, or other staple items. The contrast between what these individuals purchased and the others was striking. At least a third, possibly half of those who could readily be identified as blue-collar workers came into the store and paid cash for their fuel. But, regardless of how they paid for their gas, a majority of those who came into the store purchased beer, cigarettes, smokeless tobacco, candy, or other snack foods.

The difference between each group's purchases reminded me of the old adage, "Which came first, the chicken or the egg?" I don't mean to criticize anyone, because there was a time when I wore muddy boots and work clothes and stopped off on the way home for beer and cigarettes too, but I was fortunate enough to learn some valuable lessons at a young age. I learned that what you do with money is far more important than how much of it you make. Tracking your spending is just one of the things you must do if you expect to truly keep up with your finances. That's why I mentioned using one of the computer programs mentioned above so you don't lose track of where you are spending your money.

As I described in Chapter 23, early in my career, I always seemed to come to the end of the money before I came to the end of the month. I wasn't alone in this predicament; most of my friends were experiencing the same problem. I didn't view myself as a spendthrift, but for some reason, no matter how much I made, it always seemed to slip away, and I just couldn't seem to get ahead.

Without being too repetitive, I decided to find out what was really happening with my money. This was during the time I was learning from having tracked my mortgage loan and other debts. Remember how I described buying a small spiral-bound notebook that would fit in my shirt pocket and writing down every penny I spent . . . and I mean every penny. If I bought a soft drink, I wrote it down. If I bought a candy bar, I wrote it down. Everything! Groceries, gas, cigarettes, clothes, bowling, even a piece of bubble gum, I wrote it down. At the end of a month, I did a simple analysis; I categorized each expenditure as either necessary or unnecessary.

Loan payments, utilities, food, and similar expenditures fell into the necessary category. Unnecessary were the things I wanted enough to purchase, but things I could have done without. Cigarettes, candy, soft drinks, records, a new pocketknife, and a new bowling ball were things that showed up on this list. If you choose to try this, you have to be honest with yourself when making the categorizations. Also, you can categorize your spending in much more detail using one of the computer accounting programs mentioned earlier.

When I totaled my list and discovered that in just one month, my unnecessary expenditures came to more than $600, I learned that I could change my life by changing what I did with the money I was spending on unnecessary items.

Back to the steady stream of working people coming and going from the convenience stores; they were blowing their hard-earned money on feel-good items that did nothing to improve their lives. I couldn't help but wonder if their spending habits would change if they really understood how much money they were wasting. With more discipline and better spending habits, they might be the ones driving better cars, wearing nicer clothes, and possibly getting the higher-paying jobs.

Whether you're struggling or not, can you see the value of tracking your finances? If you owe money, keep a record of how you are paying off the debt. Keep a record of your savings too. Balance your bank accounts. On regular intervals measure your progress by subtracting what you owe from the value of what you own. (I do it annually.) The difference is your net worth. If it is growing, you're making progress and you are on the right track. If it's declining or is a negative, you need to give yourself a checkup from the neck up and re-evaluate your lifestyle and spending habits. Regularly tracking your financial progress keeps you out of trouble and separates you from those who don't. When I started doing it, within a year, my finances were dramatically improved and I was on my way to financial independence. And the most remarkable part was I hardly noticed the changes I made to make it all happen.

Key points from this chapter:

- Tracking the progress as a loan is paid down is rewarding and an excellent way to keep yourself motivated.

- Tracking the repayment of credit card debt creates direct awareness of how your balance is affected by new purchases, results in better decision making, and increases your likelihood of paying off the debt.

- Bounced checks and overdraft fees only add insult to injury and reduce your ability to get ahead of your financial situation.

- Mistakes happen! Don't pay for the bank's miscalculation by keeping sloppy records. Don't rely on the bank to keep up with your money; balance your accounts and catch the mistakes before they get the best of you.

- Keep a record of every transaction: checks, deposits, ATM transactions, automatic drafts, etc. That way you'll always know how much money you have without having to call the bank or go online.

- Programs like Quicken and Microsoft Money are a great way to track your spending and balance your accounts.

- By tracking your spending you can detect little spending "leaks" in your purchasing habits on feel-good items that don't really do anything to improve your life. If these frivolous spending habits are changed, the extra money can be the difference between a paycheck-to-paycheck lifestyle and the road to a more financially secure and successful life.

34

You Must Visualize Success Before You Can Achieve It

Napoleon Hill's *Think and Grow Rich* is probably the great-granddaddy of all self-help books. Napoleon Hill was a newspaper editor and later a speechwriter for President Franklin Delano Roosevelt. It was Hill who wrote the famous sentence: "Let me assert my firm belief that the only thing we have to fear is fear itself."

The book came about because industrialist Andrew Carnegie hired Hill to write a book about his success principles. Carnegie had come to the United States penniless from Scotland and had worked as a telegraph operator for the Pennsylvania Railroad for 12 years. He became the richest man in the world because he saw the potential of steel beams for railway-bridge construction, rather than wooden trestles. This simple insight led to his starting the Carnegie Steel Company, which he sold to U.S. Steel for $250 million in 1901.

It's fascinating that we human beings tend to forget the difficulties of accomplishment once we've reached our objective. Once we've done something, we tend to look at others and think, "Why are you having so much trouble? It's not that hard." We do that regardless of the difficulty we may have had when we first tried it. Carnegie felt that way about making money.

During his rise to power, I'm sure Carnegie faced incredible difficulties, but after his success, he couldn't understand the poverty that he saw all around him. It astounded him that so many people were having trouble surviving in a country that had given him a fortune.

He wanted to endow the world with his secrets of success. A high school dropout, he lacked the education to write a book, so he hired Napoleon Hill to write it for him.

Hill says in the preface:

In every chapter of this book, mention has been made of the money-making secret that has made fortunes for hundreds of exceedingly wealthy men whom I have carefully analyzed over a long period of years.

The secret was brought to my attention by Andrew Carnegie, more than half a century ago. The canny, lovable old Scotsman carelessly tossed it into my mind, when I was but a boy. Then he sat back in his chair, with a merry twinkle in his eyes, and watched carefully to see if I had brains enough to understand the full significance of what he had said to me.

When he saw that I had grasped the idea, he asked if I would be willing to spend 20 years or more preparing myself to take it to the world, to men and women who, without the secret, might go through life as failures. I said I would, and with Mr. Carnegie's cooperation, I have kept my promise.

Hill followed Carnegie around for many years, watching everything the billionaire did. From this experience he wrote *Think and Grow Rich.* If you haven't already done so, I urge you to read it or to listen to Earl Nightingale's brilliant audio condensation. It amazes me that everyone doesn't read and covet this book, which is available at Amazon.com for around $8 new and $3 used. The book will make an incredible difference in your perspective. As Earl Nightingale says, "The hand that puts this book down after finishing it is a different hand." The book fascinates me because Hill never spells out Carnegie's success secret.

In the preface of the book he assures you that by reading it, you'll learn the secret of accumulating wealth. "The secret to which I refer has been mentioned no fewer than 100 times throughout this book. It has not been directly named . . . if you are ready to put it to use, you will recognize this secret at least once in every chapter." So you can't turn to a page and find the secret carefully outlined in a little box. Nevertheless, you'll understand the secret as soon as you've finished the book because you will have planted it in your subconscious mind. This was consistent with Andrew Carnegie's feelings that you have to make people work for their own success. As he said, "There is no use whatever trying to help people who do not help themselves. You cannot push anyone up a ladder unless he is willing to climb himself." Although it may be cheating, I'm going to tell you the message that's buried in that book.

In his day, Carnegie had an opportunity to rub shoulders with hundreds of self-made millionaires. As he got to know them, he realized that there was a common denominator among all of them. What they all shared was that even in the earliest days of their careers, these millionaires knew what they wanted and what it would feel like to be successful. They experienced their success long before they achieved it.

They could create a visual image in their minds of their success. They could experience the feeling of stepping into their Cadillac and sinking into the fine leather seats long before they had the car. They knew what it would be like to wear the world's finest clothes and have dozens of employees at their disposal years before it came to pass. They knew how it would feel to walk into the boardroom of a corporation they owned and have everyone present rise in respect. They knew what it would be like to enter a ballroom filled with people who would turn and be awed by their approach.

Hill called this ability to mentally experience the future "imagizing." These high achievers were able to imagine—to create in their mind—the feel of success. When Carnegie first looked at a wooden-trestle railway bridge and visualized how steel beams could replace all that wood, he didn't see himself as a steel salesman. He saw himself owning a great steel mill.

Napoleon Hill taught us that to become successful we must first change our subconscious thoughts. To achieve financial independence, you must first "imagize"—project onto your subconscious mind—the experience of having great success.

Can you really visualize and hold in your mind the image of yourself not having to worry about paying your bills? Can you experience this successful feeling before you achieve it? Can you "imagize" the day when petty fears and worries no longer influence you, and when every day is an exciting adventure? Can you see yourself driving the car you've always wanted, living in the house of your dreams, or any of the other things you might associate with financial independence? Can you?

Harry Belafonte used to wash dishes in a restaurant in Harlem. What a tragedy if a limiting self-image had stopped him from sharing his true talent with the world. What if you had that kind of talent within you and never explored it?

At the height of her career, Barbra Streisand risked everything to produce and direct the movie *Yentl*. "Why on earth would you do such a thing?" her friends asked her. "It had nothing to do with the desire for fame and fortune," she said. "I already had all that. I did it because one night I dreamed that I had died, and God revealed my true potential to me. He told me about all the things I could have done, but didn't because I was afraid. That was when I decided that I had to create *Yentl* even if it cost me everything I had."

For a really chilling story of a positive self-image lost and regained, listen to bestselling author Og Mandino tell the story of hitting rock bottom one day in Cleveland. Thirty-five years old, he'd lost his family, his home, his job, and his self-respect. He stood in front of a pawnshop window in the rain, with his last $30 in his pocket, looking at a handgun for sale, thinking of ending his life. He could never say why, but he was drawn instead to a library down the street. There, a self-help book by W. Clement Stone captured his interest. The book was *Success Through a Positive Mental Attitude,* and reading it saved Mandino's life. He put his life back together, eventually went to work for Mr. Stone at his insurance company, and later became the editor of his magazine *Success Unlimited.* He went on to write *The Greatest Salesman in the World* and eventually sold over 15 million self-help books.

So "imagizing" your success is the way to start changing your self-image. Learning to mentally experience success will help you to achieve it.

The next step is to change your self-talk from negative fears to positive expectations. Eliminate "I can't do this," and "It'll never work," and "Other people are just lucky." Replace them with "I can do this," and "No problem, I'll make it work," and "I'm the lucky one." Soon you'll find your image of yourself changing—you'll see yourself as a different person and then gradually you'll become a different person.

I play a little game with this positive-thinking approach. Each time I drive into the parking lot of a restaurant or large store, I say to myself, "There is someone getting ready to pull out of the parking space closest to the door because they know I'm coming and it belongs to me." Amazingly, more than 90 percent of the time that's just what happens. Recently I visited the local Sam's Club just two days before Christmas. The parking lot was filled to capacity. I noticed people turning off the highway and immediately heading to the far corners of the lot where a few parking spaces remained. "Hum!" I jokingly said to myself. "I guess they are going there so I can have my space at the front." I drove directly to the front of the store just in time to see a car pulling out of the space closest to the front door. I know positive thinking really does work!

Did positive thinking make the parking space magically appear? Of course not! That would be metaphysical madness! The parking space was always there, but only a positive thinker goes to look for it. As Mei Li sings in Rodgers and Hammerstein's *Flower Drum Song*: "A hundred million miracles are happ'ning every day, and those who say they don't agree are those who do not hear or see."

Many people beside Andrew Carnegie have promoted the idea that if we are to change our lives, we must first change our self-image. The bestselling talking record of all time is Earl Nightingale's *The Strangest Secret*. Earl was a successful radio personality on WGN in Chicago with his own daily commentary show. He did so well that he was able to achieve financial independence and retire at the age of 35. One of his investments was a life-insurance company and he got in the habit of attending its sales meetings and giving the salespeople a motivational talk. When he was leaving for a vacation, his sales manager begged him to record a message for him to play to the salespeople when Nightingale was away. Legend has it that Nightingale sat down and at one sitting recorded the message that was to sell more than a million copies and win a gold record.

Unlike Napoleon Hill, who preferred to bury the secret of success in his book, Earl Nightingale revealed it in the first two paragraphs:

Why do men with goals succeed in life . . . and men without them fail? Well, let me tell you something, which, if you really understand it, will alter your life immediately. You'll suddenly find that you seem to attract good luck. The things you want just seem to fall in line. And from now on, you won't have the problems, the worries, the gnawing lump of anxiety that perhaps you've experienced before. Doubt . . . fear . . . well, they'll be things of the past.

Here's the key to success and the key to failure: WE BECOME WHAT WE THINK ABOUT. Let me tell you that again. WE BECOME WHAT WE THINK ABOUT.

His theory that we become what we think about has changed the lives of millions. If a person thinks all day long about becoming rich, he or she will become rich one way or another. If a person is single and thinks all the time about being married, it won't be long before he or she will marry. Conversely, if a person with a negative self-image thinks constantly of nothing but becoming poorer, that will probably happen too. In other words, a self-image is self-fulfilling.

Every self-image psychologist agrees that before you can change your life dramatically, you must first change your self-image. You must train your mind to "imagize" the person you want to become. Self-image psychology explains why the lives of people who become financially independent often seem charmed. It seems they can do no wrong. Success washes over them in gigantic tidal waves. Good things happen to them much faster and in larger quantities than seems possible. Napoleon Hill put this beautifully in the first chapter of *Think and Grow Rich* when he said:

We believe you are entitled to receive this important suggestion. When riches begin to come, they come so quickly and in such great abundance that one wonders where they have been hiding during all those lean years.

This is an astonishing statement, especially considering the popular belief that success comes only to those who work long and hard.

People who achieve financial independence know you can change your whole life by changing the way you think about yourself. They learn to experience success—to taste it and smell it—long before they actually achieve it. Every step of the long journey to accomplishment, they carry an image of what they want to be. They change their own mental image of themselves, and in doing so, make the rest of their lives a stage on which they act out a fascinating and fulfilling script. I attribute most of my success to being so concentrated on reaching the goal I set for myself that it caused me to change my self-talk and start thinking of myself as a millionaire instead of a poor factory worker.

From this moment on, I urge you to stop thinking of yourself as someone who *could* become financially independent. Think of yourself as already being financially independent. I don't care how little money you have in the bank, and I don't care how much in debt you may be. I don't care how down-and-out you feel. Once you begin to think of yourself as financially well off, you'll be amazed at how adept you'll become at accumulating wealth and influence. Once it becomes part of your psyche, the obstacles that loom so large to negative-thinking people become mere bumps in the road to your success.

One myth that I want to dispel is that wealth brings stress, which is unhealthy. I was recently part of a program on wealth building at a large national convention. Following the program, I was confronted by one of the participants who wanted me to know that there was more to life than building wealth. I listened intently as he told me about the people he knew or had known that had ruined their health or died at an early age from stress because they were constantly trying to earn more money. He said that given the choice, he would prefer to be poor and healthy than rich and not able to enjoy it. Obviously, he could not "imagize" himself as being financially independent.

My first thought was that he didn't understand the difference between earning a living and building wealth. I invited him to join me at an empty table because I wanted to hear more about his way of thinking. Once we were seated, I asked him to explain what wealth had to do with health. For the next several minutes he told me about how hard he was working, how much he was making, and how he had learned to be happy with what he had. He said he wasn't interested in working any harder, but he did add that he could always use some extra money. The longer he talked. the more he confirmed my original thought.

I wanted to jump in and say, "Wait a minute; you're talking about earning a living, not building wealth," but he was on a roll. He told me a story about his friend James who had moved his family into an expensive home in an exclusive neighborhood and was working two jobs in order to make the payments. He said his friend never had time to play golf, go boating, or do any other fun things, and he was concerned that he was going to have a heart attack because of all the stress he was under.

He finished that story and went right into another one about a friend who had recently died from a stroke. He said he had always considered his friend wealthy because he seemed to have so much and appeared to be living a charmed life. After his death, he learned that his friend was heavily in debt and in serious danger of his home being foreclosed upon at the time of his death. Had it not been for a life insurance policy, his family would have been forced out of the home. The gist of our conversation was that he had learned to be happy living within his means and wasn't interested in adding stress to his life by working harder or going into debt.

I commended him on being financially responsible but told him I still couldn't understand why he thought having wealth was unhealthy. When I asked what percentage of his income he was saving each month, it was obvious I had touched a nerve.

"I'm saving very little right now," he replied, "but I'm not going into debt either. We're living comfortably, but it takes nearly everything I make to do so, which is why I don't want to add more stress by trying to act wealthy."

This gave me an opening to point out that wealth comes from the money you save and invest, not from how much you spend. We both agreed that striving to earn more and more could be very stressful, but when I explained that investing could produce income without having to work for it, I saw a light go off. What seemed to trip the switch was when I explained to him that I had increased my standard of living only from the income my investments produced, not because I was working harder and earning more. I jokingly asked him how stressful could it be to wake up each morning knowing the day was paid for whether you earned any money or not.

Because he couldn't "imagize" himself as being wealthy, he thought it was fine to spend everything he made maintaining his current lifestyle, because he wasn't going in debt. I explained that his image of the future was resigning himself to work the rest of his life and that could become quite stressful in his senior years. That made the light that had gone off in his head burn a bit brighter and led to a discussion about how starting early, living on less than what he made, and investing the difference could enable him to reach the point where his investments would earn enough so he didn't have to work at all unless he just wanted to.

The secret is being able to "imagize" becoming financially independent. That's what encourages you not to spend all of today's earnings, but to save and invest and watch the investments move you toward the goal. It becomes even more encouraging when you come to the realization that becoming financially secure could happen at age 30, 40, or 50. There's no age limit on achieving financial independence. What's important is that you develop the habit of saving and investing early enough to allow your investments to enjoy the benefits of compounding growth.

There are a variety of ways to get started. Many people begin by simply making regular deposits to a savings account. Others buy stock, bonds, and other publicly traded securities. Some invest in their own businesses. My favorite has become investing in rental real estate. What happens with most people is that once they develop the habit of saving and investing, and learn to visualize themselves as financially successful, they quickly start learning ways to improve their rates of return.

The method you choose isn't nearly as important as getting started early. The sooner you start and the longer you keep at it, the more financially secure you will become. As your investments begin to produce income, the pressure to keep earning lessens. Remember, wealth is not measured by how much you earn, but by the length of time you can maintain your standard of living if you suddenly can't work and earn. When you no longer have to work a job to live the standard of life you want, stress levels fall dramatically. That's why I say wealth is a stress reducer; it's the quest for higher earned income that produces stress.

Key points from this chapter:

- Read and reread Napoleon Hill's book *Think and Grow Rich*.

- Everything seems to be harder the first time you do it.

- The common denominator of all successful people is that way before they were successful, they could "imagize" themselves as being successful.

- Listen to Earl Nightingale's recording of *The Strangest Secret*, available from Nightingale.com. Learn how to "become what you think about."

- You have to see yourself as financially independent before you can become so.

- High income and wealth are not the same.

- Wealth relieves stress; striving for higher income causes stress.

- Take a few minutes each day to close your eyes and "imagize" yourself living the lifestyle of your dreams. The more you see yourself in that role, the quicker you will get there.

35

Debt and the Most Important Decisions You Will Make

Probably the most important part of achieving financial independence is the ability to make smart decisions. We are where we are today because of the choices that we've made up to this point. Think back to the stories of my upbringing and the way the decisions I made affected everything that was to follow. The decision to run away from my abusive stepfather! The decision to find the father I had never known! The decision to leave home and sell encyclopedias! All of these substantially affected the person I am today, but by far the decisions that made the most impact on my financial status were the decisions I made regarding the use of debt.

Although I grew up in an age of rampant drug use, I was fortunate enough to be at the very front of the baby boom generation, and unlike many of my younger friends, I missed the addictive consequences of drugs. Much has been written about the problems associated with drug abuse, but the affliction that has had an even more adverse impact on society than drugs is our addiction to debt. Just as no one sets out to become a drug addict, people don't make their first loans with the goal of filing bankruptcy. So what happens?

It starts small. You get a credit card with a small limit, you take out student loans to go to college, you get a loan to buy a car, and before you know it, you are spending a substantial portion of your earnings paying off debt. The have-to-have-it-now mentality of today's youth has created a wider gap between young adults and their parents than at any time in history. As few as five years ago, 20-somethings were carrying an average debt of more than $16,000. Today, according to a study by

PNC Financial Group, millennials carry an average of $45,000 of debt. Student loans are the most common culprit, followed by credit card debt and car loans. When you are trying to get started in life, the mental anguish this debt burden places on you can be crushing. The negative effects caused by late payments, higher interest rates, and bankruptcy can be devastating.

Just as individuals who started out experimenting with drugs and alcohol didn't set out to become addicts, students using credit cards and obtaining student loans to get through college don't see it as a trap that may lock them into a cycle of consumer debt that can last a lifetime. Many 20-somethings graduate from college with $50,000 or more in debts and are shocked by the meager-paying jobs their expensive education brings. Frequently they find that it takes $3,000 to $10,000 per year in pretax earnings just to make their loan payments. That's a real shocker!

Payments on credit cards and student loans, when coupled with soaring housing costs, have produced what many are calling the boomerang generation: young adults who, after graduating, are moving back home to live with parents while they struggle to overcome mounting debts. Parents, who thought they would be free to enjoy life when their kids got through college, suddenly find themselves coping with adult children who don't obey the way they did when they were little children, and new tensions often erupt. Unfortunately, this phenomenon is becoming a reality in an increasing number of American homes.

The squeeze is coming from a number of places. Tuition costs are skyrocketing at both public and private universities. Housing costs have far outstripped inflation. Soaring energy prices soak up a significant portion of earnings, and health care that Obamacare is forcing on everyone is taking another big bite out of 20-somethings earnings. As bleak as the picture may seem, these factors may ultimately combine to shift behavior from the buy-now-pay-later mentality of the last few decades to the more fiscally sound save-first-then-spend method used by earlier generations. If this happens, it will go a long way toward breaking the cycle of debt addiction that is currently strangling many individuals and our country.

Unlike their parents, who expected Social Security or company pension plans to care for their needs in retirement, today's 20-somethings are increasingly skeptical about the future and openly express doubts about how they will fare as seniors. Of the recent college graduates with whom I have talked, less than a third expect they will ever see a dime from Social Security. With frequent stories about major companies eliminating retirement plans from their benefit packages, the pressure on young adults to behave in a more financially responsible manner will continue to grow.

Making a transition from spend-now-pay-later to save-first-then-spend will be a daunting task for society. It's taken several generations for the debt addiction to take hold, and I expect it will take generations before it releases its grip. It certainly won't happen overnight. It may even necessitate an extraordinary event like 9/11 or Pearl Harbor to get large segments of society to make the kind of sacrifices that will be required. I predict that extraordinary event is just beginning to arrive in the form of retirement by the baby boom generation.

As this large segment of the population fully enters retirement, it will place demands never before experienced on the Social Security System and other retirement plans. As the retirement age is extended, benefits are cut, and private plans face crisis after crisis, today's 20-somethings will experience a level of stress and anxiety their parents never faced.

Rather than waiting for financial disaster to strike and force behavioral changes, wouldn't it be better if both parents and children could recognize that as a country we can't continue to pile up mounting debts and expect to maintain a decent standard of living. A national debt now approaching $20 trillion is catastrophic. Parents willing to be frugal during their child-rearing years and set aside money to help with education expenses will enjoy more freedom and a better life once their children graduate and become able to support themselves. Children willing to work and help with expenses while going to school will not only have the opportunity to develop work habits that will help them obtain better jobs after graduation, but they will also be helping themselves to avoid entering the workplace with a big debt-monkey on their backs.

Let's explore some of the debt traps that lure people into perilous situations. One of the biggest is the enticing ads for zero interest and low payments. Have you noticed the number of ads for cars, RVs, furniture, appliances, and other big-ticket items that no longer promote the price, only the payment amount? Television is full of ads from car dealers that never once tell you how much the vehicles cost. There is a used-car dealer in the market where I live who advertises how much his cars cost less than new ones. He never once tells you how much his vehicles cost, only what the monthly payment will be.

These ads often have one or more attractive smiling young ladies giving out payment amounts while some gruff-looking salesman is waving car after car into the picture then motioning it to drive away so the next one can be displayed. A few of the ads use celebrities instead of the attractive females, but the message is the same, "Buy this car now, and you'll only pay $____ per month." Whatever your comfort level, there's a payment to fit your budget . . . if you even have one. Some even offer weekly payment options to make the payments look even smaller.

Oh, don't forget the low interest rates being offered and all those cash-back opportunities. Speaking of cash back, I still have trouble understanding how it's a deal to be overcharged and then get some of your money back. But what really gets me are the ads with the option to take a low or zero percent interest or get money back if you pay cash. Aren't these just deals where the interest is built into the purchase price? If you don't finance, the money you get back is the interest you won't be paying.

Furniture and appliance dealers are just as bad with their buy-now, pay-later promotions. FREE financing! No down payment and no interest for two years, maybe more. Some offer no payments and no interest for months or years. Many of these special offers are coupled with a requirement to open a new credit card account. What is going on? Why all the advertising to entice customers to go in debt? Isn't it the same approach as a drug dealer giving free samples to get you hooked, knowing you'll become a long-term customer once you're addicted?

These offers seem too good to be true until you read the fine print and learn that most of them are lenders gambling that you will lack the discipline to follow their strict payment guidelines. The consequence of a misstep may be penalties, late fees, and interest rates of 25 percent or more. Unfortunately for buyers, these gambles pay off far more frequently than not. America has become such a society of debtors that many people don't even bother to ask the price anymore. All they want to know is can the payments be structured to make buying seem easy.

With public schools failing miserably when it comes to teaching students about money management and consumer finance, it's no wonder that today's young people are such easy prey for all these credit gimmicks. As I've mentioned before, I grew up before the age of credit cards and easy financing. If I didn't have the cash to buy something, I had to save for it.

One option many merchants used in the past was to offer layaway plans. This let you select items you wanted to purchase and lay them aside, and then allowed you to make payments until the purchase was paid in full. Although this was a form of forced savings, it wasn't all bad. Instead of getting the product now and being charged interest while you paid for it, the merchant held the product while you made payments on your layaway. If you found that you couldn't make the agreed-upon payments, the items went back into inventory and your money was refunded minus a fee for handling the transaction. This taught people to be patient and kept them from buying things they couldn't afford. Even more importantly, it taught discipline. You paid on a layaway because you wanted to, not because you had to.

High fuel prices, the collapse of the real estate market, and tighter credit are putting a spotlight on some of the problems that come with debt. These tougher times could be why we are seeing so many of these payment ads that don't tell the price. When money is tight, a car payment of $299 per month sure looks better than a price of more than $21,000, even though you might have to make those payments for seven long years. No money down and no payments for a year for that new high-definition television might look good today, but at the end of the year, if you can't come up with the full amount, you could be assessed a huge amount of interest for the year at a time when you can least afford it.

Think about this! When money is tight, there are very few things in life you can't live without. Tough times require tough decisions, and one of the toughest is to say no to easy credit when you want to buy things you don't really need. The joy that comes with a new purchase fades rapidly, but the agony of making payments drags on for months or years. When the urge to go into debt hits, step back and let common sense dictate action. You wouldn't jump off a diving board without first checking to see if there's water in the pool, and you shouldn't take on debt to finance purchases for which you can save and pay cash even though it causes you to have to wait a while to make the purchase.

Be patient! Try out the payments initially by making them to a special bank account to see if you can comfortably handle them; treat it like a personal layaway plan. If you find they are a burden, you're not locked into a debt that may ruin your credit and put you under undue stress. See if you have the discipline to sacrifice other things in order to save for a purchase you may not need. After a few months of setting aside the money, you may find that the purchase is not such a necessity after all.

The economy is very unsettled right now and may remain that way for years. That's another reason you are seeing so many opportunities to buy on credit. When people aren't flush with cash and times may get tougher before they get better, it's a good time to keep in mind the words of Dr. Robert Schuler, "Tough times never last, but tough people do." Be tough! Don't get sucked into situations you may regret. If you save first and buy later instead of buying now and paying later, you'll be much happier in the long run.

Let me digress a bit to tell you a story to which you may be able to relate. When teenagers graduate from high school, they are young and naive, especially when it comes to knowing how the real world works. Some will continue their education in college or technical school, but many will enter the workplace feeling 10 feet tall and bulletproof. Their zeal and enthusiasm for life will have them looking into the future and visualizing themselves living in a comfortable home, driving a nice car, and prospering financially. Unfortunately, by age 30, reality sets in and outlooks change . . . unless they understand and follow a simple lesson from Economics 101.

Let's use Mary and John as examples. Both are 18 years old, have just graduated from high school, and have entered the workforce. Both have found jobs paying $15 per hour and will realize a 3 percent-per-year pay increase until age 30. Mary decides to save 5 percent of her gross income and put it in an investment account earning an average of 6 percent per year, compounded monthly. John decides to take a different path. He has the attitude that you only live once so you should enjoy yourself as much as possible. After all, you may not make it to retirement age. Let's follow Mary and John during the next 12 years until they turn 30.

As soon as he starts his job, John gets a credit card with a $1,000 credit limit. The credit card's interest rate is 18 percent, and it has a minimum payment of $10 or 2 percent of the outstanding balance, whichever is greater. The first month he spends his entire income plus an additional $100 that he puts on the credit card. Mary deposits $130, which is 5 percent of her gross pay into an investment account and lives on what's left.

John and Mary are close friends, so in one of their conversations, he tells her that he got to enjoy the $100 he charged to his credit card, while she didn't get to enjoy the $130 she put in her investment account. That means he had $230 more enjoyment the first month than she did. He also points out that his minimum payment the next month will only be $10, and he can handle that with no problem. This continues month after month. John isn't extravagant, but he keeps overspending about $100 per month. Gradually his credit card payment increases because his balance grows large enough that the 2 percent minimum is more than $10, but he isn't worried. It's still just a small payment that he hardly misses.

Interestingly, as his balance nears its $1,000 credit limit, John receives a nice letter from the bank informing him that due to his excellent payment record, they are increasing his credit limit to $5,000. He also begins receiving solicitations from other banks that want his business, and they offer him additional credit cards. Eventually he opens several more accounts with credit limits that total more than $25,000. Now he really feels successful!

Watching John live it up is difficult for Mary. He seems to always get to do more than she does, but she continues to religiously deposit 5 percent of her gross earnings into her investment account. Because of her sacrifice, Mary eventually notices that the interest she is earning on her savings is growing significantly. She doesn't mention this to John, but it sure makes it easier for her to keep saving.

By the time they reach their mid-20s, John's spending habits haven't changed. He is still spending an average of $100 per month more than he makes, but he isn't quite as enthusiastic as he was at 18. Their conversations are now center around how he uses one credit card to pay off another so he doesn't have to use so much of his paycheck to make the payments. Although he always seems to have more and be able to do more than Mary, her savings are growing, while his debt keeps increasing.

Eventually, they reach age 30, and John has an epiphany. He isn't doing as well as he thought. His credit card debt has grown to more than $10,000, and his payments exceed $200 per month. In contrast, Mary's investment account contains nearly $23,000, and she is earning $160 per month in interest for which she doesn't have to work. Mary points out that if she wanted, she could increase her standard of living by $160 per month for the rest of her life without ever having to touch her principal. John realizes that he will have to reduce his standard of living for years in order to pay off his debts. In actuality, Mary now has $360 more per month she could enjoy than John has because $200 of his salary is going to make the payments on his credit cards.

The overall impact of living these two very different lifestyles between ages 18 and 30 is quite revealing. John averaged overspending $100 per month for a total of $14,400 over the 12 years. By funding this with his credit cards and paying 18 percent interest on the money, it cost him more than $12,300 in interest and left him $10,000 in debt. While John was "living it up," Mary's investment account earned more than $9,600 in interest. Mary could buy anything she wants with her $9,600, but John has paid out $12,300 in interest that bought him nothing. The combined total of the interest John paid and the interest Mary earned was more than $21,900. That's the price of impatience and should be a lesson for all young people . . . and most adults too. You can't borrow your way to prosperity!

The above story reduces the debt problem down to a personal level, but when you look at the big picture, it's much greater. In 2008, the stock market was in chaos, banks and insurance companies were failing, and there was plenty of talk about the problems created by sub-prime loans and mortgage-backed securities. With the news filled with talk about things like derivatives, LIBOR, CDOs, GSEs, and more, who could expect average working people to know what was going on? During this time, whenever you turned on the television news or picked up a newspaper, there were stories about how the economy was taking a beating. It brought to mind the old fable about Chicken Little claiming, "The sky is falling." Granted, the financial structure in this country is extremely complicated and can't be taken lightly, but just as from a tiny acorn, a mighty oak tree grows, there has to be a seed from which our current mess has grown.

Could that seed be consumer debt as described in John's and Mary's stories? I'm not talking about money borrowed to invest in income-producing assets that bring in more than enough to pay off the loan. I'm talking about debt that has to be paid from your earned income. It's the debt that you use to elevate your standard of living above what your earned income will support, as John did. Let me add that I don't consider home-mortgage debt bad unless it is excessive in relation to your income, because everyone has to pay to live somewhere, whether it's rent or mortgage payments.

Just for fun, let's go back to a not-so-distant time when things were rosy and there was no such thing as consumer debt. Jerry and Bill were neighbors who worked in the same industry and had identical salaries. Bill thought he must be doing better than Jerry until he discovered that Jerry was saving a substantial portion of his income. In fact, when he learned that Jerry had several thousand dollars in cash, he approached him about borrowing some money to buy one of those newfangled contraptions called a television.

Jerry, being the good neighbor that he was, loaned Bill $1,000, and Bill agreed to pay him 10 percent interest on the money. Bill used the money to buy a television and became the envy of everyone in the neighborhood. Whenever friends came to watch Bill's television, they wanted to know how he could afford it. Bill explained that Jerry had loaned him the money to buy it. Suddenly others started asking Jerry for a loan so they could get one too. It wasn't long before Jerry had so many neighbors making payments to him that he was able to buy his own television with just the interest he had received.

As time passed, more and more people came to Jerry for loans so they could buy the latest gadgets that everyone else was getting. Eventually Jerry became the banker for his entire community, and his original meager savings grew to become millions. The problem was, things weren't as rosy anymore. People who had been his friends called him a fat cat and resented having to make payments to him each month. They said it wasn't fair that he had so much money and they didn't. Sound familiar?

I know this is a simple scenario, but imagine situations like this playing out in communities all across the country. Gradually the few people who saved, invested, and earned interest grew increasingly wealthy, and those living on debt found it progressively more difficult to maintain their standard of living. Those who used debt to live above their means gradually grew poorer, and the rich got richer. The reason is simple; money is borrowed from the rich, not the poor. Interest is a transfer of wealth. The borrowers pay interest. The rich receives interest. Interest paid buys nothing but time, but interest received can be used to purchase anything the lender wants to buy.

I realize that this is an oversimplification of what our nation has been experiencing for decades. Subprime loans, mortgage-backed securities, and derivatives are just a few of the complicated ways lenders have found to raise and loan money to a society living above its means. The problem may have started with small loans to people with good credit, but, gradually, as borrowers became addicted to the higher standard of living that debt brought, it evolved into a frenzy of lending without regard to the borrower's ability to repay. Greed trumped common sense.

The problem we have today is that individuals, companies, cities, states, and especially the federal government have all been borrowing. Total debt is in the trillions. Almost everyone has been living above his or her means, and it has created a house of cards that is on the verge of collapse. The growing gap between the rich and the poor can be traced directly to debt. Interest paid on debt is the vehicle through which wealth is transferred from the poor to the rich. My fear is that government's attempt to solve the problem with more debt may turn out to be like throwing gasoline on a fire.

Warning bells have been sounding for years, yet we keep borrowing. Individually, we are in a growing financial crisis because credit has become more difficult to obtain, but that may not be all bad. We have already spent our children's inheritance and robbed them of the lifestyles we have enjoyed. The questions become, Are we going to start repaying the debt, or just keep piling on more?

If you're wondering who is at fault for the current problems, ask yourself this question. Is part of your paycheck going to make payments other than a reasonable mortgage payment? If the answer is yes, then you're part of the problem! It means you've been living above your means and borrowing part of tomorrow's income to pay for today's spending.

I know I've bounced around in this chapter, but it's important to show that the predicament is widespread. It's a problem that we're never going to solve with continued borrowing. Years ago, if a child got sick, he and all his siblings got a good dose of Castor Oil. It tasted terrible, but it worked. I believe that what our country needs today is a good dose of economic castor oil. Forcing people to pay off debt and live within their means won't be pleasant, but unless we do it, we're never going to break the debt addiction.

If you're just starting out in life, my advice is to pay yourself first! Set a savings goal and meet it first. Treat your savings as money you never received. Forget about it! Adjust your lifestyle to live on what's left after you pay yourself. This may seem difficult to do when you're young and have a bad case of the "I wants," but if you develop the discipline to do it, you will ultimately be far more financially successful in life than those who spend first and plan to save later.

If you're already buried in debt, your first focus needs to be on getting the debt paid off. When you're in debt, it means you've already dug yourself a financial hole. You have to get out of the hole (pay off your debt) and get back on level ground before you can start building for the future. If you aren't in debt, resolve to keep it that way, and focus on saving so you can pay as you go through life without having to mortgage your future just to have more fun today.

I know it's a difficult subject, but I urge parents to open a dialogue with their children about financial responsibility at an early age and continue the discussion until they mature. Some parents avoid talking about money, and it often gives youngsters a skewed outlook on the way life really works. Talking about financial difficulties as well as successes helps children learn that life is filled with ups and downs. The better prepared they are to deal with life's responsibilities, the better future they will have when Mom and Dad aren't around to handle things.

Key points from this chapter:

- The decisions you make regarding the use of debt may be the biggest decisions of your life.
- Debt addiction can ruin a life as much as or more than drug addiction.
- The United States is facing a growing debt addiction that will have to be curbed to avoid financial disaster.
- Think of saving first and paying later as a personal layaway plan.
- Credit card debt can become more addictive than drug or alcohol addiction.

- You can't borrow your way to prosperity.
- The rich get richer and the poor get poorer because interest is a transfer of wealth. The rich earn interest, and the poor pay interest.
- Set a savings goal and meet it first.
- If you are in debt, do whatever it takes to pay it off as quickly as possible.

[36]

Plan Time to Allow for Wealth-Building Tasks

As I pointed out in Chapter 7, the one thing we all have in common is time. Young, old, rich, or poor, everyone has 24 hours in a day and seven days in a week. It's what you do with your time that determines how quickly, if ever, you reach financial independence. It's critical for four important reasons:

1. Time management enables you to become more efficient and get more done in less time. Doing so allows you to free up a few hours each week to devote to wealth building. Those who lack an understanding of time management approach their week with dread. They spend the entire week scurrying around doing busywork and complaining about how hard they are working and why they don't have time for anything else. If you manage your time well, you can often get more done in an hour than many people can all day.

Your willingness to work long hours may be noble, but I don't want you spending all of your time working. If you're like most people, after eight to 10 hours on the job, you're getting tired and just want to get home and rest. That's fine, but with good time management, you can schedule time for rest plus all those little things around the house that need to be done and still have a few hours to devote to wealth building.

2. Good time management takes the pressure and stress out of

working, thereby making it more fun. Tasks like budgeting, planning, and tracking your financial progress all take time and aren't real exciting, but they are critically important to achieving the happiness that comes with financial independence. When you plan ahead to spend time on wealth building tasks, you'll not only look forward to accomplishing your other objectives for the week, but will feel even better knowing that part of what you are doing is contributing to your goal of becoming financially independent.

3. Time management enables you to plan time for recreation and family life, which enriches your overall life experience. You may think that a good manager of time is someone who is capable of taking on monumental amounts of work and still getting everything done. My perspective of someone who manages time well conjures up the vision of a parent fishing with his or her children on a Saturday afternoon because he or she finished all their wealth-building tasks on Saturday morning. My youngest son Matt paid me the greatest compliment I've ever received when he was addressing a group and said, "Most of you know that I have been an athlete all through my years in school. What you may not know is the fact that from youth league all the way through college, my dad never missed one of my games." I'd like to think that was the result of properly managing my time.

4. Good time management enables you to develop an incredible reputation for reliability. If you say you'll call your financial adviser for an update at 9:45 Saturday morning, he or she can count on it. The adviser will be sitting by the phone with the information you need. If you say you'll mail someone information, then the person can expect it. If you say you'll take care of a situation, then the person you told doesn't have to waste time following up on you to see if you remembered to do it. People with whom you do business will admire you so much for your reliability that they will be drawn to you. The people you hire to work for you will soon learn that if they committed to complete a project for you, they should do it on time or you will be right behind them, following up. They'll learn that you live by the motto, "People do what you inspect, not what you expect," and this will cause them to become more responsible.

Eight Rules for Good Time Management
Rule number one: Concentrate on one thing at a time. Good time managers know that the key element to getting control of their life

is to constantly be breaking projects down into pieces small enough that they can concentrate on one thing at a time. Writing this book seemed like a daunting task until I broke it down into chapters and then concentrated on writing one chapter at a time. I would focus on getting all my thoughts for a chapter down on paper without regard for grammar or punctuation as one task, and then I would go back later to revise, edit, and correct spelling and punctuation as another task. As I kept performing these small tasks, the manuscript for the book slowly but surely began to materialize. Had I started out with the single task of writing well over 120,000 words on financial security, I would have been overwhelmed and may have given up.

Let me pose this question to you: If, when you were born, someone had magically appeared in front of you and told you all the things you'd have to face throughout life—all the problems, the trials, the tribulations that a lifetime would bring you, you'd probably have crawled back into the womb, wouldn't you? You would have looked up at the doctor that was hanging you by your ankles, and said, "Get me out of here!" However, taking one day at a time, look at all the things you've been able to accomplish. The old saying, "inch by inch, it's a cinch" is so true. You can handle just about anything when you tackle it in small, manageable tasks.

Learning how to concentrate on one thing at a time takes a great deal of personal discipline. A good time-management system will encourage you to concentrate on each task separately. It will break down all of your responsibilities into pint-size pieces so you can concentrate on "one thing at a time." You will come to trust your system to bring the right thing to your attention at the right time.

Rule number two: Use a daily planning system that you customize to complement the way you work. Don't attempt to change the way you work to fit a prepackaged time management system. If you're like most people, you've had the experience of getting so frustrated by being disorganized that you went out and bought an expensive time-management system. You probably spent hours learning how to use it and days setting it up. Then you found that it was more trouble than it was worth. It simply didn't match the way you work or the type of work you do. There are computer-based time management systems that have the flexibility to be adapted to fit your individual needs, but even if you use nothing more than a simple sheet of paper, whatever system works for you and that you will use is better than no system.

Rule number three: Prioritize your work. Before you do anything, it is essential that you prioritize your tasks. It's the only way that you'll force yourself to do the most important things first. If you don't prioritize your tasks, you'll find yourself looking down your list and gravitating to one of two categories:

1. The most enjoyable things. "I have to call my real estate agent and see what came on the market this week," you might think, because you enjoy talking to your real estate agent. It's not a threatening situation to you. So you follow that phone call up with another call to a friend and after that you read your emails. When you do this, you soon realize that you never got to the most important things.

2. Doing those things that take the least time. You say, "It'll only take me a minute to read my emails, so I'll do that first." Then you'll spend the first 15 minutes of your day reading spam, which is probably the least important thing you need to do. This task will always be near the bottom of a prioritized list.

You may have heard the story of Ivy Lee and Bethlehem Steel, but if not, it bears repeating. Charles Schwab was the president of the company and a very successful business manager. He was the first man ever to earn a salary of more than $1 million a year, and that was back in the 1930s when a million dollars was a great deal of money. (Incidentally he died penniless, after spending the last few years of his life on borrowed money. He didn't have a copy of *The Financial Security Bible*.)

Ivy Lee was a management consultant who wanted a contract with the company. Schwab rebuffed him, saying that they already knew more about producing and selling steel than Lee would ever know. Then he gave Lee a challenge that would go down in business folklore. Schwab told Lee that the only thing he lacked was the time to implement all the ideas he had and that if Lee would show him a way to get more things done with his time, he would pay him any fee within reason.

According to management expert Donald Schoeller, Lee replied, "Write down the most important tasks you have to do tomorrow and number them in order of importance. When you arrive in the morning, begin at once on Number 1 and stay on it till it's completed. Recheck your priorities; then begin with Number 2. If any task takes all day, never mind. Stick with it as long as it's the most important one. If you don't finish them all, you probably couldn't do so with any other method, and without some system, you'd probably not even decide which one was most important. Make this a habit every working day. When it works for you, give it to your men. Try it as long as you like. Then send me your check for what you think it's worth."

What he was saying is so unbelievably simple that you may find it hard to grasp its importance. Charles Schwab loved it. He sent Ivy Lee a check for $25,000, calling the advice the most profitable lesson he'd every learned. He credited this system with turning Bethlehem Steel around and making it, in its day, the biggest independent steel producer in the world. Business experts later chided Schwab for his extravagance in sending Lee so much more than he expected, but Schwab insisted that it was the best investment he'd made all year, saying that it was only when he'd adopted this system that he found all of his people doing the most important things first.

Rule number four: Give yourself deadlines by scheduling blocks of time. Have you noticed that when you're up against a deadline, you can get an incredible amount of work done? If you have bills to pay that will be due in a few days and you plan to leave for a trip that will keep you away from your office for a week, you can skim through a large pile of work that might otherwise take you all day . . . if you had all day. C. Northcote Parkinson's Law says, "Work expands so as to fill the amount of time available for its completion." So a key to getting more done is to work against a self-imposed deadline. If you have a stack of mail to answer, allocate an hour to it, and when the hour is over, set it aside for another day. Don't let meetings be open-ended. If you've scheduled a meeting with your property manager or stockbroker, tell that person how long you've allocated for the meeting and that he or she will have to work hard and stay on track to get everything done in that amount of time.

I disagree with Ivy Lee that you should stick with one task all day if you have to. If you take that approach, you find other issues piling up so much that it may take you several days to climb out of the hole you've dug for yourself. Better to say, "I'm going to take the hour after lunch to get caught up on my other work, but at exactly 2:00 p.m., I'm going to return to this task." Forcing yourself to work against deadlines like this can dramatically increase your effectiveness.

Rule number five: Get comfortable with voice mail. This has been a tough one for me. I like to talk directly with people, not machines, but I've had to learn that instead of cursing that I can't reach the person, I've started valuing a system that allows me to leave a detailed message in a short amount of time. I once received a call from a friend who left the message to call him back as soon as I could. I returned the call but got a message machine, so I left a message that I had returned his call. For two weeks we played phone tag until we finally got to talk to each other.

All my friend wanted was to see if I would like to take a short motorcycle trip that he and several of my other friends were going on . . . over a week before. Look how much time and effort it would have saved if he had left a message saying, "We're taking a motorcycle ride Sunday afternoon, and I wanted to see if you would like to join us. If so, call me back or just meet us at Denny's at 1:00 p.m. ready to ride." My first return message could have been, "I'd love to go. See you at Denny's Sunday afternoon at 1:00."

Rule number six: Read a sheet of paper only once. Break the habit of reading a sheet of paper more than once. Here's what typically happens: The morning's mail includes a letter from someone with whom you do business, and they're asking you for some action. You say, "Okay, I'll need to take care of that later on today," and you put it into your pending basket. Then later in the day, you'll go through your pending basket and see the letter again and say, "Oh, how urgent was that?" So you read the letter again, and maybe then, you'll schedule it for some positive action. However, very often you'll find yourself reading the same letter three or four times.

Here's a system to break that bad habit. Every time you read a piece of paper, tear off a corner. It will amaze you how often you'll tear off all four corners before you get around to taking action on that particular item.

Instead of wasting time by rereading letters like that, get into the habit of quickly reviewing what you need to do and making a decision about when and how you're going to do it. Then make a quick notation on your time management system as to when you will take care of it. When the time comes up for completion, handle it and then move on. Don't keep reading and rereading the same thing over and over. Reading it only once will free up a tremendous amount of time.

Rule number seven: Don't ask for time to think things over. You either have enough information to make a decision, or you don't. A basic fundamental of good decision making is that you first determine if you have enough information to make a decision. If you don't have enough information, don't ask for more time—ask for more information, and be as specific as possible about what information you want. If you have enough information, stop procrastinating and make the decision. If the decision involves doing something you don't want to do, using "let me think it over" is nothing but a way to avoid saying NO. It not only wastes your time, but the time of everyone else involved as well.

Rule number eight: Develop a daily planning system that works for you. When you develop a system that you believe in and trust, you will find it easier to always use the system. There are many good computer time-management programs that work and make it easy for you to keep your to-do list on your computer. If, on the other hand, you don't like using a computer, develop a system that you feel comfortable using. Even little notes tucked away in pockets are better than nothing. One good thing about computer systems is that they eliminate writing down phone messages on odd scraps of paper. If your answering machine gives you six messages that require action, you can immediately transfer them to your Daily Plan. If you made notes as you listened to the message, immediately add them to your computer file so you'll have them when you tackle the matter.

A good computer program enables you to mark the date when an issue needs to be done. Be sure to allocate the estimated time it will take you to handle each project, and don't schedule more in one day than you think you can reasonably get done. If you find yourself looking at the list and groaning at the thought of all the work you have to do, that's a good indicator that you're attempting too much for that day. Move some of the projects to future days. Don't overload yourself. It's essential that you feel comfortable that you can get everything done, because during the day other things will come up and you need to have enough cushion in your plan to be able to take care of them too.

Some of the things you'll need to schedule may not be for tomorrow or the next day, even if you would have time to do them then. These are things that need to be done at a future date, for example, a reminder to call someone when he or she returns from vacation. In that case, simply move forward to the day they are to be done and list them there.

Prioritizing your commitments

The next thing to do is to prioritize the commitments you have. I find that three levels are enough.

1. "Highest" projects are those that you must accomplish today, although they may not always be the most important commitments. For example, something as simple as making a deposit to your checking account may be a "Highest" priority, while calling a real estate agent about a new listing that came on the market, which may be more important, is just a "High" priority. Here's why. If the deposit to your checking account must be made today to avoid bouncing checks, it is a higher priority than the call to the Realtor, which could wait until tomorrow.

2. "High" priorities are those projects you'd like to get done today, but if they get pushed back until tomorrow, it won't result in costly or dire consequences.

3. "Normal" priorities are those projects it would be nice to get done today but which aren't essential.

Be sparing with your "highest" priorities. Only include the truly critical things in the "highest" category, things you must do, or else. These are projects that failure to complete on time will cause problems that can't be corrected. Attending your child's award ceremony this afternoon can't be put off until another day. Any task like this that is time-critical falls into the "highest" priority category.

When you're prioritizing, don't give something a "high" priority just because it has been sitting on your desk for ages. When prioritizing, keep two things in mind:

1. Will tackling the projects bring you to your long-term objective?
2. What will be the consequence if you don't get it done today?

Having prioritized "Highest," "High," and "Normal," now go back and number them for importance. "Highest—1," for example, would be the most important thing to do that day. "Highest—2" is the second most important and so on. Again, think strictly about moving yourself closer to your objective, instead of how many people are bugging you to get it done.

1. Prioritize the "Highs" only when you've completed all the "Highest."
2. Prioritize the "Normals" only when you've completed all the "Highest" and the "Highs."

At this point you may be thinking, "I'm much too busy to go through that prioritizing process. It would take me at least 15 minutes a day." Perhaps it will, but remember that if you want to spend a few hours each week on wealth building, it takes only a small improvement in efficiency to free the time to do so. When you look at it this way, doesn't taking those 15 minutes a day to prioritize the use of your time make it a good investment?

Once you've prioritized your list, start immediately with "Highest—1." Don't go back and reread the list. You've already done that. Just begin your day with the most important task, and work on it until it's completed. When you've done that, automatically move on to task "Highest—2." From there, move to "Highest—3" and so on. That's another point on which I disagree with management consultant Ivy Lee.

Remember that he told Charles Schwab at Bethlehem Steel: "Begin at once on No. 1 and stay on it till it's completed. Then recheck your priorities, and begin with No. 2." I find that rechecking your priorities really slows you down because it is distracting. You can certainly reorder your priorities if something happens that makes it necessary, but don't do it just because you completed No. 1. Your system needs to be able to accommodate changing events; therefore, you must be flexible enough that you don't become a slave to it. In the absence of an unforeseen event popping up, I'm sure you'll find that you get much more done if you move right on to the next task without rechecking priorities once they've been set.

There may be a project that you're not able to complete as scheduled. Perhaps you need to set it aside for a while until you can get more information. If that's the case, you should renumber it on today's priority list or reassign it to another day for completion. Here's a caution: Don't jump around on your list. Consider and deal with each item in order. Don't worry if you have 15 "highest" priorities on your list and you get only five of them accomplished; at least you'll have done the five most important things on your schedule that day.

Here's another caution: Don't assign tasks a low priority just because they're things you'd rather not do. If you have an unpleasant job to do, such as calling your banker to let him or her know that you're going to be late with your payment this month, get that task off your list first thing in the morning. Then it will be easier to complete the rest of your tasks without that unpleasant one hanging over you all day.

When you give your worst jobs the highest priority, it will release you from dreading them all day long. As my friend Danny Cox says, "If you have a frog to swallow, the quicker you swallow it the better. If you have more than one frog to swallow, start with the biggest one first!"

Reviewing the 'Things to Do' list at the end of the day

At the end of your day, review your entire list of Things to Do. If you have tasks that you didn't complete during the day, move them forward. You might want to move them all to the next day, or portion them out over the next week. The important thing is that you keep them entered into your time-management system until you complete them. With a complete list of everything you need to do, all in one place, the end of the day is a great time to set up your priority list for the following day. Then you don't have to waste time doing it in the morning when you are rested and more productive.

When you're prioritizing, every task will fall into one of four categories: Urgent and Important; Urgent but not Important, Important but not Urgent, or Neither Urgent nor Important. Think about each of these categories as you begin prioritizing.

I know this system may seem a bit complicated and reading about it is probably a bit boring too, but developing good time-management habits is a real key to achieving financial success. Nothing is more important than how you use your time. It's the one thing that no matter how rich and successful you become, you'll never be able to buy any more of it. Queen Elizabeth I said on her deathbed, "I'd give everything I own for one more moment of time." At some time or another, that thought will occur to each of us. Football coach Vince Lombardi used to say he could win every game if only the clock never ran out. Think about it, you could accomplish anything in life if you had an endless supply of time. Time is the one and only thing in our lives that is non-negotiable. You can't buy it or sell it, and other people can't give it to you. You can only use it, and the more organized you become, the more you can accomplish with it. It may seem difficult in the beginning, but like everything else in life, the more you practice time management, the better you will become at it.

Remember, if you can take control of your time, you can take control of your life and channel your internal energy into building financial independence. Learning to organize your time better is what enables you to get the most out of every minute of every day. It's one of the greatest secrets to becoming successful financially or otherwise.

Key points from this chapter:

- Time is the one thing we all have in common. We cannot make time, save time, or buy time.

- Good time management enables you to use more of it for important things like creative thinking and strategic planning.

- Time management takes the stress out of life and makes working more fun.

- Time management enables you to plan for more recreation and family life.

- Time management enables you to develop a reputation for reliability.

- Learn to concentrate on one thing at a time.

- Develop and use a daily planning system that you can customize to complement the way you work.

- Prioritize your work so that you're spending your limited time on the most important things first.

- Accomplish more by giving yourself deadlines to complete specific projects.
- Read things just once.
- Don't ask for time to think things over; either ask for more information or make a decision.
- Do the job you dread most first so you don't have to think about it the rest of the day.
- Develop a daily planning system that works for you.

37

Learning the Difference Between Consumers and Investors

When I work with new investors, one of my big challenges is to get them to think like investors, not consumers. If they have not yet built any investment capital, it's usually because they have spent virtually all of their income on consumer items and set aside very little for investment. In the old days I would call that being broke. Nowadays, with the overabundance of consumer credit, being broke is just a marker on a long, slippery slope. You can zoom past being broke these days and still have plenty of money to spend.

Let's a take a look at an ordinary family: The couple has been married for 20 years, and makes about $70,000 a year. They've got 2.2 kids, a barking dog, and a yard with a picket fence. They are filling out a financial statement at a bank, perhaps because they need to borrow money for a college loan for their youngest son. They start out listing their assets, which might include a home, a car, a life insurance policy, furniture, and electronic items such as televisions, appliances, and computers. Wanting to put the best possible light on things, they would list the home at the price the one down the street is listed at and would put a value on the furniture and appliances close to what they paid for them. This side of the financial statement looks pretty good. Perhaps they have $200,000 or more in assets.

Then comes the depressing side, the liabilities. They refinanced the home a couple of times, so there isn't much equity there, and they haven't even figured out what it would cost to sell the home if they were forced to do so. By the time they've fixed the home up for sale and paid the real estate broker, there may be no equity at all. They owe more on the car than it's worth, and they have credit card debt that totals $50,000. They come to the reluctant conclusion that they have no net worth.

How could that be? They are good people. They work hard. In the last 20 years they have earned more than $1 million, but they have nothing to show for it. What went wrong? The answer is simple: they spent the last 20 years thinking and acting like consumers and not investors.

Investors think, "How I can I make money from the money that I invest?" Consumers think, "Can I afford the payments to buy the things I want?" (Unfortunately, many of them don't even give it that much thought!)

When they receive new information, investors think, "How can I use what I just learned to make money?" Consumers think, "What's that going to cost me?" Here's an example: Both the investor and the consumer read in the local newspaper that the city council is discussing building a bridge from an island that will hook up to the freeway. The investor thinks, "How can I make money from this? What's going to happen to property values on each side of the bridge if this happens?" The consumer thinks, "There go our taxes again. How much is this going to cost us?" or worse yet, "Who's getting money under the table on this one?"

When I reflect back on my life, I am reminded of a situation that may have been my first experience with capitalizing on an opportunity. It was late spring of 1959, the year after we'd moved from the small coal-mining town of War, West Virginia, to the big city of Bluefield, Virginia. I'd just turned 13, and like most teenagers, I was looking forward to getting out of school for the summer and spending time riding my bike and playing with friends, but an opportunity presented itself that I couldn't resist.

The city had a new water filtration plant under construction near where I lived, and a crew of workmen was laying lines from it to serve communities throughout the area. The way lines were put in the ground back then was totally different from the way it is done today. All of the ditching was done by hand. A foreman oversaw a crew of men who dug the ditches, laid the pipes, and then refilled them. It was an interesting process.

The men were stretched out along the ditch line for several hundred feet. The lead man, wielding a mattock or pick would loosen the dirt down four to six inches, and the second man would shovel the loose dirt out of the ditch. Then behind this pair, two more were doing the same thing, and the ditch would get a little deeper. More pairs of ditch diggers followed until the ditch reached the desired depth. The men in each pair would trade jobs periodically to spell each other or to break the monotony of the work.

Once the ditch was deep enough, the pipe layers followed behind joining new sections of pipe to extend the line. Behind the pipe layers were additional two-man teams filling in the ditch. In these teams, one man would shovel in about six inches of dirt and the second man would follow with a heavy tamp, packing down the loose soil. Additional two-man teams would repeat this process until the ditch was completely refilled and compacted. In total, there were about 30 men on the work crew, and depending on the soil they could install from a few feet to a couple of hundred feet of line each day. It was this exhausting, hot, dirty work that presented me an opportunity to make some extra money that summer.

Unlike my friends, who all received allowances from their parents, I had to earn whatever spending money I had. I guess this instilled a bit of entrepreneurial spirit in me, because when I saw these men toiling in the hot sun, with sweat streaming off their bodies, an idea came to mind. I had a sturdy bicycle, with a large basket that I'd used to deliver newspapers when we lived in War. What if I offered to bring them ice-cold soft drinks to go with their lunch instead of the lukewarm water they got from a container on the crew bus. Was there a way I could do this and earn a few dollars?

To try out my idea, I took one of my mother's quart canning jars and filled it with ice. I poured water over the ice until the jar was full and then poured the water off into a measuring cup. It measured just less than a pint. With this knowledge, I went to a nearby store and bought a quart bottle of Coca-Cola. I took it home, filled two quart jars with ice, and used it to make two quarts jars of ice-cold Coca-Cola that I took down to the work site just before lunchtime. I offered them to the workmen for $0.50 each and sold both immediately.

I waited around while they ate lunch and then got back my jars when they finished. Both men asked if I would bring them another drink the next day as did eight others on the crew. I was in business! The quart drinks cost me less than $0.25 each, I borrowed my mother's fruit jars, and the store let me have ice for free. Since one bottle made two drinks, I was making more than $0.75 on each bottle, which was not bad money for 1959. Soon I was riding my bike to the worksite each morning, taking orders, going back, and preparing what each man wanted and then delivering the drinks just before their lunch break. Within a month, nearly everyone in the work crew was buying drinks from me daily.

My friends all laughed and made fun of me, but while they were out playing, I was making money and learning about business. While they were getting a couple of dollars a week allowance and doing nothing, some weeks I was making $5 to $10, and by the end of the summer had made several hundred dollars. Had I turned my back on this opportunity because of their criticism and negative comments, I would have missed both the experience and the money. Unfortunately, too many people let peer pressure derail their financial success.

Before you can start thinking like an investor, you have to be willing to seize opportunities to improve your financial position without worrying about what others think. It's your life, not theirs, that's being affected. Opportunities are all around you if you will just look for them. When you start thinking creatively about ways to turn those opportunities into cash, not only will your financial picture improve, but so will your knowledge and confidence, and you will be earning money that can be invested.

Whether that one experience at age 13 gave me the confidence to start my own business later in life, or whether it was the series of similar ventures I attempted as a child, the bottom line is I never doubted my abilities or let fear or peer pressure control me. When you start with successes in small ventures, especially ones that others aren't willing to attempt, you gain knowledge and build self-confidence, and those are the keys to becoming successful in almost any endeavor. Look around! Are there any opportunities that you are passing up?

My first challenge is to get you to stop thinking like a consumer. This will involve three field trips.

Field Trip 101. Drive down to your local Walmart or Target store and spend an hour looking carefully at all the merchandise piled up in there. Keep repeating to yourself, "My goodness, look at all the stuff in here that I don't need." If at the end of the hour you are able to walk out of the store without buying something and still thinking, "There's nothing in there that I need," you may move on to Field Trip 201.

Field Trip 201. If you're a man, spend an hour at a Home Depot or a Lowe's Home Improvement store. If you're a woman spend an hour at Nordstrom or another top department store. Imagine that you have been given a $500 gift certificate to the store. If you can spend an hour in the store and still come out thinking, "There is nothing in there that I really need," you may move on to Field Trip 301.

Field Trip 301. (Don't try this until you've graduated from the first two field trips. It could be disastrous!) Think of your dream car, perhaps a bright red Ferrari or a gleaming white top-of-the-line Lexus. Go take it for a long test drive. If you can walk away from the showroom thinking, "Wow, I would love to have that car, but not now. I'm an investor; I spend money only on things that will show me a return. I will wait to own that car until I can pay for it from my investment earnings rather than from the sweat of my brow." Now, my friend, you are thinking like an investor!

From this moment on, I want you to think of yourself only as an investor. Before spending a penny, ask yourself, "Will this show me a return on my investment?" If it won't, figure out a way to avoid spending that penny and look for something that will show you a return.

Here are some differences between investors and consumers. Consumers think: "What does it cost?" Investors don't worry what it costs. Their only concern is with the return on investment. A consumer might say, "I'm not going to pay $300,000 for that rental house. I remember when I could have bought it for only $150,000." An investor doesn't think like that. To an investor it doesn't matter what it costs. What matters is what the return on investment will be.

When you purchased this book, I hope that you weren't thinking, "This should be an interesting way to spend a couple of hours." I hope you were thinking, "Will reading it enable me to learn enough to get back my money and will I be able to use what I learn to get back my investment many times over?" If so, congratulations! Now you're beginning to think like an investor, but I don't want you to become obsessed with wealth building to the point that it keeps you from enjoying life.

In Chapter 24, I talked about an experience I had with a participant in a session on wealth building at a large national convention. As I explained to him, the reason I want you to start thinking or "imagizing" like an investor is because if you spend everything you make today, even though you aren't going into debt, you will be forced to work the rest of your life. I know I'm being redundant, but I want to keep drumming in the message that if you start early, live on less than what you make, and invest the difference, chances are very good that over time your investments will grow to the point where you become financially independent. That's when your investments earn enough so you don't have to work at all unless you just want to. Again, I remind you that there is no age limit on when you can reach this point. Depending on the amount you save and how well you invest, this could happen at age 30, 40, or 50. What's important is that you develop the habit of saving early enough to allow your investments to enjoy the benefits of compounding interest.

There are a variety of ways to get started. As I have mentioned in previous chapters, many people begin by simply making regular deposits to a savings account. Others buy stock, bonds, and other publicly traded securities. Some invest in their own businesses. My favorite has been investing in rental real estate. What happens with most people is that once they develop the habit of saving and investing, they start learning how to improve their rates of return.

Whichever method you choose, the sooner you see yourself as an investor and get started and the longer you keep at it, the more financially secure you will become. As your investments begin to produce income, the pressure to keep earning lessens. Wealth is not measured by how much you earn, but by the length of time you can maintain your standard of living if you suddenly can't work and earn. When you no longer have to work a job to live the standard of life you desire, stress levels fall dramatically. That's why I believe wealth reduces stress instead of causing it and makes it possible for ordinary working people to build wealth and be happy.

Key points from this chapter:

- Don't spend so much on consumer items that your liabilities stay ahead of your assets.
- Think: "How much money can I make from the money I spend?"
- Don't think: "How can I make the payments to pay for what I want?"
- View each new event as an opportunity to think like an investor: "Is there a way I could make money from this?"
- Look around for opportunities that others aren't willing to tackle.
- Don't allow criticisms from others to deter you from seizing opportunities when they arise.
- Spend an hour at Walmart looking at all the stuff you don't need.
- Spend an hour in Nordstrom or Home Depot looking at all the stuff you don't have to have.
- Take a dream car for a drive and come away thinking: "Not until my investments are able to pay for it."
- Never think, "What does it cost?"
- Always think, "What will my return on this investment be?"
- Don't confuse building wealth with earning a living.
- The earlier you start thinking and acting like an investor, the sooner you will be able to enjoy the happiness that comes with achieving financial independence.

PART VI

Getting Started—Putting It All Together

Throughout this book I have shared experiences that helped shape my life and develop a mindset that has produced happiness and financial security. Several times I've urged you to keep a notepad nearby and make notes if any of my stories reminded you of events from your past. If you're sitting there now reading this with no notes, shame on you, because I urged you to do it several times throughout the book. You're already behind those who followed the recommendation. If you heeded my advice, now it's time to get out your notes and begin the process of developing your own plan to achieve financial security.

You may have noticed as you read my stories that I discovered important lessons buried in everyday experiences. Not all of these experiences were good, not all of them were bad, and I had far too many for me to tell them all, but I learned from each one. The reason I learned so much from these was because I was looking for ways to achieve my goals, not excuses for failing to do so. When people gave me advice, I listened; I didn't summarily disregard it because others said it wouldn't work. When advice worked, I improved upon it; when it didn't, I looked for the reasons why and learned from those experiences too.

As you begin constructing your roadmap to happiness and financial security, I hope you will recognize that all the things you need to build wealth and achieve happiness, fame, or anything else you desire from life is all around you; everything is there except the desire to look for it. That comes from within. Your journey to happiness and financial security expands in direct proportion with your ability to create that inner desire and eliminate excuses. In other words, it's up to you. What you do and how you act determines what you accomplish. I am amazed at the number of people who think they can buy books, audio programs, and other learning materials, put them on their shelves, and expect great things to happen. It reminds me of the old Chinese proverb, "Man sit in chair with mouth open for very long time waiting for roast duck to fly in."

Being happy and creating financial security is like building a solid brick house: it's done by laying one brick at a time. Changing your thinking, building emotional security, and financial independence is done the same way: one step at a time. There aren't any shortcuts, so the sooner you get started, the quicker you will begin to see results. I call this book *The Financial Security Bible* because it contains all the guiding principles you will need to become happy and financially independent. There are nuggets of information on every page that you can put to work if you so choose. The book contains everything you need except the desire to use it.

In this final section, I'm not only going to teach you how to create desire and eliminate excuses, but how to get started doing so immediately. Remember, you have to create the desire, and a few suggestions on how to do it may be all you need to get started.

Now get out your notepad, go to the next page of this book, and let's create some desire.

38

Desire and Its Role in Achieving Success

Everyone knows that unless you're motivated to do something, chances are you aren't going to do it. People rarely do things for no reason, which is why motivation is so important. To motivate means to provide a reason or motive for doing something, but that can span a broad spectrum. I've had many people ask me, "What can you do to get me motivated?" Seldom do I hear them say, "How can I motivate myself?" And therein lies the difference between ordinary people and extraordinary people, the difference between those who achieve happiness and become financially secure and those who live paycheck to paycheck and complain most of their lives.

Motivation has two extremes: fear and desire. The closer you get to either extreme, the more intense the motivation becomes. Let's look at an example that illustrates this phenomenon. Suppose a group of children are playing ball in the middle of a seldomly used highway. Over the course of several minutes, one mother comes out and tells her child to stop playing in the road and come in for dinner, another also scolds hers for playing in the road and says it's time to come in and do homework, and still another sees her children in the highway and starts running after them trying to get them out of the road. All the while the children are procrastinating and making excuses as they continue playing their game. Dinner, homework, or even mad parents should all be good reasons for the kids to get out of the road, but none of these reasons are close enough to either extreme on the motivational spectrum to get them moving.

Suddenly a huge tractor-trailer rig comes barreling around the curve at a high rate of speed; the driver sees the children playing in the roadway and knows he can't stop. He slams on the brakes, reaches up, and pulls the cord that blows the air horn. When the children hear the screeching of tires and the ominous blast from the horn, they instantly dive for the ditch on the side of the road. They don't even look to see if it's full of rocks or mud or snakes or anything else. They'll deal with whatever is in the ditch later. At the moment, their fear of death is greater than anything else. They are motivated! They have just experienced fear motivation to the extreme. (Many parents use fear motivation to a lesser extreme with their threats to spank or ground their children.)

But, back to the children in the highway. Let's suppose they are fully engrossed in their game, when one of them spots another child petting a baby deer in the back yard of the house next to where they are playing. He screams, "Look everybody! There's a baby deer in Johnny's back yard, and he's petting it. Let's go pet it too!"

The rest of the children instantly drop everything and start running for Johnny's back yard. They clear the roadway just as quickly as if a tractor-trailer truck was bearing down on them but do so for a totally different reason. None of them have ever seen a baby deer before, especially one they could pet. They practically knock each other down trying to be the first to get to it. They are motivated! They have just experienced desire motivation at a high level.

Can you see from these examples that while the results were the same, the motivation was entirely different? In both instances, the children got out of the road as quickly as possible, but with the truck, it was because they feared for their lives, while with the baby deer, it was because of inner desire. With the truck, the motivation came from the outside, from the fear of being physically harmed. On the other hand, the desire to see and pet the baby deer came from within. Neither little Johnny nor the deer applied any outside force to get the children out of the road. Their inner desire was enough motivation to get them to react as quickly as if their life had been threatened. Very interesting, isn't it?

Fear and desire form the extremes of motivation, but they aren't limited to just fear from the outside and desire from the inside. The roles can be reversed, and when they are, it can be counterproductive. The internal fear of failure, ridicule, criticism, loss, harm, or even the fear of success can restrain a person from developing the motivation needed to tackle and solve problems. Fear can be just as strong a factor when it resides inside you, but when it is, it kills motivation and keeps you from enjoying great success. I'm sure you've been around people who are afraid to try anything new or different. On the other hand, attempts to create desire created from the outside can also be counterproductive. The old carrot-on-the-stick approach to get the donkey to pull the cart doesn't work long term unless the donkey gets to eat the carrot occasionally. Employers are often guilty of using this approach when they dangle big bonuses in front of employees to encourage them to reach for unrealistic goals. It takes only a few times of employees' busting their butts reaching for someone else's goals and coming up short, for the promised rewards to lose their value.

The desire that is created by setting your own goals, if they are meaningful, can provide the motivation needed to overcome almost any obstacle that stands in the way.

I learned this at a very early age when I wanted my first bicycle. The day my mother told me, "Honey, I'm sorry we can't afford to get you a bicycle, but if you really want one, I'll bet you can find a way to get it" was a turning point in my life. As I described in Section II, my desire for the bicycle was greater than any of the obstacles I encountered in the process of getting it. How do I know? It's simple; I got the bicycle. Sure, I had to solve a lot of problems and overcome some difficulties, but my desire was strong enough to carry me through the tough times. The way to determine if your desires are strong enough is just as simple. If your goals are always on your mind and you are consistently striving to reach them, they are. If you find your mind wandering and your actions toward reaching your goals inconsistent, they aren't.

So, how do you create this kind of intense desire? That's where your notes come into play. Did any of my stories remind you of times when you wanted something so much that you sacrificed to get it? If so, great! What I'm trying to find out is, "Have you ever sacrificed today in order to get something that you really wanted, weeks or months into the future?" If so, I want you to think about how you felt during the time you were sacrificing in comparison with the way you felt once you finally got it. Wasn't the thrill of accomplishment worth the sacrifice?

Now think back about the times you wanted something and weren't willing to wait or to sacrifice for it. Times such as when you bought a new car and went in debt so you could have it now. Within months the new smell was gone, and it had probably picked up a few scratches and dings, but those payments kept coming relentlessly. By the time it was paid off, you were probably sick of writing the checks, that is, unless you traded up and rolled the remainder of the debt into a new loan and started over again. But even if you paid off the loan, by the time the last payment was made, the car was probably close to being worn out, and that's depressing. (Go back and review the story about the Chevrolet and Cadillac in Chapter 4.)

Your journey to financial security begins when you develop the ability to create desires strong enough that they keep you on track even when temptations arise. This is done by starting with small goals, experiencing some successes, and then gradually moving on to larger and larger goals. It also involves learning to rebound from setbacks and disappointments without giving up on your dreams. With each accomplishment, your confidence will grow and your desire to succeed will become stronger. Likewise, if you encounter an obstacle and give up on a goal, you will find it more difficult to set another one for fear of failing again. That's why you should start with smaller goals but make them goals that when accomplished will move you closer to your big goals. Try to see yourself reaching whatever goal you set. Visualize how you will feel when you reach the goal.

If you haven't yet done so, stop now, sit down with a notepad, and jot down a list of significant events from your past. If you have already made your list, great. What I want you to do now is study this list. Think about each incident. Whether the experiences were good or bad is not important. Think about what made them memorable and what you learned from them, and try to write it down. If you can't define what made an experience memorable or what lesson you learned from it, your first task will be to start paying more attention to what's going on around you. You'll never be able to create strong desires if you are just floating meaninglessly through life. You have to learn to recognize and deal with the problems and challenges in your surroundings.

In Chapter 22 I described an incident between me and another gentleman that occurred while we were bowling. Had I not learned to grasp what was taking place around me, I would have probably missed the lesson I learned from this encounter, a lesson that created a very strong desire to control my emotions. Creating desire is not about coming up with a wish list. It's developing a craving to always be thinking two or three steps ahead; it's about anticipating the outcome of your actions and having alternative actions ready if you get less than the desired results. Desire is strengthened by successes; the more of them you have, the more you want.

Small successes strengthen desire because with each success, your confidence grows and you see yourself ultimately achieving your big goals. It's important that you start with small goals as you strive to build your financial future. Yes, you need big long-term goals, but you have to break these down into small short-term goals that are easier to accomplish, but ones that when achieved move you closer to your big goals. Successfully reaching each small goal gives you a feeling of accomplishment and allows you to measure your progress. You might want to think of each small accomplishment as climbing another rung on the ladder to success.

Success can be a subjective term that is hard to define. As I mentioned in the beginning, when I refer to success in this book, I am primarily talking about financial success. I acknowledge that there are many different types of success, but desire is something that is required to achieve any type of success. Desire has to come first, followed by effort, before success can be realized. The kind of desire that motivates, which leads to effort, which leads to success, must come from within; otherwise, success is just a fleeting dream.

People react totally differently to fear and desire motivation, and therein lies one of the secrets to developing happiness and financial security. Fear motivation doesn't work, because people motivated by fear never do any more than it takes to eliminate the fear. On the other hand, there is no limit to what desire can propel you to accomplish. Nothing I can say or do, either in this book or in person, will create the inner desire you will need to become financially independent; only you can do that. The old saying, "If it's going to be, it's up to me," is so true. Throughout the book I've discussed accepting personal responsibility, developing a pattern of investing, repelling negative influences, and many other traits you need to be happy and financially secure, but all success has to start with desire. Unless your desire for financial independence, or any other goal, is strong enough to keep you hungry and make you receptive to learning, you probably won't get there. Unless you are willing to employ every legal and ethical method of achieving success, you will find yourself making one excuse after another, which leads me to the next chapter, where I will discuss eliminating excuses.

Key points from this chapter:

- The two extremes of motivation are fear and desire.
- The closer you get to either extreme, the more intense the motivation becomes.
- Fear often comes from outside you, while desire comes from inside you.
- Internal fear can kill your motivation.
- You can't rely on desire artificially induced from the outside by others, because it is depressing and will kill your motivation when you reach for someone else's goals and come up short.
- If you aren't consistently reaching your goals, it's because your desire is not strong enough.
- Crank up your desire by setting small goals that you can consistently

achieve but make them goals that move you closer to achieving larger goals.

- You must accept responsibility for creating and nurturing your inner desires.

39

Commitment Is the Key to Eliminating Excuses

Just as desire comes from within, so do excuses, but the difference between them is huge. Desires form the foundation of happiness and financial security, but excuses are the termites that devour it if you allow them to do so. The term "good excuse" may be life's biggest oxymoron. There is no such thing as a good excuse. As long as your goals are realistic, the only reason for not reaching them is you. That may sound harsh, but it's true. If your commitment is lacking, you will make up any excuse to justify failure.

Most people never set goals and the few that do are often reluctant to share them. Sharing your goals exposes you to ridicule, especially if you lack the commitment to see them through to a successful completion. As a result, people often start making excuses as soon as obstacles begin to appear. I believe they do this because they confuse excuses with reasons. Their excuses are nothing but face-saving ways to avoid having to admit they lack the commitment and willingness to learn how to overcome the obstacles.

Excuses start simple enough and creep into all walks of life. You oversleep, so you call your employer and say, "My alarm clock didn't go off and I overslept, so I'll be a few minutes late today." Then on the way to work you get caught in heavy traffic, you end up having to park at the far side of the parking lot because all the nearby spaces are already taken, and then you have trouble getting into the building because you rushed out and left your security pass at home. You've just arrived, and it's already been a rough day. As you pass the boss' office, you stick you head in the door and say, "I've finally made it; you wouldn't believe what

I've been through this morning. It started when my clock didn't go off, and then I got caught in a traffic jam, and blah, blah, blah."

Do you think the boss cares? No! All the excuses do is help you rationalize in your own mind why you weren't at work when you were supposed to be. If you had 50 excuses, it doesn't change the fact that you were late to work.

Setting and reaching goals works the same way. Either you reach the goal or you don't. If you don't, all the excuses in the world won't change that. How many times have you heard people say, "I would have done _____ (you fill in the blank), but . . ." Whatever follows the "but" is usually an excuse, especially when it is something they could have controlled.

The difference between an excuse and a reason is who controls the situation. Obstacles over which you have no control or ability to overcome are reasons, but these are few and far between.

Someone tells you, "I could have been a marathon runner, but I lost my leg in a car accident." Try telling that to Denny Chipollini of Skippack, Pennsylvania. He was in a car accident that severed both his legs. Doctors reattached them, but eventually his left leg had to be amputated due to massive injury and infection. Ask him about this, and he'll tell you that he refers to the accident as a "gift" because it changed his life for the better. Four years after the accident, he ran a five-kilometer race on his artificial leg. By 2001, he had run in the Pittsburgh, New York City, and San Diego marathons. He founded a nonprofit organization that he called Generation Hope and used his "gift" to inspire people to overcome adversity with his "no excuses and no limits" attitude toward life. This proves that even an amputee can run marathons, because if his desire is strong enough, he will find a way to do it. Imagine the "good excuses" Denny Chipollini could have used to have chosen a miserable "woe is me" attitude rather than a superbly positive "I can do it" one.

Doesn't that put excuses into perspective? I want you to make the commitment today to quit making excuses and start feeding yourself reasons to be successful. Acknowledge the fact that excuses are inexcusable. If you don't reach your goals, all the excuses in the world won't change that. The only thing that will change it is eliminating the excuses and creating the desire to be successful. Understand that setbacks are merely part of the learning process.

The first step on your journey to happiness and financial independence is to pledge that from this moment on you will never, ever, blame anyone else for what's going on in your life. You alone are responsible for setting your life's goals, and you alone are responsible for attaining them. No number of excuses changes failure to success.

The most well-known example of setting and achieving a goal of which I am aware began on May 25, 1961, with President John F. Kennedy's Special Message to Congress on Urgent National Needs. In his speech, he said, "I believe that this nation should commit itself to achieving the goal, before this decade is out, of landing a man on the moon and returning him safely to Earth." The key word in this statement is "commit." This became a goal that galvanized the nation. It was specific, "to land a man on the moon and return him safely to Earth." It had a timeframe, "before this decade is out." And he didn't add any qualifiers like, unless one of our rockets blows up, some of our astronauts are killed, or we encounter some other unforeseen events that cause problems. He simply said we will do it by the end of the decade.

All of the above mentioned obstacles and many more occurred, but commitment to the goal kept us focused. When the setbacks and disappointments arose, we learned from them and kept moving forward. Each one brought more intense study that resulted in better technology. Then right on schedule, July 20, 1969, the world heard the words, "Houston, Tranquility Base here. The Eagle has landed."

As exciting as the landing was, it was merely one more step toward successfully reaching the goal President Kennedy had set eight years before. Not until four days later, on July 24, 1969, when the command module splashed down in the Pacific Ocean and the crew was safely aboard the USS *Hornet*, was the goal declared accomplished. The mission objective for Apollo 11 was very simply stated, "Perform a manned lunar landing and return."

Think of the excuses that could have been given to abort the mission; President Kennedy was assassinated, the mission was extremely expensive, astronauts died while preparing for it, NASA chief James Webb was opposed to it, there were political disagreements over funding, and the list could go on and on. But none of these was even considered as an excuse to stop. With each small step, we drew closer to the goal and the commitment grew stronger. **Commitment is the key to eliminating excuses.**

Now go back to your notes and review your list of memorable life experiences. Think about the commitment level you had during the ones that were successful and compare this with the commitment level you had during the ones when you didn't succeed. First, think about the successful ones. Did the obstacles you encountered and were able to overcome strengthen your resolve and make you more determined to succeed? Now compare this with the ones when you didn't succeed. Did

310

you turn those obstacles into excuses? Be honest! I know how easy it was when you succeeded to take credit for the victories, but when you failed, did you accept personal responsibility for the failures or did you try to blame the outcome on others?

Before you can become truly happy and financially secure, you have to learn to eliminate excuses and accept full responsibility for your life. When you do so, it toughens you like an old piece of leather so you can bend without breaking. You learn to treat your goals like games that aren't over until you win. You don't give up when you encounter obstacles; you learn to go over, under, around, or through them until you achieve your objectives. Failure ceases to be an option.

In the last chapter I described how desire must come from within. Well, so does eliminating excuses. It is these two characteristics that separate successful people from ordinary people. But the exciting part is that **ordinary people can achieve extraordinary success**. Anyone willing to make the commitment can become very happy and financially secure. But first you have to get started, and that's what I'm going to show you how to do in the next and final chapter.

Key points from this chapter:

- Don't allow lack of commitment to cause you to make excuses.
- There is no such thing as a good excuse.
- The difference between an excuse and a reason is this: Who controls the situation?
- Even an amputee can run marathons if his desire is strong enough.
- Never, ever, blame anyone else for what's going on in your life.
- Commitment is the key to eliminating excuses.
- Vow to eliminate excuses and accept full responsibility for your life.
- Constantly remind yourself that ordinary people can achieve extraordinary success.

40

Getting Started: Putting It All Together

The final chapter of any good self-help book should be titled "Getting Started." I hope you've learned a great deal from the time you've spent with me getting to this point in the book, but unless you put what I've taught you to work, you've wasted it. Throughout these chapters, I included stories and anecdotes to tie the lessons I was sharing to the real-life events from which I learned them. I feel this approach makes for more enjoyable reading and can help you better relate these lessons to events from your own life. The message I want to leave you with is that anyone can build wealth and be happy. One is not mutually exclusive of the other, and, yes, even **ordinary people can achieve extraordinary success** when they create enough desire to be successful and fully commit themselves to becoming so.

When I was starting out, nobody would have thought that I would become financially successful. I was raised in a dirt-poor coal-mining town in Southern West Virginia. Many of the youngsters I grew up with are still living there today and are either on some form of public assistance or struggling to eke out a meager existence. The journey I've taken from poverty to financial independence has been frustrating at times, filled with potholes and bumps in the road, but I wouldn't trade it for anything. If a kid with little education, growing up in a place where more than 80 percent of the people are on some form of public assistance can do it, I know you can too!

By now, you should know the things you need to do; the only thing left is to get started, right? That's the impression given by many motivational gurus, but I disagree. I know there's much more to it than that. Sure, you have to get started, but don't we all start things that we never finish? It takes more than just starting and having good intentions to build wealth and be happy. The secret is, it's not how you start, but how you finish that makes the difference. I want to close with another story that illustrates what can happen once you develop this type of thinking.

As I've mentioned a number of times, I am a licensed multi-engine airplane pilot. What I haven't told you is that I quit flying in 1990 for medical reasons. I suffered a serious renal infarction (that's like a heart attack, only it involves the arteries to the kidneys) with no apparent cause, and did not fly again until 2002. After 12 years had passed with no recurrence of the problem, I decided it was time to get back in the air. I made an appointment with an FAA medical examiner to renew my medical certificate and then visited a local flight school based at the Asheville airport to begin the process of getting checked out to fly again. I took my first flight on May 1, 2002, in a small single-engine Cessna 172. This was quite a switch from the much larger twin-engine propjet I had flown several years prior to 1990.

It took less than two hours to be checked out in the 172 and signed off to take it up solo and start building some flying hours. During the month of May, I rented the 172 five more times and practiced the instrument approaches and other procedures with which I had once been so familiar. I was surprised that my flying skills came back so quickly, and before the end of the month, I was itching to buy an airplane. To my astonishment, when I inquired about getting insurance on another propjet, no insurance company would even consider writing liability coverage, let alone insuring the plane against damage. They all wanted me to have 100 to 200 hours of multi-engine time before they would consider it.

With my traditional find-a-way-not-an-excuse mentality, I considered my options and then began to formulate a plan. I made several calls to insurance companies and finally found one that would write liability insurance for me to fly a Beechcraft Duke, provided I would get five hours of instruction prior to flying solo. I inquired about a Duke because I had owned one of these in the early 1980s and had logged about 1,000 hours of time in that same make and model airplane. Although the Duke is a pressurized twin-engine plane with turbocharged piston engines, it was an inexpensive airplane that could fill the bill for what I needed. Just as I had in the 1980s, I decided it would be a good interim plane in which to build up enough hours to get back into a propjet.

Although the Duke was an older airplane, I was able to find one that had been completely refurbished, including having the latest avionics installed. I took it for a test flight and quickly discovered that navigation had changed dramatically in the 12 years I had been out of flying. The Loran and RNAV instruments I had used before were now obsolete, and this plane was equipped with a new digital GPS navigation system, including a Multi-Function Display that would actually display airways, airports, navigation stations, terrain, and even the instrument approach procedures on a video screen installed in the instrument panel. It could even show the airplane's location on the map as it tracked across the screen. Great equipment, but I didn't have a clue how to use it. Another obstacle!

After taking it for the test flight, I agreed to buy the plane and. without delay. put it into a maintenance facility for a complete inspection and to have my own registration number N65MS painted on the tail. While the plane was in the shop, I went to work on the obstacle. I took the manuals for the new navigation instruments home, and they became my reading materials for several days. Needless to say, they were far more technical and difficult reading than this book.

When the work was completed and the plane was ready to fly, I hired an instructor to give me the five hours of refresher training the insurance company required. That was interesting, because both the instructor and I had to learn how to use the new instrumentation. It was so new that the instructor hadn't seen it either. Between us, we gradually figured it out and by the end of the five hours, I had been checked out on the plane's systems, received a biennial flight review and an instrument competency check, and was ready to fly it solo.

As the months passed, I made several flights in the Duke and was becoming more proficient with each one, but I was still anticipating the day I could be back in a turbine engine propjet. During this time, my good friend and negotiating expert Roger Dawson paid me a visit. He wanted me to co-author a book with him on real estate investing. I wanted to talk flying at the time, and the fact that I had purchased a plane led to Roger's asking me if I would take him for a ride in it. I jumped at the opportunity, and we headed to the airport. When he saw the plane, Roger was quite impressed. I think he had been expecting to go for a ride in a little two-passenger Piper Cub, not a plane that could cruise at 25,000 feet and fly more than 270 miles per hour.

I invited Roger to join me in the cockpit, and as we were going through the start, taxi, and departure checklist, I shared my goal of flying the Duke for a couple of years and then moving back into a propjet. As we taxied past a row of planes, I pointed out a Beechcraft King Air like the one I eventually planned to buy. I shared this goal with my good friend without fear of ridicule or criticism. After nearly 20 years of friendship, Roger had learned not to doubt me.

When we returned from the sightseeing flight, Roger went back to work on his goal: getting me to co-author a real estate book with him.

Just to humor him, I joined him in preparing an outline for the book, and before his visit was over, Roger was able to get me to agree to join him in writing it if he found a publisher. I gave my commitment lightly and assumed that would be the end of it. But Roger didn't take it that way, and within a few weeks, a contract from McGraw-Hill Publishing Company landed on my desk for our first book *The Weekend Millionaire's Secrets to Investing in Real Estate*. It turned out to be a huge bestseller and eventually led to us joining forces to write three more books in what became the Weekend Millionaire Series. Roger had accomplished his goal and more, but what about me and the propjet?

First, you need to understand that we are very different people with very different goals in life. Please be sure that you are pursuing goals that excite and motivate you, not someone else. Roger is an accomplished boat captain and owns a lovely sailboat but wouldn't think of getting behind the controls of an airplane. I, on the other hand, feel right at home in the air but could care less about going sailing. (My one trip with Roger, getting soaked by ocean spray and nearly freezing to death, was enough to cure me.) Roger loves to travel and earns his living traveling around the world teaching negotiating skills to some of the world's largest corporations. I prefer to stay closer to home and devote most of my time to overseeing my real estate holdings. Although I speak occasionally at special events, speaking is not my primary source of income as it is with Roger. While very different, we are both very goal oriented and committed to achieving what we set out to do. We are also perfect examples of two ordinary people who have achieved extraordinary success. And I say ordinary, because neither of us comes from affluent backgrounds nor holds university degrees . . . unless PhDs from the University of Hard Knocks count.

Now back to my goal of once again flying a propjet. I did just what I set out to do and flew the Duke for a couple of years, accumulated the needed hours to get insurance, and then went to work looking for a Beechcraft King Air. After an extensive search, I found just the right airplane. It was a Beechcraft King Air E-90, smaller that the B200, but just the right size for me, and it included the extended range fuel tanks. Shortly after I bought it, I put larger brand-new factory engines on it, which gave me nearly the same speed as the B200 at much lower cost. I also had all the old avionics removed and installed the very latest digital glass cockpit with a new digital autopilot, and today it is one of the nicest King Airs in the fleet. Oh, by the way, I called Roger to remind him of what I had told him that day we took the flight in the Duke.

When I told you in the beginning of this chapter that it takes more than just starting to achieve financial independence, I did so for a reason.

I want you to understand that whatever your goals, until you can picture yourself accomplishing them, you aren't ready to start. I could already see myself in the King Air while I was flying the Cessna 172 when I was just getting back into flying. When you set your goals, you need to believe in yourself enough to be able to see yourself crossing the finish line. No excuses!

That's the kind of desire Roger had, when he set a goal to get me to write a book with him. He could see us doing it, he believed in himself, and he never doubted his ability or let me talk him out of his goal. That's also the kind of desire I had at the same time when I set a goal to once again own and fly a Beechcraft King Air. Neither of us wavered in our quest to reach our goals, and thanks to Roger, I've come to enjoy writing. I never knew it could be so much fun to share what I've learned with the world. As I said in the first sentence of this book, "I believe the greatest injustice successful people can do to their fellow man is to go to their graves and take with them the knowledge that brought them success."

Granted, my goals today may be different from what most ordinary people set in the beginning, but they serve as perfect examples of what can happen to ordinary people when they start setting and reaching goals. One success leads to another and another. Confidence grows, and things that seemed unattainable in the beginning become very doable as your knowledge grows, your successes mount, and your desire increases. Remember starting is important, but it's how you finish that really matters. I challenge you to get started today and then, in the words of Sir Winston Churchill, "Never give in. Never, never, never, never . . . Never give in."

Thank you for taking this journey with me. Throughout these pages I have tried to help you view success from a different perspective. I hope you have enjoyed reading about my journey to financial independence and hope that seeing how I learned from my experiences and overcame obstacles will inspire you to greater achievements. I want to wish you my best as you begin your journey and encourage you to keep this book nearby. Use it as a reference whenever you have doubts or just need a little encouragement. You will hit some rough spots, just as I did. There will be some tough times, and you may even feel like quitting, but before you do, stop and look up in the sky. If you happen to see a beautiful white propjet with blue and gold striping flying over, wave. It may just be me flying in to give you **a kick in the pants and to remind you that you CAN build wealth and be happy.**

Here's to YOUR wealth and happiness!
Mike Summey

successtips@aol.com

Key points from this chapter:

- Even ordinary people can achieve extraordinary success when they have enough desire to be successful and fully commit themselves to becoming so.

- Set your goals, and then as the Nike ads say, "Just do it!"

- If I can do it, you can too!

- It's not how you start, it's how you finish that counts.

- Be sure that you are pursuing goals that excite and motivate you, not someone else's.

- Once you start, never, never, never give up.